D0705671

Restoring Justice

Daniel Van Ness
Karen Heetderks Strong

since 1887

anderson publishing co.
p.o. box 1576
cincinnati, oh 45201-1576
(513) 421-4142

Restoring Justice

Copyright © 1997 by Anderson Publishing Co./Cincinnati, OH

All rights reserved. No part of this book may be reproduced in any form or by any electronic or mechanical means including information storage and retrieval systems without permission in writing from the publisher.

ISBN 0-87084-890-0
Library of Congress Catalog Number 97-71386

Ellen S. Boyne *Editor*
Elizabeth A. Shipp *Assistant Editor*

Cover design by Edward Smith Design, Inc./New York

Foreword

This book has been a decade in writing. It began in the mid-1980s when the organization we worked for undertook development of a model of criminal justice built on what was then a largely unknown and incomplete theory called *restorative justice*. The organization was Justice Fellowship, a criminal justice reform organization affiliated with Prison Fellowship Ministries (both of us now work for other affiliated organizations in the Prison Fellowship movement).

We and our colleagues began by articulating what we felt were the principles of restorative justice. This took months of work, and involved not only the staff of Justice Fellowship but also criminal justice practitioners, researchers, elected officials, academics, theologians and concerned laypersons. After working sessions and multiple drafts, we settled on three basic principles, similar to those proposed in Chapter Three. Then began a three-year project to research and write systematically about the theory undergirding restorative justice, the principles for its application, and particular programs to bring it into being. These were developed using a similar approach of working sessions, multiple drafts and external review.

The purpose of this exercise was to help Justice Fellowship focus its reform efforts. But as time passed, we became convinced that it would be useful to a wider audience. So we began a lengthy process of revision, incorporating the growing research and literature on restorative justice, and writing for a broader audience. This book is the result.

We are indebted, therefore, to the many team members and contributors involved in the process since 1987. Although some of these individuals will not agree with all of our conclusions, their contributions have enriched and strengthened this work.

Specifically, we would like to thank former colleagues at Justice Fellowship who helped research and write the previous work, "Restorative Justice: Theory, Principles, and Practice," printed and copyrighted by Justice Fellowship in 1989 and 1990. Ideas and portions of these manuscripts are reflected in this book, by permission from Justice Fellowship and our co-authors. As we prepared this volume, we were continually reminded of the formative and highly meaningful interaction among these individuals as we worked together to challenge, articulate and refine ideas about restorative justice and their implications. Thomas Crawford poured himself into the project, cultivating personal and intellectual excellence in the process, and gaining hope for a criminal justice future tempering compassion with accountability and opening pathways for renewal and forgiveness. Lisa Barnes kept asking tough questions and pressing for clarity. David R. Carlson played a crucial role in the formulation of the three Justice Fellowship principles of restorative justice and the development of "Restorative Justice: Theory." Kimon Sargeant and Claire Souryal assisted in researching and writing "Restorative Justice: Principles and Practice." Dorothea Jinnah has been invaluable as a precise, resourceful and ever-thoughtful researcher and colleague. Thanks, too, to Ed Hostetter for his online searches and project help. We are indebted to these co-laborers (and others, too many to name) for their hard work and insightful perspectives.

We are also thankful for and appreciative of the persistence of Mickey Braswell at Anderson Publishing Co., who cajoled, encouraged and constructively criticized as we completed the manuscript. His colleague, Ellen S. Boyne, used her adept editing and refining skills to good effect. We have enjoyed working with them both.

Excerpts from other previously published works by Daniel Van Ness have also been used by permission in this volume. These works and publishers are as follows:

"Preserving a Community Voice: The Case for Half-and Half Juries in Racially-Charged Criminal Cases," *John Marshall Law Review* 28, 1 (1994) is used courtesy of The John Marshall Law School.

"New Wine and Old Wineskins," *Criminal Law Forum* 4, 2 (1993) and "Anchoring Just Deserts," *Criminal Law Forum* 6, 3 (1995) are used courtesy of *Criminal Law Forum,* Rutgers Law School.

Adapted excerpts from "Restorative Justice" in *Criminal Justice, Restitution, and Reconciliation,* edited by Burt Galaway and Joe Hudson (1990) and from "Restorative Justice and International Human Rights" in *Restorative Justice: International Perspectives,* edited by Burt Galaway and Joe Hudson (1996) are used with permission from Criminal Justice Press, P.O. Box 249, Monsey, New York 10952.

In the following chapters we present our arguments for why criminal justice is in need of a new vision, and we propose that this need may be met by restorative justice. Further, we explain our understanding of what restorative justice means, and explore the foundational underpinnings upon which we can build restorative justice into policy and practice. We end the book with a chapter on steps toward bringing the new vision into reality.

We do not claim to be the first or only proponents of restorative justice. Indeed, the term has grown into wide usage in the last decade. We are encouraged by the growth of interest in restorative justice worldwide, and the many and diverse examples of its practice. Therefore, it is our desire that this volume may contribute substantively to the growing literature on restorative justice, and may encourage greater practical use of its vision.

Table of Contents

Part One

The Vision of Restorative Justice

Chapter One

Visions and Patterns:

Why Patterns of Thinking Obstruct Criminal Justice Reform

The young woman watched intently as the man who raped her was sentenced to prison. But as the rapist was escorted from the courtroom, it was clear to Justice John Kelly that she was no less distraught than she had been throughout the court proceedings. So before the next case was called, Justice Kelly asked the victim to approach the bench. He spoke with her briefly and quietly about what had happened, and concluded with these words: "You understand that what I have done here demonstrates conclusively *that what happened was not your fault.*" At that, the young woman began to weep and ran from the courtroom. When Justice Kelly called the victim's family several days later, he learned that his words had been words of vindication for the woman; they marked the beginning of her psychological healing. Her tears had been tears of healing.

A short time later this Australian judge spoke at an international conference on criminal law reform held in London.[1] Speaking to 200 judges, legal scholars and law reformers from common law countries, he laid aside his prepared comments and spoke with great feeling about the need for criminal law practitioners to see themselves as healers. A purpose of criminal law, he said, should be to heal the wounds caused by crime. Since "healing" is not a word frequently heard in legal gatherings, he illustrated what he meant by

---

[1] This conference led to the formation of the Society for the Reform of Criminal Law and is described in "Conference Report: Reform of the Criminal Law," *Crim. L.F.* 1 (1989): 91.

recounting the story of the rape victim for whom even the offender's conviction and sentencing had not been enough.

The rehabilitation model of criminal justice has been by far the most influential school of thought in American criminology since at least the Civil War period.[2] Although the model has fallen into disrepute in the past 25 years, opinion surveys suggest that the desire to rehabilitate offenders remains strong among members of the general public,[3] and even among many crime victims.[4] At a fundamental level we recognize that criminal justice should consider not only whether accused offenders have violated the law but also why they have done so. But even when rehabilitation programs are helpful in addressing the underlying problems that led to the decision to commit a crime, those programs fail to address all the injuries surrounding the crime. Crime is not simply lawbreaking, it is also injury to others; it is not simply the manifestation of an underlying injury, it is also the creation of new injuries. A purpose of criminal justice should be, in Justice Kelly's words, to heal those injuries.

As we will see, these injuries exist on several levels and are experienced by victims, communities and even offenders. But the current policies and practice of criminal justice focus almost entirely on the offender as lawbreaker, filtering out virtually all aspects of crime except questions of legal guilt and punishment. This is because a set of assumptions, or pattern of thinking, structures our perception of crime and consequently our sense of what a proper response should be. Howard Zehr's description of paradigms is pertinent here: "They provide the lens through which we understand phenomena. They shape what we 'know' to be possible and impossible. [They] form our common sense, and things which fall outside . . . seem absurd."[5]

---

[2] *See* Chapter Three, "The Rise of Rehabilitation," in Francis T. Cullen and Karen E. Gilbert, *Reaffirming Rehabilitation* (Cincinnati: Anderson Publishing Co., 1982).

[3] In the 1995 publication titled *Seeking Justice: Crime and Punishment in America*, the Edna McConnell Clark Foundation cites key findings from 12 different national or state public opinion polls and surveys conducted between 1989 and 1995. They conclude that "studies show the American public still holds rehabilitation as a primary goal of criminal justice," consistently supporting drug treatment for addicted offenders and community-based correctional approaches for the nonviolent. William M. DiMascio et al., *Seeking Justice: Crime and Punishment in America* (New York: Edna McConnell Clark Foundation, 1995), 44-45.

[4] In fact, when crime victims are asked about their view of punishment, they often respond that they hope something will happen to the offenders to help them emerge as better people who will not hurt others. *See* Mark Umbreit et al., *Victim Meets Offender: The Impact of Restorative Justice and Mediation* (Monsey, NY: Criminal Justice Press, 1994).

[5] Howard Zehr, *Changing Lenses: A New Focus for Crime and Justice* (Scottsdale, PA: Herald Press, 1990), 86-87. Some (including the authors at various times) have referred to the move to a restorative perspective as a paradigm shift. However, after considering the issue, Howard Zehr argues that, at this stage at least, restorative justice does not amount to a paradigm. We agree, and consequently are using "patterns of thinking" as a way to express the revolutionary dimension of restorative justice.
   A paradigm is more than a vision or a proposal. It requires well-articulated theory, combined with a consistent grammar and a 'physics' of application—and some degree of consensus. It need not solve all problems, but it must solve the most pressing ones and must point a direction. I doubt that we are there yet. (*Changing Lenses*, 180).

Patterns of thinking are necessary because they give meaning to the myriad bits of data we must deal with in life. Edward de Bono illustrates this using the example of a person crossing a busy road: "If, as you stood waiting to cross the road, your brain had to try out all the incoming information in different combinations in order to recognize the traffic conditions, it would take you at least a month to cross the road. In fact, the changing conditions would make it impossible for you ever to cross."[6] To avoid this problem, the brain uses "active information systems" to develop patterns of thinking that organize the data around us.[7] It is how we make sense out of the chaos of information that would otherwise overwhelm us. A pattern of thinking is like the collection of streams, rivulets and rivers formed over time in a particular place by the rainfall there; once the pattern of water runoff is established, rainwater will always flow there, and nowhere else.[8]

However, the reason for their usefulness is also a fundamental weakness of patterns: they limit the data we even perceive. We simply do not recognize "absurd" information; we see only what makes sense. Therefore, one sign that a pattern of thinking has become deficient is that we increasingly encounter troublesome data that do not fit; we are then forced to make a choice: disregard that evidence or seek a new pattern. For example, at one time scientists believed that the Earth was flat and that the universe revolved around it. But as astronomers recorded the actual movement of heavenly bodies, this model became less and less satisfactory. When Copernicus proposed that the Earth revolves around the sun—not the other way around—his model offered a much more satisfactory explanation of observable data.

We believe that a similar shift may be underway in criminal justice. The current pattern of thinking channels us to see crime as law breaking, to focus our energies on the offender and to value punishment when it deters, rehabilitates, incapacitates or denounces. But nagging questions continue to surface, prompted in part by data that regularly seem to fall outside the pattern.

1. *Why does the criminal justice system seem so ineffective in its efforts to combat crime?* In spite of increasing powers, government seems less and less capable of solving the problem of crime in our communities. Although state and federal jurisdictions incarcerate more people than ever before, the people of the United States continue to express high levels of fear and concern about crime. And

---

[6] Edward de Bono, *Conflicts: A Better Way to Resolve Them* (New York: Penguin Books, 1991).

[7] Ibid., 12-13.

[8] Ibid., 13.

while the United States incarcerates a larger percentage of its population than any other major country, its crime rate remains one of the world's highest.

2. *Why do prisons make offenders worse, rather than reha-bilitating or deterring them?* The RAND Corporation, in its report *Prisons versus Probation in California*, found that recidivism (repeat offender rates) are actually more serious for convicted offenders who have been sent to prison than for similar offenders who were simply put on probation. This was particularly true for property offenders,[9] and is true in spite of the fact that the United States is spending more money (and relying more) on prisons than ever before.

3. *Why are victims so dissatisfied with how the criminal jus-tice system treats them?* The injustice of failing to include the victims' interests is becoming more and more appar-ent. Victims suffer a perverse kind of double jeopardy, victimized once by the criminal and then again by the criminal justice system, that excludes them and their needs almost from the moment a crime is committed. As a result, victim rights groups have sprung up across the country to force the system to deal with victims' needs. This is true in spite of the fact that civil suits (the tradi-tional method for private citizens to bring cases to court) remain an option for victims.

For two centuries, Americans have experimented with waves of new programs to address these chronic problems. Every such attempt has ended in apparent failure. We believe a major reason is that the way we think about crime is inadequate; by defining crime only as law-breaking and then concentrating on the resulting adversarial rela-tionship between government and the criminal offender, the existing pattern of thinking fails to address—or even recognize—the other dimensions involved. Consequently, adding new programs to the old way of thinking is not enough; what is needed is a different way of thinking about crime. That is what this book proposes.

It is certainly not novel to consider alternative patterns of think-ing in responding to crime; at one point in Western history, justice was based on a perspective that viewed crime as an offense against victims, their families and the community. The goal of the justice process was to make things right by repairing the damage to those parties, whether the damage was physical, financial or relational. As

---

[9]   Joan Petersilia, Susan Turner and Joyce Peterson, *Prison versus Probation in California: Implications for Crime and Offender Recidivism* (Santa Monica: RAND, 1986).

we have seen, the more recent approach views crime as an offense against the government. Its goal is crime prevention, initially through rehabilitation (changing criminals into law-abiding citizens). In recent years, however, there has been increasing pessimism regarding whether this can be achieved. Clamping down on crime through deterrence, punishment and incapacitation is now the dominant policy. In Figure 1.1 (below) the approaches to crime of these two models are presented. These contrasts are discussed further in the paragraphs that follow.

Figure 1.1

	Ancient Pattern	Current Pattern
Crime	Injury to victims and their families in the context of the community	Violation of the law
Parties	Victims, offenders, community and government	Offenders and government
Goal	Repair damage and reestablish right relationships	Reduce future lawbreaking through rehabilitation, punishment, deterrence and/or incapacitation

Let us look at these patterns more closely.

The Ancient Pattern

The early legal systems forming the foundation of Western law emphasized the need for offenders and their families to settle with victims and their families. Although crime breached the common welfare so that the community had an interest in—and responsibility for—addressing the wrong and punishing the offender, the offense was not considered primarily a crime against the state, as it is today. Instead, crime was viewed principally as an offense against the victim and the victim's family.[10] Consequently, offenders and their fam-

---

[10] In his book on what he calls "primitive law," E. Adamson Hoebel wrote: "The job [of primitive law] is to clean the case up, to suppress or penalize the illegal behavior and to bring the relations of the disputants back into balance, so that life may resume its normal course. This type of law-work has frequently been compared to work of the medical practitioner. It is family doctor stuff, essential to keeping the social body on its feet." E. Adamson Hoebel, *The Law of Primitive Man: A Study in Comparative Legal Dynamics* (New York: Atheneum, 1973), 279.

ilies were required to settle accounts with victims and their families. This view can be seen in the legal codes of these civilizations. The Code of Hammurabi (c. 1700 B.C.E.)[11] prescribed restitution for property offenses, as did the Code of Lipit-Ishtar (1875 B.C.E.). Other Middle Eastern codes, such as the Sumerian Code of Ur-Nammu (c. 2050 B.C.E.) and the Code of Eshnunna (c. 1700 B.C.E.), required restitution even in the case of violent offenses. The Roman Law of the Twelve Tables (449 B.C.E.) required thieves to pay double restitution unless the property was found in their houses; in that case, they paid triple damages; for resisting the search of their houses, they paid quadruple restitution. The Lex Salica (c. 496 C.E.), the earliest existing collection of Germanic tribal laws, included restitution for crimes ranging from theft to homicide. The Laws of Ethelbert (c. 600 C.E.), promulgated by the ruler of Kent, contained detailed restitution schedules that distinguished the values, for example, of each finger and its nail.[12] Each of these diverse cultures responded to what we now call crime by requiring offenders and their families to make amends to victims and their families—not simply to ensure that injured persons received restitution but also to restore community peace.[13]

Ancient Hebrew justice also aimed to restore wholeness.[14] This can be seen in the language of the Hebrew Scriptures, in which the word *shalom* is used to describe the ideal state in which the community should function.[15] It meant much more than absence of conflict; it signified completeness, fulfillment, wholeness—the existence of right relationships among individuals, the community and God.[16] Crime was understood to break *shalom*, destroying right relationships within a community and creating harmful ones. Restitution formed an essential part of the restoration process, but restitution was not an end in itself. This is suggested by the Hebrew word for "restitution," *shillum*, which comes from the same root as *shalom* and likewise implies the reestablishment of community peace. Along

---

[11] B.C.E. and C.E. replace B.C. and A.D., respectively. B.C.E. stands for "Before Common Era" and C.E. stands for "Common Era."

[12] Daniel W. Van Ness, "Restorative Justice," in Burt Galaway and Joe Hudson, eds., *Criminal Justice, Restitution, and Reconciliation* (Newbury Park, CA: Sage Publications, 1990).

[13] Hoebel, *supra* note 10, at 279.

[14] Van Ness, *supra* note 12, at 9.

[15] We distinguish *shalom* from the irrational belief that the world is basically a safe and just place in which to live. Psychologist Melvin Lerner has concluded that humans need to believe that people basically get what they deserve, and that the world is a just and safe place to live, even when events suggest otherwise. This self-delusion, Lerner argues, is necessary in order for people to function in their daily lives. Melvin J. Lerner, *The Belief in a Just World: A Fundamental Delusion* (New York: Plenum Press, 1980), 11-15. But the Hebrew word *shalom* does not imply a delusional belief that all is well. To hold healing and *shalom* as goals for society's response to crime is to recognize that hurt and injustice do exist, and that they must be healed and rectified.

[16] G. Lloyd Carr, "Shalom," in R.L. Harris et al., eds., *Theological Wordbook of the Old Testament* (Chicago: Moody Press, 1980), 931.

with restitution came the notion of vindication of the victim and the law itself. This concept was embodied in another word derived from the same root as *shalom* and *shillum*: *shillem*. *Shillem* can be translated as "retribution" or "recompense," not in the sense of revenge (that word comes from an entirely different root) but in the sense of satisfaction or vindication.[17] In short, the purpose of the justice process was, through vindication and reparation, to restore a community that had been sundered by crime.

This view of justice is not confined to the distant past. Many precolonial African societies aimed less at punishing criminal offenders than at resolving the consequences to their victims. Sanctions were compensatory rather than punitive, intended to restore victims to their previous position.[18] Current Japanese experience demonstrates a similar emphasis on compensation to the victim and restoration of community peace.[19] The approach (as we will see later) emphasizes a process that has been referred to as "confession, repentance and absolution."[20] Indigenous populations in North America, New Zealand, Australia and elsewhere are experimenting with ways in which their traditional approaches to crime, which are restorative in intent, may exist in the context of the dominant Western legal system.[21]

A Shift in Thinking

For all of its tradition, the restorative approach to criminal justice is unfamiliar to most of us today. For common law jurisdictions, the Norman invasion of Britain marked a turning point away from this understanding of crime. William the Conqueror and his succes-

---

[17] How is it that a root word meaning "wholeness and unity, a restored relationship" could produce derivatives with such varied meanings in the Hebrew Scriptures? "The apparent diversity of meanings . . . can be accounted for in terms of the concept of *peace being restored through payment* (of tribute to a conqueror, Joshua 10:1), *restitution* (to one wronged, Exodus 21:36), or *simple payment and completion* (of a business transaction, II Kings 4:7). The payment of a vow (Psalm 50:14) completes an agreement so that both parties are in a state of *shalom*. Closely linked with this concept is the eschatological motif in some uses of the term. *Recompense for sin, either national or personal, must be given. Once that obligation has been met, wholeness is restored* (Isaiah 60:20, Joel 2:25)." Carr, *supra* note 16, at 931 (emphasis added).

[18] Daniel D.N. Nsereko, "Compensating Victims of Crime in Botswana," paper presented at the Society for the Reform of Criminal Law Conference on "Reform of Sentencing, Parole, and Early Release," Ottawa, Ontario, Canada, Aug. 1-4, 1988.

[19] *See, e.g.,* Daniel H. Foote, "The Benevolent Paternalism of Japanese Criminal Justice," *Cal. L. Rev.* 80 (1992): 317.

[20] John O. Haley, "Confession, Repentance, and Absolution," in Martin Wright and Burt Galaway, eds., *Mediation and Criminal Justice: Victims, Offenders, and Community* (Newbury Park, CA: Sage Publications, 1989), 195.

[21] Carol LaPrairie, "Conferencing in Aboriginal Communities in Canada: Finding Middle Ground in Criminal Justice," *Crim. L. F.* 6 (1995): 576. D.B. Moore and T.A. O'Connell, "Family Conferencing in Wagga Wagga: A Communitarian Model of Justice," in Christine Alder and Joy Wundersitz, eds., *Family Conferencing and Juvenile Justice: The Way Forward or Misplaced Optimism?* (Canberra: Australian Institute of Criminology, 1994); Robert Yazzie, "'Life Comes From It': Navajo Justice Concepts," *N.M. L. Rev.* 24 (1994): 175.

sors found the legal process an effective tool for establishing the pre-eminence of the king over the church in secular matters, and in replacing local systems of dispute resolution.[22] The *Leges Henrici Primi*, written early in the twelfth century, asserted royal jurisdiction over offenses such as theft punishable by death, counterfeiting, arson, premeditated assault, robbery, rape, abduction and "breach of the king's peace given by his hand or writ."[23] Breach of the king's peace gave the royal house an extensive claim to jurisdiction:

> [N]owadays we do not easily conceive how the peace which lawful men ought to keep can be any other than the Queen's or the commonwealth's. But the King's justice . . . was at first not ordinary but exceptional, and his power was called to aid only when other means had failed. . . . Gradually the privileges of the King's house were extended to the precincts of his court, to the army, to the regular meetings of the shire and hundred, and to the great roads. Also the King might grant special personal protection to his officers and followers; and these two kinds of privilege spread until they coalesced and covered the whole ground.[24]

Thus, the king became the paramount crime victim, sustaining legally acknowledged (albeit symbolic) injuries. Over time, the actual victim was ousted from any meaningful place in the justice process, illustrated by the redirection of reparation from the victim in the form of restitution to the king in the form of fines.[25] A new model of crime emerged, with the government and the offender as the sole parties. This model brought with it a new purpose as well: rather than centering on making the victim whole, the system focused on upholding the authority of the state. Instead of repairing the past harm, criminal justice became future-oriented, attempting to make offenders and potential offenders law-abiding. It is not surprising, then, that restitution, which is both past-oriented and victim-centered, was eventually abandoned, with fines, corporal punishment and the death sentence taking its place as the central response to wrongdoing.[26] Whipping, using the stocks, branding and other forms

---

[22] Harold J. Berman, *Law and Revolution: The Formation of the Western Legal Tradition* (Cambridge: Harvard University Press, 1983), 255-256.

[23] *Leges Henrici Primi* 109 (L.J. Downer ed., & trans., 1972).

[24] Frederick Pollock, "English Law Before the Norman Conquest," *Law Q. Rev.* 14 (1898): 291, 301.

[25] "In the hands of the royal administrators after the Conquest [the King's peace] proved a dynamic concept, and, as Maitland once expressed it, eventually the king's peace swallowed up the peace of everyone else. . . . Already by the time of Bracton, in the thirteenth century, it has become common form to charge an accused in the following terms: 'Whereas the said B was in the peace of God and of our lord the king, thus came the said N, feloniously as a felon,' etc." George W. Keeton, *The Norman Conquest and the Common Law* (New York: Barnes and Noble, 1966), 175.

[26] For a detailed history of the use of corporal and other punishments, see Norval Morris and David Rothman, eds., *The Oxford History of the Prison: The Practice of Punishment in Western Society* (New York: Oxford University Press, 1995).

of public retribution not only inflicted physical pain on offenders but served to humiliate them as well.[27]

Partially in reaction to this increasingly brutal treatment of offenders, reformers began to call for a new approach to the punishment of offenders. In the early decades of the United States' existence, these reformers convinced policymakers to implement a new rehabilitative model of sentencing. With this model emerged an institution that, while novel at that time, has become a symbol of the criminal justice system itself: the prison. Prior to 1790, prisons were almost exclusively used to hold offenders until trial or sentencing, or to enforce labor while a person worked off debts.[28] The Quakers in Philadelphia, aghast at the cruelty of contemporary punishments and jail conditions, and stirred by the belief that criminals were the products of bad moral environment, succeeded in persuading local officials to turn the Walnut Street Jail into what they called a "penitentiary" or place of penitence. As expressed in the 1787 preamble to the constitution of the Philadelphia Society for Alleviating the Miseries of Public Prisons, they sought not only to save offenders from dehumanizing punishment, but also to rehabilitate them.

> When we consider that the obligations of benevolence, which are founded on the precepts of the example of the author of Christianity, are not canceled by the follies or crimes of our fellow creatures . . . it becomes us to extend our compassion to that part of mankind, who are the subjects of these miseries. By the aids of humanity, their undue and illegal sufferings may be prevented . . . and such degrees and modes of punishment may be discovered and suggested, as may, instead of continuing habits of vice, become the means of restoring our fellow creatures to virtue and happiness.[29]

Prisoners at this penitentiary were isolated in individual cells, away from the immoral elements of society. They were given a Bible and time to contemplate it. Yet by the early 1800s, prisons were already

---

[27] John Braithwaite, who has argued for the restoration of what he calls "reintegrative shaming" to the criminal justice system, contends that the humiliation of public punishment which characterized that period was counterproductive. "Public exhibitions of state acts of brutality against other human beings perhaps did as much to legitimate brutality as it did to delegitimate crime. In differential association terms, they involved the state in communicating definitions favorable to violence. More critically to the present analysis, most of the shaming was stigmatizing rather than reintegrative. . . ." John Braithwaite, *Crime, Shame, and Reintegration* (New York: Cambridge University Press, 1989), 59. See discussion in Chapter Seven.

[28] Morris and Rothman, *supra* note 26.

[29] Blake McKelvey, *American Prisons: A History of Good Intentions* (Montclair, NJ: Patterson Smith, 1977), 7. Cullen and Gilbert, *supra* note 2, maintain that the intent of the Walnut Street Jail reformers was punishment, not rehabilitation. But we suggest that their intent was for the structure of the punishment to lead to reformed character and lives—in effect, rehabilitation.

being denounced. "Our state prisons as presently constituted are grand demoralizers of our people," concluded a New York lawyer.[30] This, however, did not discourage prison advocates; if isolation did not achieve the goals of repentance and rehabilitation, then perhaps other measures would work. Succeeding generations of prison reformers moved from theories of repentance to those of hard work, then of discipline and training, and eventually of medical and psychological treatment.[31] Each generation of reformers was disappointed as many prisoners proved to be unchanged by their particular model of rehabilitation. As a result of this history, since the mid-1970s, many criminal justice policymakers have concluded that rehabilitation is simply an impossible goal, and that pursuing it is a failed policy.

What Went Wrong?

Commentators have offered a variety of practical and conceptual explanations for why rehabilitative programs have not met the expectations of their advocates.[32] The practical explanations have ranged from inadequate funding to improper screening of participants. A challenge to the conceptual underpinnings of the model has been that it reflected an overly optimistic view of human nature— that people are morally good and make bad choices only because of their circumstances. The rehabilitation model was predicated on an assumption that if an individual's social environment improves or psyche becomes healthy, that person will naturally make the right choices. Further, it assumed that the state could identify those deficiencies and force the individual to receive treatment that would be effective even though compelled.

Unfortunately, contemporary rejection of the rehabilitation model did not lead to rejection of the perspective that crime is simply an offense against the state. Instead, it has prompted states to impose increasingly repressive and punitive sanctions against those who commit crimes, with the claimed goals of punishing and incapacitating criminals. This wave of "get tough" measures has been no more successful than the rehabilitation model in controlling crime, and by contributing to prison overcrowding it may be contributing to the breakdown of the criminal justice system itself.

---

[30] Morris and Rothman, *supra* note 26, at 115.
[31] Cullen and Gilbert, *supra* note 2.
[32] Ibid.

Changing the goal of the justice system from rehabilitation to retribution and incapacitation has not solved the crisis in criminal justice; nor will it, because a major cause of the crisis is the way we think about criminal justice. We have constructed elaborate institutions under this pattern of thinking, and because the pattern itself is wrong, we have given them impossible tasks. It is no wonder they fail. Crime is not merely an offense against the state, and justice is more than punishment and incapacitation. To find lasting solutions we will have to rebuild the criminal justice system from its foundations. The first step will be to construct a new pattern of thinking about crime and justice.

Chapter Two

Explorers:

The Search for a New Pattern of Thinking

Pre-Copernican astronomers were right that the sun and planets move through the heavens, but they were wrong about one fundamental premise: the Earth is *not* the stationary center of creation; it too swirls through the universe. Likewise, current criminal justice policy is built on the partial truth that crime involves lawbreaking. That policy's flaw is that it ignores another critical dimension of crime—that it causes injuries to victims, the community and even to offenders. As a consequence, criminal justice policy is preoccupied with maintaining security—public order—while trying to balance the offender's rights and the government's power.[1] These are, of course, important concerns, but order and fairness would be only *part* of society's response to crime if its overall purpose included healing the injuries caused by crime.

What other responses might there be? Over the past decades a number of them have emerged. Some grew out of critiques of the

---

[1] Herbert Packer has described these as the crime control and due process models of criminal justice. He has maintained that all of the practices of the criminal justice system lie along a continuum with crime control values at one end and due process values at the other. Herbert Packer, *The Limits of the Criminal Sanction* (Stanford: Stanford University Press, 1968), 153. Although his universal claims have been criticized (*see, e.g.,* John Griffiths, "Ideology in Criminal Procedure or A Third 'Model' of the Criminal Process," *Yale L.J.* 79 (1970): 359; Peter Arenella, "Rethinking the Functions of Criminal Procedure: The Warren and Burger Courts' Competing Ideologies," *Geo. L.J.* 72 (1883): 185, 209-228; and Mirjan Damaska, "Evidentiary Barriers to Conviction and Two Models of Criminal Procedure: A Comparative Study," *U. Pa. L. Rev.* 121 (1973): 506, 574-577), the crime control/due process dichotomy is a useful expression of the conventional policy options available under the pattern of thinking that crime is lawbreaking.

current system; others out of political, philosophical and theological concerns. While there is diversity in their underlying premises as well as in their conclusions, they also show a surprising agreement on certain fundamental premises, as we will see in the next chapter. Together they form streams of thought that contribute to restorative justice theory. It is our intention in this chapter to identify those sources. This is an undertaking that we can approach only in a sketchy fashion; a more comprehensive story of the development of restorative justice—one that suggests how and why these influences intersected—must wait for another time.

We will begin by describing a series of movements whose critiques have been key to the development of the restorative critique. Then we will sample recent attempts to articulate restorative justice theory.

Movements

A number of movements predate and have contributed to restorative justice theory. In some instances, such as the reconciliation/conferencing movements, they have flowed fairly directly into the restorative justice movement. In many others, they have not necessarily converged, although there are many points of intersection. We do not claim to offer a complete description of any of these movements, nor to include all of their proponents.[2] We will attempt, however, to give a sufficient outline so that it will be clear in what ways the movements have contributed to restorative justice theory.

Informal Justice

This movement emerged in the 1970s with the recognition by legal anthropologists that legal structures and ways of thinking about law are specific to particular times and places, and that in virtually all societies justice is pursued in both formal and informal proceedings.[3] Because the legal system confronted a growing crisis of confidence in the legitimacy of formal legal structures, a series of proposals followed for informal alternatives, with "an emphasis on

---

[2] For another attempt at this analysis, *see* Gordon Bazemore and Mark Umbreit, "Rethinking the Sanctioning Function in Juvenile Court: Retributive or Restorative Responses to Youth Crime," *Crime & Delinq.* 41(3) (1995): 296-316.

[3] Roger Matthews, "Reassessing Informal Justice," in Roger Matthews, ed., *Informal Justice?* (Newbury Park, CA: Sage Publications, 1988), 3. This book contains a good overview of the arguments for and against informal justice as an alternative to formal justice systems.

(a) increased participation, (b) more access to law, (c) deprofession-alization, decentralization and delegalization and (d) the minimiza-tion of stigmatization and coercion."[4] Two of the leading proponents of informal justice were Jerold S. Auerbach (whose *Justice Without Law?*[5] argues forcefully for the need to deprofessionalize the justice system) and Nils Christie.

Christie, a Norwegian, suggests in the 1977 article, "Conflict as Property" in *The British Journal of Criminology* that conflict is not in fact something to be "solved" but something to be possessed. The criminal justice system is an instance in which a victim's conflict is stolen by the state. This represents a real and a serious loss:

> This loss is first and foremost a loss in *opportunities for norm-clarification*. It is a loss of pedagogical possibilities. It is a loss of opportunities for a continuous discussion of what represents the law of the land. How wrong was the thief, how right was the victim? Lawyers are, as we say, trained into agreement on what is relevant in a case. But that means a trained incapacity in letting the parties decide what *they* think is relevant. It means that it is difficult to stage what we might call a political debate in the court.[6]

In his subsequent book on punishment, *Limits to Pain*, Christie shows the connection between this "theft" and the use of punish-ment. In criminal law, values are clarified by graduated punishment. "The state establishes its scale, the rank-order of values, through variation in the number of blows administered to the criminal, or through the number of months or years taken away from him."[7] Rather than being clarified through conversation among the partici-pants—the "owners" of the conflict—values are communicated by the state through the infliction of pain. He proposes participatory justice as a better response to crime, a response characterized by a process of direct communication between the owners of the conflict leading to compensation.[8]

Related to the informal justice movement have been studies and reflections on specific examples of customary or indigenous approaches to justice. Of particular interest to researchers have been

---

[4] Ibid., 4.

[5] Jerold S. Auerbach, *Justice Without Law?* (New York: Oxford University Press, 1983).

[6] Nils Christie, "Conflict as Property," *Brit. J. Criminology* 17(1) (1977): 1, 8.

[7] Nils Christie, *Limits to Pain* (Oslo-Bergen-Tromsø: Universitetsforlaget, 1981), 94.

[8] Ibid.

the procedures found in Native American views of justice,[9] African customary law[10] and the approaches found in the Pacific Islands.[11]

Restitution

The restitution movement grew out of the rediscovery in the 1960s that paying back the victim is a sensible sanction. Several rationales were offered for restitution, and these have significantly influenced the development and influence of this movement: (1) the rediscovery of the victim as the party harmed by criminal behavior, (2) the search for alternatives to more restrictive or intrusive sanctions such as imprisonment, (3) the expected rehabilitative value for the offender of paying the victim, (4) the relative ease of implementation, and (5) the anticipated reduction in vengeful and retributive sanctions that would come when the public observed the offender actively repairing the harm done.[12] Evaluations conducted in the 1970s and 1980s questioned whether restitution programs have lived up to all of those expectations.[13] Nonetheless, restitution appears to be increasingly ordered and collected.

---

[9] See, e.g., Robert Yazzie, "'Life Comes From It': Navajo Justice Concepts," N.M. L. Rev. 24 (1994): 175; Karl Llewellyn, "Anthropology of Criminal Guilt," Jurisprudence: Realism in Theory and Practice (Chicago: University of Chicago Press, 1962); Carol LaPrairie, "Conferencing in Aboriginal Communities in Canada: Finding Middle Ground in Criminal Justice?," Crim. L.F. 6 (1995): 576; The Church Council on Justice and Corrections, Satisfying Justice: Safe Community Options that Attempt to Repair Harm from Crime and Reduce the Use or Length of Imprisonment (Ottawa, Ontario: The Church Council on Justice and Corrections, 1996); John Pratt, "Colonization, Power and Silence: A History of Indigenous Justice in New Zealand Society," in Burt Galaway and Joe Hudson, eds., Restorative Justice: International Perspectives (Monsey, NY: Criminal Justice Press, 1996); Robert Yazzie and James W. Zion, "Navajo Restorative Justice: The Law of Equality and Justice," in Burt Galaway and Joe Hudson, eds., Restorative Justice: International Perspectives (Monsey, NY: Criminal Justice Press, 1996); Curt Taylor Griffiths and Ron Hamilton, "Sanctioning and Healing: Restorative Justice in Canadian Aboriginal Communities," in Burt Galaway and Joe Hudson, eds., Restorative Justice: International Perspectives (Monsey, NY: Criminal Justice Press, 1996); Barry Stuart, "Circle Sentencing: Turning Swords into Ploughshares," in Burt Galaway and Joe Hudson, eds., Restorative Justice: International Perspectives (Monsey, NY: Criminal Justice Press, 1996); and Marianne O. Nielsen, "A Comparison of Developmental Ideologies: Navajo Peacemaker Courts and Canadian Native Justice Committees," in Burt Galaway and Joe Hudson, eds., Restorative Justice: International Perspectives. (Monsey, NY: Criminal Justice Press, 1996).

[10] Daniel D.N. Nsereko, "Compensating Victims of Crime in Botswana," paper presented at the Society for the Reform of Criminal Law Conference on "Reform of Sentencing, Parole, and Early Release," Ottawa, Ontario, Canada, Aug. 1-4, 1988; Samuel O. Gyandoh, "Tinkering with the Criminal Justice System in Common Law Africa," Temp. L. Rev. 62 (1989): 1131.

[11] See, e.g., Jim Consedine, Restorative Justice: Healing the Effects of Crime (Lyttelton, NZ: Ploughshares Publications, 1995); Gabrielle Maxwell and Allison Morris, "The New Zealand Model of Family Group Conferences," in Christine Alder and Joy Wundersitz, eds., Family Conferencing and Juvenile Justice: The Way Forward or Misplaced Optimism? (Canberra: Australian Institute of Criminology, 1994).

[12] Elmar Weitkamp, "Can Restitution Serve as a Reasonable Alternative to Imprisonment? An Assessment of the Situation in the U.S.A.," in Heinz Messmer and Hans-Uwe Otto, eds., Restorative Justice on Trial, (Dordrecht, The Netherlands: Kluwer Academic Publishers, 1992), 82, 83. Other works on restitution include Alan T. Harland and Cathryn J. Rosen, "Impediments to the Recovery of Restitution by Crime Victims," Violence and Victims 5(2) (1990): 127, 132; Alan T. Harland, "Monetary Remedies for the Victims of Crime: Assessing the Role of the Criminal Courts," UCLA L. Rev. 30 (1982): 52; Margery Fry, "Justice For Victims," London Observer, 7 July 1957; Joe Hudson and Burt Galaway, eds., Restitution in Criminal Justice (Lexington, MA: D.C. Heath and Company, 1977); and Burt Galaway and Joe Hudson, eds., Criminal Justice, Restitution and Reconciliation (Monsey, NY: Criminal Justice Press, 1990).

[13] See, e.g., Joe Hudson and Burt Galaway, "Financial Restitution: Toward an Evaluable Program Model," Canadian J. of Criminology 31 (1989): 1-8.

One of the earliest and most consistent proponents of restitution was Stephen Schafer, who made a comprehensive and influential case for the historic precedence of restitutionary sanctions.[14] In his writings he describes the era of compensatory justice prior to development of centralized governments in Europe as the "golden age of the victim" because it was a time in which the victim's interests and freedom of action were given great deference.[15] He proposes that compensation could once again become a means of sanctioning offenders, either in conjunction with or as an alternative to imprisonment.

Charles F. Abel and Frank A. Marsh, in their 1984 book *Punishment and Restitution*,[16] argue that restitution offers an approach to punishment that is ethically, conceptually and practically superior to contemporary criminal justice. In their model, imprisonment would be used only as a last resort for offenders who pose a danger to the community, and those who were imprisoned would be given the opportunity and obligation to work for wages and to compensate the victim (and the state for the cost of their incarceration). Most offenders, however, would live outside prison under varying degrees of supervision as necessary, working and paying restitution.

Randy Barnett and John Hagel argue in *Assessing the Criminal*[17] that criminal law should be abolished and replaced with the civil law of torts. They suggest that restitution constitutes a new paradigm of justice, one that is preferable to criminal justice. Crime is defined by exploring the rights of the victim, not by examining the behavior of the offender. The rights of society are satisfied, they contend, when the rights of individual victims within it are vindicated through restitution.

The Victims' Movement

As we saw in the last chapter, until recent years the interests and needs of victims were ignored by modern criminal justice systems. The contemporary "rediscovery of crime victims" is the result of an accumulation of criticisms and reforms by individuals and groups who were frustrated and angry at being ignored.[18] The movement has focused on three broad thrusts: (1) increasing services to victims in

---

[14] Stephen Schafer, *Victimology: The Victim and His Criminal* (Reston, VA: Reston, 1968). *See also* Stephen Schafer, *Compensation and Restitution to Victims of Crime* (Montclair, NJ: Patterson Smith, 1970); Stephen Schafer, "Victim Compensation and Responsibility," *S. Cal. L. Rev.* 43 (1970): 55; and Stephen Schafer, "The Restitutive Concept of Punishment," in Joe Hudson and Burt Galaway, eds., *Considering the Victim* (Springfield, IL: Charles C Thomas, 1975).

[15] Ibid., 5.

[16] Charles F. Abel and Frank A. Marsh, *Punishment and Restitution: A Restitutionary Approach to Crime and the Criminal* (Westport: Greenwood Press, 1984).

[17] Randy E. Barnett and John Hagel, eds., *Assessing the Criminal: Restitution, Retribution, and the Legal Process,* (Cambridge, MA: Ballinger Publishing Co., 1977), 1, 15. See Chapter Six for a critique of this position.

[18] Andrew Karmen, *Crime Victims: An Introduction to Victimology* (Pacific Grove, CA: Brooks/Cole Publishing Company, 1990), 15-41.

the aftermath of the crime, (2) increasing the likelihood of financial reimbursement for the harm done, and (3) expanding victims' opportunities to intervene during the course of the criminal justice process.

Morton Bard and Dawn Sangrey, in *The Crime Victim's Book*,[19] address the range of needs that crime victims may confront, and give practical suggestions for how those needs might be met. It offers advice not only for crime victims, but for those who are close to them or who might serve them professionally as well. Albert Roberts subsequently surveyed victim services programs that had sprung up across the United States, often affiliated with various departments in the law enforcement system and funded by state or federal grants. He describes and evaluates these programs in *Helping Crime Victims*.[20]

Robert Elias has demonstrated that the harm resulting from victimization can be extensive. Not only can there be direct and indirect financial losses, but there may be physical injury as well.[21] Furthermore, there are psychological harms: personal guilt, blame and pain, and individual and public fear.[22] In addition are the resultant costs of prevention: financial expenditures for insurance and security, often accompanied by psychological and behavioral costs in the form of changed patterns, increased precautions, avoidance and protection. When these costs still fail to offer security, the result might be futility.[23] Elias demonstrates that victim compensation programs (through which governments provide financial assistance to crime victims) generally fail to adequately address these losses.[24] As we have seen, the restitution movement offered an additional remedy—one that required reimbursement by the offender.

The third major strand in the victims' movement has worked to increase the opportunities for victim participation in the criminal justice process. William McDonald edited a collection of articles in 1976 that provides a comprehensive survey of the opportunities for, and the barriers to, victim participation during that process.[25] Beginning with the victim's decision regarding whether to call the police and concluding with issues related to the victim and correctional policy, McDonald and his colleagues describe the alienating effects on victims of an essentially offender-oriented system.

---

[19] This was subsequently re-issued as Morton Bard and Dawn Sangrey, *The Crime Victim's Book*, 2d ed. (Secaucus, NJ: Citadel Press, 1986).

[20] Albert R. Roberts, *Helping Crime Victims: Research, Policy, and Practice* (Newbury Park, CA: Sage Publications, 1990).

[21] Robert Elias, *The Politics of Victimization: Victims, Victimology and Human Rights* (New York: Oxford University Press, 1986), 108-110.

[22] Ibid., 116-118.

[23] Ibid., 111-112, 124-128

[24] Robert Elias, *Victims of the System: Crime Victims and Compensation in American Politics and Criminal Justice* (New Brunswick, NJ: Transaction Books, 1983).

[25] William F. McDonald, ed., *Criminal Justice and the Victim* (Beverly Hills, CA: Sage Publications, 1976).

Reconciliation / Conferencing [26]

This movement has had two major strands. The first, victim-offender reconciliation/mediation, brings together victims and offenders to discuss their crime and the harm that resulted from it. Then, with the aid of a mediator/facilitator, they formulate a course of future action that permits the offender to "make things right."[27] One of the earliest and most prolific writers on victim-offender reconciliation/mediation is Mark Umbreit. Building on his work with early programs in the United States, and applying social science research methodologies, he has produced a series of articles and books explaining and evaluating victim-offender reconciliation/mediation,[28] including the use of such programs in cases of violent crime.[29] He has demonstrated that victims and offenders are generally more satisfied when they have used victim-offender reconciliation/mediation than when their cases are processed routinely through the courts.[30] He has also shown that these cases can be used in cases of violent and serious crime, provided that appropriate screening and preparation are used.[31]

Two other early practitioners of victim-offender reconciliation/mediation were Howard Zehr and Ron Claassen. Both are deeply involved in the Mennonite Church, and each came to these programs as a result of their work within that faith context. They argue that church-based programs offer greater potential than others for building toward genuine healing. Claassen, in particular, has for the last 15 years run a victim-offender reconciliation program that is supported entirely by local churches. Its finances and volunteer mediators are contributed from local churches, although its case referrals come through the criminal justice system. Claassen and Zehr argue that this community base strengthens the vitality of victim-offender reconciliation/mediation, and that it is preferable

---

[26] *See* Chapter 6 for a discussion concerning the use of "reconciliation," "mediation" and "dialogue" to describe these programs.

[27] For a more detailed description, *see* Chapter 6.

[28] *See, e.g.,* Mark Umbreit, *Crime and Reconciliation: Creative Options for Victims and Offenders* (Nashville: Abingdon Press, 1985); Mark Umbreit et al., *Victim Meets Offender: The Impact of Restorative Justice and Mediation* (Monsey, NY: Criminal Justice Press, 1994); Mark Umbreit, *Mediating Interpersonal Conflicts: A Pathway to Peace* (West Concord, MN: CPI Publishing, 1995); Mark Umbreit, "Restorative Justice Through Mediation: The Impact of Programs in Four Canadian Provinces," in Burt Galaway and Joe Hudson, eds., *Restorative Justice: International Perspectives* (Monsey, NY: Criminal Justice Press, 1996); Mark Umbreit, "Holding Juvenile Offenders Accountable: A Restorative Justice Perspective," *Juv. & Fam. Ct. J.* (Spring, 1995): 31-42; Mark Umbreit, "Mediating Victim-Offender Conflict: From Single-Site to Multi-Site Analysis in the U.S.," in Heinz Messmer and Hans-Uwe Otto, eds., *Restorative Justice on Trial* (Dordrecht, The Netherlands: Kluwer Academic Publishers, 1992); and Mark Umbreit, "The Meaning of Fairness to Burglary Victims," in Burt Galaway and Joe Hudson, eds., *Criminal Justice, Restitution and Reconciliation* (Monsey, NY: Criminal Justice Press, 1990).

[29] Mark Umbreit, "Victim-Offender Mediation with Violent Offenders," in Emilio Viano, ed., *The Victimology Handbook: Research Findings, Treatment, and Public Policy* (NY: Garland, 1990).

[30] Mark Umbreit, *Victim Meets Offender: The Impact of Restorative Justice and Mediation* (Monsey, NY: Criminal Justice Press, 1994).

[31] Umbreit, *supra* note 29.

(although it may be more work) to organize programs in this way rather than as a part of, or funded by, the criminal justice system.[32]

Victim-offender reconciliation/mediation programs started in North America, but have spread rapidly throughout the world. Evidence of this can be found in the literature describing the development and adaptation of these programs in Europe.[33] In the 1990s, a second branch of this movement has developed, one which grew out of the Maori tradition in New Zealand. Family group conferencing (FGC) differs from victim-offender reconciliation/mediation in several ways, but the most notable difference is that more people are included in the meetings called to deal with the crime: in addition to the victim and offender are family members and community representatives.[34] Christine Alder and Joy Wundersitz have edited a volume of papers presented at a seminar that brought together proponents and critics of family group conferencing.[35] The book follows roughly the organization of the conference. It begins with articles by program proponents, and describes the models developed in New Zealand and Australia. The second half of the book raises questions about those models from a variety of theoretical and practical perspectives. The book then concludes with an essay by John Braithwaite responding to some of the criticisms, in particular those that concern his theory of reintegrative shaming.[36]

Social Justice

A number of critiques of and proposals for change in the criminal justice system have emerged from persons and groups that, while not sharing a common perspective, have shared a common commitment to seeing their understanding of justice given practical application. These include members of various religious communities and proponents of the feminist movement.

We noted earlier that Quakers were leaders in the development of the penitentiary at the Walnut Street Jail. During the 1960s and 1970s, members of the Society of Friends began urging that the use

---

[32] Ron Claassen and Howard Zehr, *VORP Organizing: A Foundation in the Church* (Elkhart, IN: Mennonite Central Committee U.S. Office of Criminal Justice, 1989).

[33] *See, e.g.,* Martin Wright and Burt Galaway, eds., *Mediation and Criminal Justice: Victims, Offenders and Community* (London: Sage Publications, 1989); Heinz Messmer and Hans-Uwe Otto, eds., *Restorative Justice on Trial: Pitfalls and Potentials of Victim-Offender Mediation—International Research Perspectives* (Dordrecht, The Netherlands: Kluwer Academic Publishers, 1992); Burt Galaway and Joe Hudson, eds., *Restorative Justice: International Perspectives* (Monsey, NY: Criminal Justice Press, 1996).

[34] For a more detailed description, *see* Chapter 6.

[35] Christine Alder and Joy Wundersitz, eds., *Family Conferencing and Juvenile Justice: The Way Forward or Misplaced Optimism?* (Canberra: Australian Institute of Criminology, 1994).

[36] John Braithwaite, "Thinking Harder About Democratising Social Control," in Christine Alder and Joy Wundersitz, eds., *Family Conferencing and Juvenile Justice: The Way Forward or Misplaced Optimism?* (Canberra: Australian Institute of Criminology, 1994).

of prisons be significantly curtailed and that other responses to crime be adopted. In part this was due to abuses in prison, abuses that seemed inherent in the institution itself and consequently not amenable to reform. But this position also grew out of a belief that criminal justice could not be achieved in an unjust society. One influential expression of this concern is *Struggle for Justice,* a report presented to the American Friends Service Committee and published in 1971.[37]

Gerald Austin McHugh's *Christian Faith and Criminal Justice* suggests that current penal models in America grew out of a Medieval Christian view of sin and punishment, but argues that this is not the only expression that has emerged from the Christian faith. He argues that this faith also proclaims values of relationship, restoration, forgiveness, reconciliation and hope, and that those values, if applied to criminal justice policy, would bring very different structures from those now in place.[38] Similar biblical reflection has been carried on by members of the Mennonite Community in North America, resulting in a wealth of literature and programs on alternatives to current approaches.[39]

Drawing from his experience as a prisoner and then as an advocate of volunteer involvement within the correctional environment, Charles Colson has offered a critique from a different theological perspective. He argues for the importance of affirming personal responsibility,[40] and the consequent need to use restitution instead of imprisonment for offenders for whom incapacitation is unnecessary.[41] His colleague Daniel W. Van Ness, in *Crime and Its Victims,*[42] argues that biblical justice is highly concerned with the needs and rights of victims, as well as with the worth of offenders. He proposes a series of public policy implications growing out of this premise.[43]

Feminist scholar M. Kay Harris has argued for a fundamental restructuring of criminal justice to reflect feminist values—"that all people have equal value as human beings, that harmony and felicity

---

[37] G. Richard Bacon et al., *Struggle for Justice: A Report on Crime and Punishment in America* (New York: Hill & Wang, 1971).

[38] Gerald A. McHugh, *Christian Faith and Criminal Justice: Toward A Christian Response to Crime and Punishment* (New York: Paulist Press, 1978).

[39] *See, e.g.,* Wayne Northey, *Justice is Peacemaking: A Biblical Theology of Peacemaking in Response to Criminal Conflict* (Akron, PA: Mennonite Central Committee U.S. Office of Criminal Justice, 1992); and Howard Zehr, *Retributive Justice, Restorative Justice* (Akron, PA: Mennonite Central Committee U.S. Office of Criminal Justice, 1985).

[40] Charles W. Colson, "Towards an Understanding of the Origins of Crime" and "Towards an Understanding of Imprisonment and Rehabilitation," in John Stott and Nick Miller, eds., *Crime and the Responsible Community: A Christian Contribution to the Debate about Criminal Justice* (London: Hodder and Stoughton, 1980).

[41] Charles W. Colson and Daniel H. Benson, "Restitution as an Alternative to Imprisonment," *Det. C.L. Rev.* 2 (1980): 523-598.

[42] Daniel W. Van Ness, *Crime and Its Victims: What We Can Do* (Downers Grove, IL: InterVarsity Press, 1986).

[43] Colson and Van Ness also collaborated on Charles W. Colson and Daniel W. Van Ness, *Convicted: New Hope for Ending America's Crime Crisis* (Westchester, IL: Crossway Books, 1989).

are more important than power and possession, and that the personal is the political"[44]—in place of the currently expressed values of control and punishment. She argues that the preoccupation with rights in dispute resolution blinds parties to the need for a caring and interdependent response as well. A recognition of the broader dimensions of justice would increase awareness of the need and opportunity for participation by all parties in order to address the needs of all.

None of these movements alone has led to restorative justice theory, but all have influenced its development, if only because many who are now preoccupied with restorative justice came to it from one of those perspectives. Furthermore, although there is significant common ground between these movements, there are also notable differences. Nonetheless, as we shall see in the following pages, much in restorative justice theory has been drawn from its predecessors.

The Term "Restorative Justice"

The term "restorative justice" was probably coined by Albert Eglash in a 1977 article in which he suggests that there are three types of criminal justice: (1) retributive justice based on punishment, (2) distributive justice based on therapeutic treatment of offenders, and (3) restorative justice based on restitution. Both the punishment and treatment models, he notes, focus on the actions of offenders, deny victim participation in the justice process and require merely passive participation by the offender. Restorative justice, on the other hand, focuses on the harmful effects of offenders' actions and actively involves victims and offenders in the process of reparation and rehabilitation.[45]

A number of persons have adopted the term "restorative justice," but have given it somewhat different meanings. Howard Zehr analogizes to a camera lens and suggests that there are two alternative lenses: retributive justice and restorative justice. Here is how he describes restorative justice: "Crime is a violation of people and relationships. It creates obligations to make things right. Justice involves the victim, the offender, and the community in a search for solutions which promote repair, reconciliation, and reassurance."[46] Wesley Cragg describes restorative justice as a process: "resolving conflicts

---

[44] M. Kay Harris, "Moving Into the New Millennium: Toward a Feminist Vision of Justice," *The Prison Journal* 67/2 (1987): 27-38.

[45] Albert Eglash, "Beyond Restitution: Creative Restitution," in Joe Hudson and Burt Galaway, eds., *Restitution in Criminal Justice* (Lexington, MA: D.C. Heath and Company, 1977), 91, 92.

[46] Howard Zehr, *Changing Lenses: A New Focus for Crime and Justice* (Scottsdale, PA: Herald Press, 1990), 181.

in a manner that reduces recourse to the justified use of force."[47] Martin Wright adds that the new model is one "in which the response to crime would be, not to add to the harm caused, by imposing further harm on the offender, but to do as much as possible to restore the situation. The community offers aid to the victim; the offender is held accountable and required to make reparation. Attention would be given not only to the *outcome*, but also to evolving a *process* that respected the feelings and humanity of both the victim and the offender."[48]

Others have chosen to use different terms. Ruth Morris speaks of "transformative justice," emphasizing that crime is not simply a violation of people and relationships, it also offers an opportunity for a transformation of those people and relationships that can deal with the causes of crime, and in that way, increase safety in the community.[49] Jonathan Burnside and Nicola Baker have used the term "relational justice," highlighting the importance of thinking of crime's relational (and not simply its legal) dimensions.[50] Marlene Young uses the term "restorative community justice" to stress both the importance of community involvement and the value and potency of community action in crime prevention.[51] Although a good case can be made for the use of each of these names, we will follow what seems to have become convention and refer to this movement as "restorative justice."

Explorers of Restorative Justice Theory

There is already a significant body of literature concerning restorative justice.[52] The following overview of books and articles gives a sketch of the approaches being taken in exploring this topic. We begin with Howard Zehr's *Changing Lenses*.[53]

---

[47] Wesley Cragg, *The Practice of Punishment: Towards a Theory of Restorative Justice* (New York: Routledge, 1992).

[48] Martin Wright, *Justice for Victims and Offenders* (Philadelphia: Open University Press, 1991), 112.

[49] Ruth Morris, *A Practical Path to Transformative Justice* (Toronto: Rittenhouse, 1994).

[50] Jonathan Burnside and Nicola Baker, eds., *Relational Justice: Repairing the Breach* (Winchester, UK: Waterside Press, 1994). This name was drawn from the Relational Movement, defined in Michael Schluter and David Lee, *The R Factor* (London: Hodder and Stoughton, 1993).

[51] Marlene A. Young, *Restorative Community Justice: A Call to Action* (Washington, DC: National Organization for Victim Assistance, 1995).

[52] A number of these are cited in this book and listed in the bibliography. Several other sources for bibliographic information on restorative justice include the National Criminal Justice Reference Service, Reference Department, Box 600, Rockville, MD 20849-6000 (Phone: 800/851-3420) and the Working Party on Restorative Justice of the United Nations Alliance of NGOs on Crime Prevention and Criminal Justice which has compiled an extensive bibliography of works on the subject.

[53] Zehr, *supra* note 46.

Zehr is director of the Mennonite Central Committee U.S. Office of Criminal Justice. To many he is the "grandfather" of restorative justice; he was certainly one of the first articulators of restorative justice theory. His interest developed during his work with victim-offender reconciliation programs, and has found expression in a number of articles as well as this book. In it he consolidates and advances his critique of criminal justice as failing to meet the needs of victims or offenders. He suggests that the current criminal justice "lens" is the retributive model, which views crime as lawbreaking and justice as allocating blame and punishment. He contrasts that with restorative justice, which views crime as a violation of people and relationships, which in turn leads to obligations to "make things right," and views justice as a process in which all the parties search for reparative, reconciling and reassuring solutions.[54]

Virginia Mackey has prepared an evocative "discussion paper" on restorative justice for the Criminal Justice Program of the Presbyterian Church (USA).[55] This document is intended to facilitate conversation within that faith community on the problems of current approaches to crime and on biblically reflective alternatives. Using Fay Honey Knopp's terminology, it proposes a "Community Safety/Restorative Model"[56] predicated on six principles: (1) that safety should be the primary consideration of the community; (2) that offenders should be held responsible and accountable for their behavior and the resulting harm; (3) that victims and communities harmed by crime need restoration; (4) that the underlying conflicts that led to the harm should be resolved if possible; (5) that there must be a continuum of service or treatment options available; and (6) that there must be a coordinated and cooperative system in place that incorporates both public and private resources.

Martin Wright, drawing from experience as both a victim and offender advocate, suggests in *Justice for Victims and Offenders*[57] that criminal justice can indeed be restorative rather than retributive. Agreeing with Christie that crime is conflict, he argues that the exclusion of victims from the process could be remedied in a restorative justice approach to crime. This would entail expanded use of compensation, restitution and mediation processes to permit greater participation by both victim and offender. He suggests that such a model might be constructed by creating two departments. The first, responsible for crime prevention, would emphasize deterrence through enforcement (which is preventive in nature, as opposed to the reac-

---

[54] Ibid., 181.

[55] Virginia Mackey, *Restorative Justice: Toward Nonviolence* (Louisville, KY: Presbyterian Justice Program, 1990).

[56] Ibid., 41-42.

[57] Wright, *supra* note 48.

tive and largely ineffective deterrence through punishment). The second department would be responsible for a just response to crimes when they do occur. This would include victim support, mediation and reparation, as well as courts that emphasize restitution.[58]

With the appearance of Wesley Cragg's *The Practice of Punishment*,[59] the discussion of restorative justice took a more philosophical turn. Cragg, a philosopher and a long-time volunteer with a prisoner advocacy and prison reform organization, revisits foundational issues concerning the role and use of punishment. He criticizes traditional justifications for punishment, but insists on the importance of formal processes in which conflict can be resolved. These formal processes may provide a framework for informal resolution and for offender acceptance of responsibility. Formal justice, in his view, need not be antithetical to virtues such as forgiveness, compassion, mercy and understanding;[60] what is antithetical is an insistence on punishment whose sole justification is to cause suffering.[61]

The potential conflict between the values of the current justice system (proportionality and due process, for example) and those of restorative justice have been discussed by several writers. Responding first to reservations about restorative justice raised by Andrew Ashworth,[62] and then to a book by Andrew von Hirsch,[63] Daniel W. Van Ness has suggested that while proponents of desert (or just deserts) theory have raised concerns about the likelihood that restorative justice will cause unwarranted disparity in sentencing, it need not necessarily do that.[64] Furthermore, the restorative justice concern with addressing the harm caused by crime may be a point of connection for desert theorists in linking crimes and punishments.[65] Van Ness has also argued that restorative justice provides a theoretical framework under which otherwise conflicting human rights proclamations may be reconciled.[66] Gordon Bazemore and Mark Umbreit also address these concerns in their argument for restorative justice as a more suitable theory of sentencing than retribution,[67] as

---

[58] Ibid., 114-117.

[59] *Cragg,* supra note 47.

[60] Ibid., 216.

[61] Ibid., 213.

[62] Andrew Ashworth, "Some Doubts about Restorative Justice," *Crim. L.F.* 4/2: (1993): 277.

[63] Andrew von Hirsch, *Censure and Sanctions* (London: Clarendon Press, 1993).

[64] Daniel W. Van Ness, "New Wine in Old Wineskins," *Crim. L.F.* 4/2 (1993). Many of the arguments in this article will be found in the next chapter.

[65] Daniel W. Van Ness, "Anchoring Just Deserts," *Crim. L.F.* 6/3 (1995).

[66] Daniel W. Van Ness, "Restorative Justice and International Human Rights," in Burt Galaway and Joe Hudson, eds., *Restorative Justice: International Perspectives* (Monsey, NY: Criminal Justice Press, 1996).

[67] Gordon Bazemore and Mark Umbreit, "Rethinking the Sanctioning Function in Juvenile Court: Retributive or Restorative Responses to Youth Crime," *Crime & Delinq.* 41(3) (1995): 296-316.

does Mark William Bakker in his exploration of the possibilities of victim-offender reconciliation/mediation in the legal context of the criminal justice system.[68]

An attempt to root restorative concepts within a larger conceptual framework was offered in a book edited by Jonathan Burnside and Nicola Baker, titled *Relational Justice*.[69] Noting the decline in the quality of relationships in Western cultures, these authors consider whether "relationalism" might offer an antidote to problems plaguing criminal justice. Although not specifically referring to restorative justice theory, the contributors write on victim-offender mediation[70] and family group conferences,[71] and suggest ways the activities of police, probation and prison authorities might be analyzed based on their capactiy to strengthen relationships.[72]

David Moore and others have also attempted to find theoretical frameworks within which to understand and analyze restorative justice. As noted earlier, reintegrative shaming is the term used by John Braithwaite for his theories concerning the causes and consequences of crime,[73] but it was not until a family group conferencing program was being organized in Wagga Wagga, a city in New South Wales, Australia, that reintegrative shaming and family conferencing were clearly and intentionally linked.[74] Moore has since proposed that the work of Silvan Tomkins and Donald Nathanson may offer a "psychology of reintegrative shaming,"[75] and further has analyzed this approach to crime and reintegration from the perspective of moral psychology/moral philosophy theory and political theory.[76] He concludes that reintegrative shaming offers a framework for theoretical analysis and evaluation of conferencing programs.

---

[68] Mark W. Bakker, "Repairing the Breach and Reconciling the Discordant: Mediation in the Criminal Justice System," *N.C. L. Rev.* 72 (1994): 1479.

[69] Jonathan Burnside and Nicola Baker, eds., *Relational Justice: Repairing the Breach* (Winchester, UK: Waterside Press, 1994).

[70] Nicola Baker, "Mediation, Reparation and Justice," in Jonathan Burnside and Nicola Baker, eds., *Relational Justice: Repairing the Breach* (Winchester, UK: Waterside Press, 1994).

[71] Fred McElrea, "Justice in the Community: The New Zealand Experience," in Jonathan Burnside and Nicola Baker, eds., *Relational Justice: Repairing the Breach* (Winchester, UK: Waterside Press, 1994).

[72] Andrew Coyle, "My Brother's Keeper: Relationships in Prison," in Jonathan Burnside and Nicola Baker, eds., *Relational Justice: Repairing the Breach* (Winchester, UK: Waterside Press, 1994); Roger Shaw, "Prisoners' Children: Symptoms of a Failing Justice System," in Jonathan Burnside and Nicola Baker, eds., *Relational Justice: Repairing the Breach* (Winchester, UK: Waterside Press, 1994); and David Faulkner, "Relational Justice: A Dynamic for Reform," in Jonathan Burnside and Nicola Baker, eds., *Relational Justice: Repairing the Breach* (Winchester, UK: Waterside Press, 1994).

[73] *See, e.g.,* John Braithwaite, *Crime, Shame, and Reintegration* (New York: Cambridge University Press, 1989). *See* Chapter 7 for a more extensive discussion of his theory.

[74] Christine Alder and Joy Wundersitz, "New Directions in Juvenile Justice Reform in Australia," in Christine Alder and Joy Wundersitz, eds., *Family Conferencing and Juvenile Justice: The Way Forward or Misplaced Optimism?* (Canberra: Australian Institute of Criminology, 1994). *See also* D.B. Moore and T.A. O'Connell, "Family Conferencing in Wagga Wagga: A Communitarian Model of Justice," in Christine Alder and Joy Wundersitz, eds., *Family Conferencing and Juvenile Justice: The Way Forward or Misplaced Optimism?* (Canberra: Australian Institute of Criminology, 1994).

[75] David Moore, "Evaluating Family Group Conferences," in David Biles and Sandra McKillop, eds., *Criminal Justice Planning and Coordination: Proceedings of a Conference Held 19-21—April 1993, Canberra* (1994).

[76] David Moore, "Shame, Forgiveness, and Juvenile Justice," *Criminal Just. Ethics* (Winter/Spring 1993): 3.

Although a number of writers have noted in passing that restorative justice principles have relevance in suggesting new strategies of crime prevention, one of the more comprehensive analyses of that aspect of criminal justice policy is offered by Marlene A. Young, Executive Director of the National Organization for Victim Assistance.[77] After proposing six principles of restorative community justice, she reviews a series of program elements that might make up a model of such a system. These include community policing, community prosecution, community courts and community corrections. The first, community policing, is becoming a relatively well-known approach to policing in which police actively build strong community bonds within the neighborhoods in which they function. The other three are similar: community prosecution involves a shift from reactive prosecution to proactive problem solving within the community; community courts increase the level of victim and community participation during adjudication; and community corrections offers communities and victims meaningful ways of participating in the correctional process.

Conclusion

Dissatisfaction with modern criminal justice has led to a number of reform movements. Some can be relatively easily incorporated into the system, but others are more difficult to reconcile. In combination, these movements suggest that there might be a new approach emerging. An increasing number of people are exploring that possibility.

---

[77] Young, *supra* note 51.

Chapter Three

Restorative Justice:

Justice That Promotes Healing

While restorative justice advocates have constructed a variety of models, there appear to be three fundamental propositions upon which most agree a restorative system should be constructed. First, restorative justice advocates view crime as more than simply law-breaking, an offense against governmental authority; crime is understood also to cause multiple injuries to victims, the community and even the offender.[1] Second, proponents argue that the criminal justice process should help repair those injuries.[2] Third, they protest the government's apparent monopoly over society's response to crime. Victims, offenders and their communities also must be involved at the earliest point and to the fullest extent possible. This suggests a cooperative effort, with government responsible for maintaining a basic framework of order, and the other parties responsible for restoring community peace and harmony. The work of government must be done in such a way that community building is enhanced, or at least not hampered.[3] Let us consider each of these premises in turn.

---

[1] See, e.g., Howard Zehr, *Changing Lenses: A New Focus for Crime and Justice* (Scottsdale, PA: Herald Press, 1990), 181-186.

[2] See, e.g., Martin Wright, *Justice for Victims and Offenders* (Philadelphia: Open University Press, 1991), 114-117 (proposing a system with the primary aim of restoring—or even improving—the victim's prior condition).

[3] The challenge to structure community-government cooperation is developed further in subsequent sections of this book.

Proposition 1. Justice requires that we work to restore victims, offenders and communities who have been injured by crime.

Crime leaves injured victims, communities and offenders in its wake, each harmed in different ways and experiencing correspondingly different needs. To promote healing, then, society must respond appropriately, considering the needs and responsibilities of each party.

Victims are those who have been harmed by the offender; this harm may be experienced either directly or secondarily. *Primary* victims, those against whom the crime was committed, may sustain physical injury, monetary loss and emotional suffering. These may be only momentary in duration or may last a lifetime. Because of the varying circumstances of victims, similar injuries may produce substantially different effects. In at least two respects, however, all victims have common needs: the need to regain control over their own lives, and the need for vindication of their rights. Being victimized is by definition an experience of powerlessness—the victim was unable to prevent the crime from occurring. As a result, primary victims often need help regaining an appropriate sense of control over their lives. As Justice Kelly discovered, victimization is also the experience of being wronged by another, bringing with it the need for vindication, for an authoritative and decisive denunciation of the wrong and exoneration of the one who was wronged. In addition to primary victims, *secondary* victims are indirectly harmed by the actions of offenders. These secondary victims can include the family members or neighbors of victims and offenders, and their injuries and needs must also be considered in constructing a restorative response to crime.

In order to consider the injuries and needs of the "community," we need to be clear about the meaning of that term. It is used in many different ways. We sometimes use it to refer to a community in geographic terms—the neighborhood in which we live, for example—a "local community." With the coming of increased mobility and transience, however, some have suggested that a more useful definition is nongeographic, emphasizing instead a "community of interest."[4] Such communities are identified by the willingness of their members "to take actions on behalf of the community not only that they would not take on their own behalf, but that are quite possibly

---

[4]   John Braithwaite discusses the relevance of expanding concepts of community to crime prevention strategies:

> This possibility comes even more to life if we consider the views of theorists who suggest that in modern urban societies the networks of individuals become less spatially localized, the locus of inter-dependency shifts from neighborhood to communities of interest based on workplace, occupation, and leisure activities. These alternative communities of interest might become alternative foci for communitarian crime control initiatives. Thus crime prevention associations might be set up in workplaces as in Japan; professional associations can be asked by government to set up monitoring and disciplinary committees to deal with fraud and malpractice in the profession; football associations can be asked to step in where the police have failed to solve problems of crowd hooliganism. John Braithwaite, *Crime, Shame, and Reintegration* (New York: Cambridge University Press, 1989): 172-173.

detrimental to their own interests."[5] They are characterized, then by a fundamental sense of duty, reciprocity and belonging.[6] Finally, the word is sometimes used loosely in everyday conversation as a synonym for society as a whole.[7] Each of these communities—the local community, the community of interest and society as a whole—may be injured by crime in different ways and degrees, but all will be affected in common ways as well: the sense of safety and confidence of their members is threatened, order within the community is threatened and (depending on the kind of crime) the common values of the community are challenged and perhaps eroded. However, the injury to the first two appear to be more direct than does the general injury to society as a whole. Consequently, when we use the term "community" we will be referring to local communities and communities of interest.[8]

Finally, the injuries of offenders must also be addressed. These injuries can be thought of as either *contributing* to the crime or *resulting* from the crime. By contributing injuries we mean those that existed prior to the crime and that prompted in some way the criminal conduct of the offender. For example, it has sometimes been argued that some victims of child abuse become abusers themselves, and that some substance abusers commit crimes to support their addictions. While these contributing injuries, these prior conditions, do not excuse the criminal choices of offenders, any attempt to bring healing to the parties touched by crime must address them.[9] Resulting injuries are those caused by the crime itself or its aftermath.

---

[5] Frederick Schauer, "Community, Citizenship, and the Search for National Identity," *Mich. L. Rev.* 84 (1986): 1504.

[6] *See* Ian R. Macneil, "Bureaucracy, Liberalism, and Community—American Style," *Nw. U. L. Rev.* 79 (1984-85): 900, 937.

[7] Macneil distinguishes between what we call the community of interest and society:
It is necessary to distinguish sharply community thus viewed from society as a whole, and particularly from any idea of Leviathan as embodying society. It is possible, of course, to lose one's self to—and gain community with—Leviathan; witness any popular war or mass movement, or indeed even the very modest loss of self in standing up during the abominably bad singing of the Star Spangled Banner at football games. But this kind of community, patriotism—particularly the sense of belonging—only rarely has any of the continuity, nonsporadic duration, completeness, and intensity of the smallest community, the family, or even of other small communities. And when it does, the world shakes. Moreover, in the modern state large scale community is necessarily a bureaucratic community, which has significant consequences both for the nature of community and for bureaucracy. (Ibid., 936-937.) (citations omitted)

[8] One of the important implications of the distinction between "community" and "victim" is that the community may not necessarily speak for the interests of the victim (*see* Chapter Eight of this book). But the opposite is also true: the victim does not necessarily speak for the community either. Kai-D. Bussmann, "Morality, Symbolism, and Criminal Law: Chances and Limits of Mediation Programs," in Heinz Messmer and Hans-Uwe Otto, eds., *Restorative Justice on Trial* (Dordrecht, The Netherlands: Kluwer Academic Publishers, 1992), 320.

[9] There are at least three occasions to address offenders' adverse circumstances. First, when those circumstances would prevent offenders from discharging their obligations (for example, they are unable to pay restitution because they are unemployed); second, when the circumstances directly contributed to the decision to commit the crime (for example, when the crime was committed to support a drug habit); and third, when the victim and offender have identified circumstances that they agree should be addressed, even though they did not contribute directly to the crime nor would they prevent completion of the sentence (for example, illiteracy).

These may be physical (as when the offender is wounded during the crime or incarcerated as a result of it), emotional (as when the offender experiences shame[10]) or moral and spiritual (since the offender has chosen to injure another). Further, offenders will likely be injured by the criminal justice system's response, which further alienates them from the community, strains family relationships, may lead to long-term employment disadvantages or prevent them from making amends to their victims.[11] Again, we are not arguing that offenders be relieved of accountability by recognizing "injuries." We are simply asserting that the injuries should be acknowledged and addressed in the response to crime. Unfortunately, there are no terms in the English language that appropriately describe this process. Consequently, we have adopted the admittedly awkward word "habilitation" to express this goal.

Proposition 2. Victims, offenders and communities should have opportunities for active involvement in the restorative justice process as early and as fully as possible.

Virtually every facet of our criminal justice system works to reduce victims, offenders and communities to passive participants. Because the current approach considers government to be the party harmed by crime, government's virtual monopoly over the apprehension, prosecution and punishment of offenders seems logical and legitimate.[12] Because of the legal presumption of innocence bestowed on all defendants, as well as the panoply of due process rights that are afforded them, defendants have few incentives to assume responsibility for their actions, and many incentives to remain passive while the government marshals its cases and their lawyers attempt to dismantle them. Because victims are not parties of interest in criminal cases, and rather are simply "piece[s] of evidence to be used by the state to obtain a conviction,"[13] they have very limited control over what occurs and no responsibility to initiate particular phases of the

---

[10] *See* Braithwaite, *supra* note 4 for an extended discussion of how shaming can be both positive and negative for offenders and the community.

[11] We do not suggest that the offender should not experience pain as a result of his or her treatment in the criminal justice system. Retribution is a part of society's response to an offender, although we will argue that the suffering caused to the offender should come as the offender is held accountable for helping repair the injuries caused by the criminal behavior (*see* Chapter Six). Our point here is that the justice system itself may create new wounds, and that these must be considered and addressed in building a restorative justice system.

[12] As we will see in Chapter Eight, this state monopoly has a relatively short history; as late as the mid-nineteenth century victims were the dominant party in the criminal justice system, responsible for initiating and prosecuting criminal cases.

[13] Juan Cardenas, "The Crime Victim in the Prosecutorial Process," *Harv. J.L. & Pub. Pol'y* 9 (1986): 371.

process.[14] Finally, the direct participation of members of the community is also very limited, consisting almost exclusively of service on grand or petit juries.[15]

Restorative justice, on the other hand, places a much higher value on direct involvement by the parties. For victims who have experienced powerlessness, the opportunity to participate restores an element of control.[16] For an offender who has harmed another, the voluntary assumption of responsibility is an important step in not only helping others who were hurt by the crime but also in building a prosocial value system.[17] Likewise, the efforts of community members to repair the injuries to victims and offenders serves to strengthen the community itself, and to reinforce community values of respect and compassion for others.[18]

Proposition 3. In promoting justice, government is responsible for preserving order and the community for establishing peace.

The term "order" is sometimes used as though it were a synonym for public safety; politicians speak, for example, of the need for "law and order" as a means of ending "crime in our streets." Safety, however, is a broader, more inclusive concept than order; to put it another way, both order and peace are required to secure public safety. As ancient Jewish law incorporated notions of "shalom," so today we must think of "peace" as a cooperative dynamic fostered from within a community. It requires a community's commitment to respect the rights of its members and to help resolve conflicts among them. It requires that those members respect community interests even when they conflict with their individual interests. It is in this context that communities and their members assume responsibility for addressing the underlying social, economic and moral factors that contribute to conflict within the community. "Order," on the other hand, is imposed on the community. It sets external limits on behav-

---

[14] While some states have retained vestiges of private prosecution on their law books (as we will see in Chapter Eight), Cardenas is correct in concluding:

In sum, the practice of allowing crime victims to hire private attorneys to participate in state prosecutions is a vestige of the English origins of American justice. English common law rested on the notion that the best way to bring a public wrong to satisfactory resolution was to vest in the family of the wronged individual the right to pursue its own concept of vengeance. Critics of private prosecution argued that a public prosecution system was necessary to regulate private revenge and to place a restraint upon the avenging party. Today, almost without exception, American jurisprudence has incorporated this view, holding that a private individual no longer has any right to prosecute another for a crime. (Cardenas, *supra* note 13, at 383.)

[15] The community does play a significant indirect role in that the criminal justice system is supported by taxes. Further, their community members have worked outside the criminal justice system to address various dimensions of crime prevention and response. Examples of this latter involvement include participation in crime watch programs and offender or victim assistance programs.

[16] *See* Chapter Eight.

[17] *See* Chapter Six.

[18] *See* Chapter Seven.

ior and enforces those limits to minimize overt conflict and to control potentially chaotic factors. Like peace, a just order is important in preserving safety, and government has both the power and mandate to establish such an order.

Both order and peace are appropriate means to achieving safety. However, as imposed order increases, personal freedom decreases; hence, peace will be sought in a society that values freedom. Security built primarily on governmentally imposed order is detrimental to a free society, as conditions in police states throughout the world demonstrate. On the other hand, when the community fails to foster peace, it may be necessary for the government to intervene and impose order. The American civil rights movement is an example of that kind of action. Desegregation of public schools was met with violent resistance on the community level, and National Guard troops had to enforce sufficient order for African-American children to enter the schools. The community, content with preserving the interests of the powerful by seeking to preserve the status quo, had failed in its role to seek peace for all members.

Of course, describing peace as the community's responsibility and order as government's is somewhat simplistic. Each plays a role in achieving peace and order, as we see when community members form "neighborhood watch" programs to prevent crime or when government programs address economic and social injustices that inhibit peace. We wish to emphasize a point that is often forgotten in the debate about crime and criminal justice: *safety comes as both government and community play their parts in upholding order and establishing peace.*

Restorative Justice: A Visual Model

A series of figures will illustrate some of the features of restorative justice theory. Figure 3.1 illustrates how contemporary criminal justice focuses exclusively on the offender and the government. The government seeks to establish order by enacting laws and punishing those who violate them. Because the government's power is so great, due process safeguards have been developed over the centuries to ensure fairness in how offenders are treated. One consequence is that the offender's posture is defensive (and often passive) during the proceedings, while the government plays the active role. Criminal courts are arenas of battle in which the government is pitted against offenders in a high-stakes contest to determine whether the law has been violated, and if so, what form of retribution should be imposed.

Figure 3.1

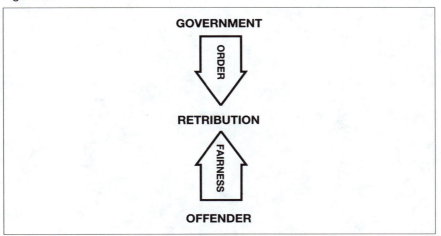

Figure 3.2 illustrates how restorative justice theory returns to the ancient view that there are actually four parties affected by crime: victim, offender, community and government. Restorative justice theory emphasizes that every crime involves specific victims and offenders, and that the goal of the criminal justice process should be to help them come to resolution (see Figure 3.3). This response to crime is largely neglected by the criminal justice system and left to the civil courts to address. Resolution requires that the rights of victims be vindicated by exoneration from responsibility for the injuries they have sustained as well as by receiving reparation for those injuries.

Figure 3.2

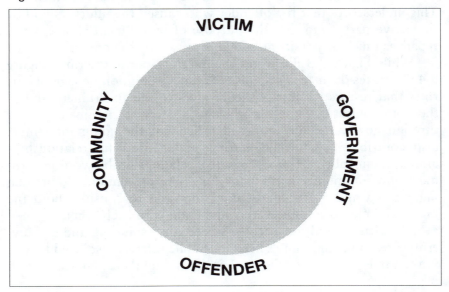

Figure 3.3

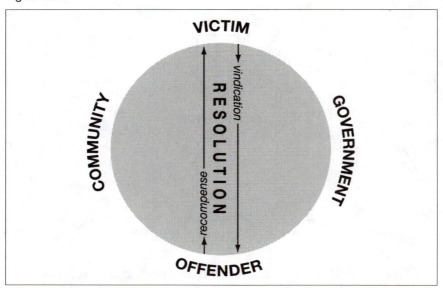

That is not all that is required. The offender must make recompense for there to be full resolution. Recompense and retribution are different. Retribution is defined as deserved punishment for evil done. The definition underscores an important aspect of a society's response to offenders, but it has two shortcomings. First, the active party, the punisher, is the government; the offender is merely a passive recipient of punishment. Second, punishment that does not help repair the injuries caused by crime simply creates new injuries; now both the victim and the offender are injured. "Recompense," on the other hand, is something given or done to make up for an injury. This underscores that the offender who caused the injury should be the active party, and that the purpose of punishment should be to repair as much as possible the injury caused by the crime.

While Figure 3.3 illustrates the micro response to crime, Figure 3.4 illustrates the macro response of crime prevention. It suggests the roles that restorative justice theory gives to the government and to the community in establishing safety. Safety is obtained in part through governmentally imposed order, but the community must also contribute by forming strong, stable, peaceful relationships among its members. This cooperative relationship between government and community is the basis for crime prevention. Combining Figures 3.3 and 3.4 reminds us of the need to consider both the micro and macro responses in conjunction with each other.

The victim's and the offender's need for resolution, and the government's and community's need for public safety, must be addressed in the same process (see Figure 3.5). This dual thrust contrasts with

Figure 3.4

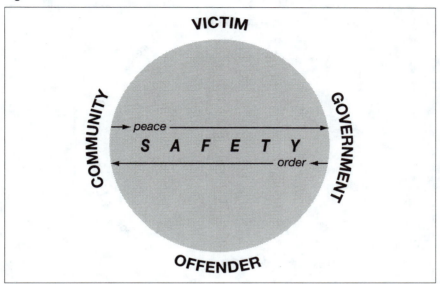

the separation of civil and criminal law in most modern jurisdictions, a separation that can force either/or choices for victims and the government in deciding whether and how to proceed against the offender. Figure 3.6 shows the restorative justice goals that govern the relationships of government with individual victims and offenders. The government helps reestablish order by ensuring that reparation takes place. It facilitates redress to victims through restitution and compensation while ensuring that offenders are treated with fairness.

Figure 3.5

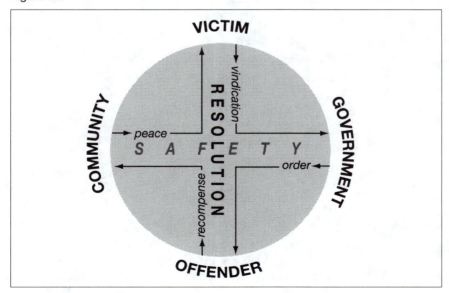

Figure 3.6

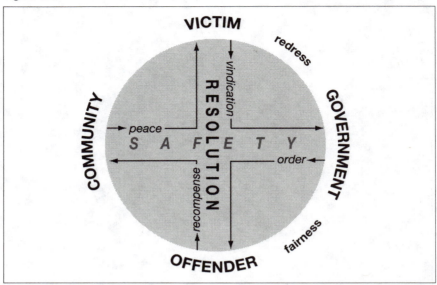

Figure 3.7 completes the circle by presenting a restorative justice perspective on the role of the community. The community seeks to restore peace between victims and offenders, and to reintegrate them fully into the community. For victims the goals can be expressed as healing; for offenders, as habilitation. The circular construction of the figures suggests the dynamic and dependent relationships that are necessary among the parties under restorative justice theory. Peace without order is as incomplete as recompense without vindication;

Figure 3.7

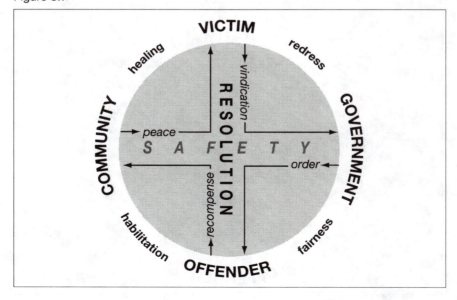

healing without redress is as inadequate as rehabilitation without fairness. A society cannot select certain features of the model and omit others; all are essential. That very comprehensiveness is a fundamental aspect of the restorative pattern of thinking about crime. Restorative justice theory seeks to address and balance the rights and responsibilities of victims, offenders, communities and the government.

Conclusion

Restorative justice, then, focuses on repairing the harm caused by crime and reducing the likelihood of future harm. It does this by encouraging offenders to take responsibility for their actions and for the harm they have caused, by providing redress for victims and by promoting reintegration of both within the community. This is done through a cooperative effort by communities and the government.

Restorative justice is different from current criminal justice practice in a number of ways. It views criminal acts more comprehensively; rather than limiting crime to lawbreaking, it recognizes that offenders harm victims, communities and even themselves. It involves more parties; rather than including only the government and the offender in key roles, it includes victims and communities as well. It measures success differently; rather than measuring how much punishment has been inflicted, it measures how much harm has been repaired or prevented. And finally, rather than leaving the problem of crime to the government alone, it recognizes the importance of community involvement and initiative in responding to and reducing crime.

Restorative justice responds to specific crimes by emphasizing both recovery of the victim through redress, vindication and healing, and recompense by the offender through reparation, fair treatment and habilitation. It seeks processes through which parties are able to discover the truth about what happened and the harms that resulted, to identify the injustices involved and to agree on future actions to repair those harms. It considers whether specific crimes are suggesting the need for new or revised strategies to prevent crime.

Restorative justice seeks to prevent crime by building on the strengths of community and the government. The community can build peace through strong, inclusive and righteous relationships; the government can bring order through fair, effective and parsimonious use of force. It emphasizes the need to repair past harms in order to prepare for the future. It seeks to reconcile offenders with those they have harmed. And it calls on communities to reintegrate victims and offenders.

Four Questions About Restorative Justice

1. **What is restorative justice?**

- It is a *different way of thinking* about crime and our response to it.
- It focuses on the *harm caused by crime*: repairing the harm done to victims and reducing future harm by preventing crime.
- It requires offenders to take *responsibility* for their actions and for the harm they have caused.
- It seeks *redress* for victims, *recompense* by offenders and *reintegration* of both within the community.
- It is achieved through a *cooperative effort* by communities and the government.

2. **How is restorative justice different from what we do now?**

- It *views criminal acts more comprehensively*: rather than defining crime only as lawbreaking, it recognizes that offenders harm victims, communities and even themselves.
- It *involves more parties*: rather than giving key roles only to government and the offender, it includes victims and communities as well.
- It *measures success differently*: rather than measuring how much punishment has been inflicted, it measures how much harm has been repaired or prevented.
- It recognizes the importance of *community involvement and initiative* in responding to and reducing crime, rather than leaving the problem of crime to the government alone.

3. **How does restorative justice respond to crime?**

- It emphasizes *victim recovery* through redress, vindication and healing.
- It emphasizes *recompense by the offender* through reparation, fair treatment and habilitation.
- It establishes processes through which parties are able to *discover the truth* about what happened and the harms that resulted, to *identify the injustices* involved and to *agree on future actions* to address those harms.
- It establishes evaluation processes through which the community and government may consider whether *new strategies to prevent crime* are needed.

4. **How does restorative justice seek to prevent crime?**

- It builds on the *strengths of community and the government*. The community can build peace through strong, inclusive and righteous relationships; the government can bring order through fair, effective and parsimonious use of force.

- It emphasizes the need to *repair past harms* in order to prepare for the future.

- It seeks to *reconcile* offenders with those they have harmed.

- It helps communities learn to *reintegrate* victims and offenders.

Chapter Four

Conceptual Impediments:

Objections to a New Pattern of Thinking

Ultimately, whole new institutional structures are likely to emerge from the restorative approach, just as the rehabilitation model gave birth to penitentiaries, probation, parole and juvenile courts,[1] and the just deserts model of fairness in sentencing gave rise to determinate sentences and sentencing guidelines.[2] One restorative initiative (discussed in Chapter Five) is victim-offender reconciliation, which permits the two parties to meet with a trained mediator to discuss the crime and its aftermath and to develop a strategy to "make things right."[3]

There is great value in model programs such as victim-offender reconciliation: they explore new horizons in criminal justice theory and provide data with which to evaluate and modify not only the programs but the theory behind them as well.[4] More than models are needed, however; there is a continuing need for analytical precision in understanding the new vision, articulating purposes and outcomes, developing strategies for accomplishing those purposes and evaluating results. It must be remembered that criminal justice his-

---

[1] *See* Edgardo Rotman, *Beyond Punishment : A New View of the Rehabilitation of Criminal Offenders* (Westport, CT: Greenwood Press, 1990), 21-57.

[2] *See* Dean J. Spader, "Megatrends in Criminal Justice Theory," *Am. J. Crim. L.* 13 (1986): 157, 180-195.

[3] For a more complete discussion of victim-offender reconciliation programs, *see* Chapters Six and Eleven.

[4] This phenomenon has been aptly described as "theory overtaking practice" in Martin Wright, *Justice for Victims and Offenders* (Philadelphia: Open University Press, 1991).

tory is filled with visionary people whose visions failed to be realized because of their failure to apply such analysis.[5] Consequently, before considering specific programs that might help reorient the criminal justice system in a more restorative direction, we must first acknowledge a series of objections and obstacles to the suggestion that a fundamental purpose of criminal justice should be to promote restoration of those touched by crime. Some of those are theoretical, others practical. In this chapter we will consider four conceptual objections:[6]

1. This means the end of criminal law.

2. Multiple parties cannot pursue multiple goals and achieve a single overarching purpose.

3. Not all harms can be identified, and of those that are, not all are of equal importance.

4. Government and community will not be able to share responsibility for public safety in the way anticipated by restorative justice theory.

Objection 1: This Means the End of Criminal Law

Currently, both the criminal law and the civil law of torts deal with intentional behavior by one person that violates the rights of another. In criminal cases, the offender is prosecuted by an agent of the government and punished; to convict, the prosecutor must prove the offender guilty beyond a reasonable doubt. In tort cases, the defendant-offender is sued by the plaintiff-victim and is required to pay damages or otherwise make right the harm done; the plaintiff must prove the defendant liable by a preponderance of the evidence.[7] But as the underlying harmful action is basically the same in criminal and tort cases, why are the two treated differently? The answer most often given is that while civil cases are concerned with the violation of individual rights, criminal cases are concerned with broad-

---

[5] *See* Blake McKelvey, *American Prisons: A History of Good Intentions* (Montclair, NJ: Patterson Smith, 1977).

[6] In Chapter Nine we will discuss three practical obstacles: (1) unsolved crimes; (2) social, economic and political inequities in society; and (3) politics as usual.

[7] For an excellent discussion of the distinctions between what he calls the criminal justice and civil justice *paradigms, see* Kenneth Mann, "Punitive Civil Sanctions: The Middle Ground Between Criminal and Civil Law," *Yale L.J.* 101 (1992): 1803-1813.

er societal rights; criminal cases should not be initiated by victims, since vindication of public policy should not depend on an individual's decision to institute legal proceedings.[8]

As we will see, excluding victims' interests from criminal cases is a relatively recent development. How does the emphasis in restorative justice on repairing the damage caused by crime affect our understanding of criminal law? Should a separate criminal law be maintained?

Randy Barnett and John Hagel, early proponents of restitution as a new paradigm of criminal justice, have argued for what would effectively be the end of criminal law, replacing it with the civil law of torts:

> A specific action is defined as criminal within the context of this theory only if it violates the right of one or more identifiable individuals to person and property. These individuals are the victims of the criminal act, and only the victims, by virtue of the past infringement of their rights, acquire the right to demand restitution from the criminal.
>
> This is not to deny that criminal acts frequently have harmful effects upon other individuals beside the actual victims. All that is denied is that a harmful "effect," absent a specific infringement of rights, may vest rights in a third party.[9]

Barnett and Hagel define crime by examining not the offender's behavior but the victim's rights, particularly "the fundamental right of all individuals to be free in their person and property from the initiated use of force by others."[10] They agree that there may be broader social goals, but they argue that settling the private dispute will "vindicate the rights of the aggrieved party and thereby vindicate the rights of all persons."[11] They conclude that, among other things, this means there can be no "victimless crimes."

But vindicating the rights of primary victims (those directly injured by the crime) and of secondary victims (those indirectly injured) does not automatically vindicate the rights of society at large.

---

[8] *See* Ibid., 1812 n.61, in which Mann argues that while this is the conventional argument for the paradigmatic distinction between criminal and civil justice, the practical distinction is blurred by RICO statutes, that authorize private prosecution, and by SEC actions, in which the government is authorized to seek compensation for private individuals.

[9] Randy E. Barnett and John Hagel, eds., *Assessing the Criminal: Restitution, Retribution, and the Legal Process* (Cambridge, MA: Ballinger Publishing Co., 1977), 1, 15.

[10] Ibid., 11.

[11] Ibid., 25.

> [C]rime imposes three distinct kinds of costs on its indirect
> victims. There are, first, the *avoidance costs* that are
> incurred by anyone who takes steps to minimize his
> chances of becoming the direct victim of crime. Installing
> locks and burglar alarms, avoiding unsafe areas, and pay-
> ing for police protection, whether private or public, all fall
> into this category. Indirect victims may also have to pay
> *insurance costs*—costs that increase as the rate of crime in
> an area increases. And, finally, "as crime gives rise to fear,
> apprehension, insecurity, and social divisiveness," indirect
> victims are forced to bear the *attitudinal costs* of crime.[12]

These costs are rarely if ever addressed directly, either in civil or
criminal proceedings. In fact, the phrase "debt to society" is misleading because it implies that there is an actual financial obligation
that the offender will be required to "pay." In practice, however, this
is simply a justification for the imposition of any sort of sentence on
the offender; there is seldom a serious effort to determine precisely
what the particular crime has cost society at large.

On the other hand, the existence of the indirect costs mentioned
above may serve as justification for the use of criminal proceedings
against an offender. Society is affected by crime. That is why, at least
in part, it prohibits certain conduct and seeks to apprehend and hold
accountable those who engage in those activities. Any sentence will
vindicate that interest, but a lack of sentence will not. This, then, is
one of the justifications of criminal proceedings, which are not
dependent on the plaintiff/victim's determination (or lack of it) to
pursue civil remedies. Civil proceedings do not adequately protect
the interests of indirect victims.

Second, criminal law offers more than vindication of individual
rights. It also provides a controlled mechanism for dealing with
those accused of crossing the boundaries of socially tolerable behavior. In a thoughtful and disturbing essay titled "Retributive Hatred,"
Jeffrie Murphy notes that crime arouses "feelings of anger, resentment, and even hatred . . . toward wrongdoers."[13] He argues that
criminal justice should restrain these feelings. "Rational and moral
beings . . . want a world, not utterly free of retributive hatred, but
one where this passion is both respected and seen as potentially dangerous, as in great need of reflective and institutional restraint."[14]

---

[12] Richard Dagger, "Restitution, Punishment, and Debts to Society," in Joe Hudson and Burt Galaway,
eds., *Victims, Offenders and Alternative Sanctions* (Lexington, MA: Lexington Books, 1980), 3, 4 (citations omitted).

[13] Jeffrie G. Murphy, "Retributive Hatred: An Essay on Criminal Liability and the Emotions," paper presented at a conference on "Liability in Law and Morals," Bowling Green State University, Bowling
Green, Ohio, Apr. 15-17, 1988.

[14] Ibid., 31.

While one may argue with his description of the desires of "rational and moral beings," few would argue that the retributive impulse must be restrained.

Third, there are procedural advantages to governmentally prosecuted criminal cases. This is borne out in the experience of European countries that permit varying degrees of victim involvement in the prosecution of criminal cases.[15] The victim typically lacks the expertise, financial resources and/or time to prosecute. Furthermore, the goals of consistency, fairness and efficiency can best be pursued by coordinated governmental action, because public prosecutors can weigh prosecution decisions in light of stated policies and rely on the help of investigatory agencies. Moreover, prosecutors are presumably less influenced than are victims by personal motivations, such as revenge.[16]

In summary, maintaining the criminal law is desirable inasmuch as it provides an effective method of vindicating the rights of secondary victims, it restrains and channels in acceptable ways retributive emotions in society, and it offers procedural efficiencies in enforcing public values.

Objection 2: Multiple Parties Cannot Pursue Multiple Goals and Achieve a Single Overarching Purpose

The overall purpose of restorative justice is the reintegration into safe communities of victims and offenders who have resolved their conflicts. This purpose can be achieved only when multiple parties (victims, offenders, communities and governments) pursue multiple goals (redress, fairness, healing and rehabilitation). Is it possible for so many parties to pursue so many goals in such a way as to achieve restoration?

The current approach to criminal justice faces the challenge of balancing multiple goals,[17] usually expressed as deterrence, incapacitation, rehabilitation and retribution (also known as "desert" or "just deserts"). The first two can be clearly classified as utilitarian— focused on crime control. The third can either be similarly classified

---

[15] *See, e.g.,* Matti Joutsen, "Listening to the Victim: The Victim's Role in European Criminal Justice Systems," *Wayne L. Rev.* 34 (1987): 95.

[16] *But see* Abraham S. Goldstein, "Defining the Role of the Victim in Criminal Prosecution," *Miss. L.J.* 52 (1982): 515, 555. Governmental prosecution of offenses also has its limitations: the prosecutor administers an agency of government with its own administrative, political, investigative and adjudicative objectives, any of which can lead prosecutors to focus less on a just resolution of the particular case and more on the effective use of limited resources. In addition, political forces may lead prosecutors to cater to, rather than restrain, retributive impulses in the community.

[17] Paul H. Robinson, "Hybrid Principles for the Distribution of Criminal Sanctions," *Nw. U. L. Rev.* 82 (1987): 19.

or be justified as a social value in and of itself. The last limits the nature and extent of the sentence, emphasizing proportionality. Practitioners and commentators alike have recognized the difficulty of constructing sentences that reflect those goals with any kind of precision. At first glance, this difficulty appears to grow geometrically under the restorative justice model, which adds such goals as recompense and vindication. However, the more holistic perspective of restorative justice may actually help society successfully manage multiple goals because it identifies restoration—not deterrence, incapacitation, rehabilitation or retribution—as the overarching goal of criminal justice.

In a helpful article on sentencing policy under current criminal justice, Paul Robinson suggests that the attempt to pursue all four goals[18] raises questions at two levels. First, should any one of them (such as crime control or proportionality) take precedence as an overarching goal of criminal justice? Second, should any of the goals be given priority in the event they cannot all be accommodated?[19] The answers to these questions could be discovered, he suggests, by adopting any of five alternative approaches.[20] Two of them are of particular interest to us.[21]

The first would be to distinguish between purposes that *determine* the sentence and those that simply *limit* the nature or duration of the sentence.[22] A "determining purpose" requires that certain features be included in the sentence; a "limiting purpose" requires that certain features be excluded.[23] While this approach does not eliminate conflict, it reduces it by clarifying the different functions of the purposes. For example, if rehabilitation were the determining pur-

---

[18] Robinson acknowledges that it is theoretically possible to choose one of the four goals as the single goal of sentencing. He argues, however, that doing so would violate traditional fundamental values of Western criminal justice. In other words, the four goals are traditionally given because each contains values and restraints that we are unwilling to give up in favor of those included in the others. Ibid., 22-25.

[19] Ibid., 25-28.

[20] Ibid., 29-36.

[21] The other three are as follows: One approach would be to assign priorities to the goals; when conflict arises because different purposes yield different sentences, the purpose with the highest priority would prevail. Robinson proposes a "simple priority," in which the priority purpose always trumps the others, or a "contingent priority," in which the priority is given only if a predetermined condition has been met. For example, one could make incapacitation a contingent priority provided that the future dangerousness of the convicted offender could be predicted with a specified level of reliability. Ibid., 29. The second approach would be simply to pick the purpose that would result in the highest sentence, as this would ensure that all purposes were satisfied. Robinson discards this on the grounds that it is incorrect to say that a sentence that is higher than that required by a purpose thereby satisfies that purpose. In fact, a higher sentence may frustrate that purpose as much as a lower sentence would. Ibid., 33. The third approach would be to identify a common overarching goal (such as crime prevention) that is shared by all the purposes, as well as a "common currency" for evaluating the costs and benefits of particular sentence formulations from the perspective of each purpose. The sentence formulation with the best combined cost-benefit ranking would be selected. The problem, Robinson warns, is that not all the purposes share the overarching goal of crime prevention nor the common currency needed to calculate the cost-benefit scores. Ibid., 32.

[22] Ibid., 29-31.

[23] Ibid.

pose and desert the limiting purpose, then a sentence would include rehabilitative features and exclude features that would make it more or less painful than sentences given for other similar offenses.

The second approach is to distinguish the *amount* of a sanction from the *method* of sanctioning. Again this approach will not end conflict between purposes, but it suggests ways in which they might coexist. For example, desert is most directly related to the question of amount, while the utilitarian sanctions address the method. Robinson suggests that the amount be expressed in terms of a number of "sanction units" (comparable in some ways with the "common currency" noted above), and the method would be selected on the basis of which purpose would be most successful in reducing crime.[24]

These approaches were designed to rank sentencing purposes under the current model of criminal justice, and they led Robinson to propose his own "hybrid" system under this model.[25] We suggest that together they may be useful for restorative justice theory as well. The following paragraphs refer to Figure 4.1.

The overarching purpose of restorative justice, and consequently of the various goals it encompasses, is the reintegration into safe communities of victims and offenders who have resolved their conflicts. As we have seen, this requires particular responses when specific crimes are committed as well as when broad-based crime prevention strategies are implemented. With regard to *specific crimes*, the determining goal will be resolution of the conflict; community safety should be a limiting goal only. This means that restitution would be presumed and that prison sentences, which effectively preclude or substantially delay restitution, should be used only as a last resort when necessary for purposes of incapacitation. Any social controls imposed on the offender should not unnecessarily obstruct the determining goal of resolution. Likewise, when looking at *crime prevention*, the determining goal of the community and government will be safety, with specific strategies limited by the need to resolve appropriately individual crimes as they occur.

Similar analysis can assist us in organizing the subsidiary goals: recompense, redress and fairness through the formal criminal justice system, and healing, rehabilitation and reconciliation through community-based programs. This may be done by distinguishing procedural goals and criteria from those pertaining to outcomes. The governmental response to specific crimes is determined by its criminal laws and by the truth of the allegations that the offender has violated those norms. The process is limited by the human rights of its citizens, particularly of those suspected, accused or convicted of violat-

---

24 Ibid., 35.
25 Ibid., 36-41.

Figure 4.1

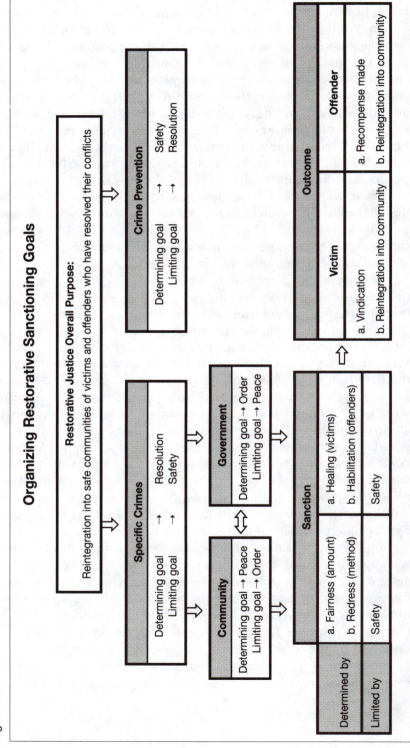

Organizing Restorative Sanctioning Goals

Restorative Justice Overall Purpose:
Reintegration into safe communities of victims and offenders who have resolved their conflicts

Crime Prevention

| Determining goal | → | Safety |
| Limiting goal | → | Resolution |

Specific Crimes

| Determining goal | → | Resolution |
| Limiting goal | → | Safety |

Community

Determining goal → Peace
Limiting goal → Order

Government

Determining goal → Order
Limiting goal → Peace

Sanction

	Determined by	a. Fairness (amount)	a. Healing (victims)
		b. Redress (method)	b. Habilitation (offenders)
	Limited by	Safety	Safety

Outcome

Victim	Offender
a. Vindication	a. Recompense made
b. Reintegration into community	b. Reintegration into community

ing those rules. Once the matter of legal guilt is resolved, new criteria apply in selecting the sentence. The *amount* of a sentence could be determined on the basis of fairness: similar offenses are given similarly onerous sanctions. The *method* by which the sanction is carried out may serve compensatory goals. The sentence is limited by the human rights protections given the convicted offender as well as by the need for public safety. Therefore, if paying $100 in restitution is as onerous as one day in jail, then the goals of fairness and of recompense are satisfied when the financial penalty is imposed unless it can be demonstrated that freedom jeopardizes public safety. Public safety, however, is only a limiting goal, not a determining one.[26]

Similarly, the community process of responding to crime focuses equally but distinctly on the needs of the victim and the offender for healing and rehabilitation. When both parties are sufficiently prepared, the next stage of reconciliation with each other—and reintegration into the community—may take place.

Objection 3: Not All Harms Can Be Identified, and of Those That Are, Not All Are of Equal Importance

Criminal justice currently gives insufficient attention to the harm resulting from the offense and focuses instead on the offender's actions and state of mind. The extent of harm to victims and their neighbors is, with some exceptions, ignored. When this form of injury is considered (for example, in offenses such as theft), it is only to establish the seriousness of the crime (misdemeanor versus felony), and the inquiry is typically limited to whether the property was worth more or less than a specific statutory amount.[27] Under recent sentencing and parole guidelines, the extent of harm also has been considered to determine the length or severity of the sentence,[28] but again the categories are broad and general, and typically they are used to determine the amount of punishment as opposed to the amount of reparation.

In a restorative justice model, however, victim reparation is a determining purpose. Consequently, calculating the amount of loss sustained by victims assumes great importance. In order to do such

---

[26] Andrew von Hirsch has made a similar proposal for ranking intermediate sanctions, in which desert determines the amount of the sanction and other purposes establish the nature and method of that sanction. Andrew von Hirsch, *Censure and Sanctions* (Oxford: Clarendon Press, 1993), 57-70.

[27] *See, e.g.,* Ill. Ann. Stat. ch 720, § 5/16-1(b) (1993) (providing that theft of property under $300 is a misdemeanor, and over that amount is a felony).

[28] *E.g.,* Albert W. Alschuler, "The Failure of Sentencing Guidelines," *U. Chi. L. Rev.* 58 (1991): 901, 908-915.

calculations there must first be clarity about the kinds and extent of harms to be considered. This means that three issues need to be addressed carefully: the kinds of victims to receive reparation, how harms should be quantified and how questions of disparity should be addressed.

1. What kinds of victims should receive reparation?

Earlier we distinguished between primary and secondary victims.[29] The primary victim is the person directly harmed by the offense—the person whose house was burglarized, for example. Secondary victims are also affected adversely by the offense, but that harm is experienced indirectly. Family members and neighbors of the victim may suffer increased fear, financial loss and emotional devastation, for example. The family and associates of the offender may experience harm as a result of that offender's actions, if only because of their relationship with the offender. Those harms can also be emotional, financial, spiritual, and so on. The criminal justice system (and the community as well) may be called on to expend resources to apprehend the offender, to determine what took place and to impose and administer sanctions if the offender is convicted.

Which of these "victims" should be considered for reparation? Answering this question requires us to establish priorities. It also requires us to think carefully about what we mean by "harm" (we will discuss this issue in more detail below). We suggest that priority should be given to those who have been directly harmed by the crime. Secondary victims may also receive reparation, but the indirectness of their harms creates two problems. While their injury may be connected to the action of the offender, the connection is more tangential, which means that the harm may have been increased by factors other than the offender's act. Second, the indirectness of the injury also means that it was probably less foreseeable by the offender than the direct injury to primary victims. Consequently, for reasons of efficiency and fairness, we suggest that emphasis be placed on the harm experienced by primary victims. Immediate family members of a homicide victim may be considered both primary and secondary victims. As "representatives" of the deceased primary victim, they should be able to pursue reparation on that victim's behalf. As relatives, they will have experienced acute loss that may be manifested in various ways, and they should be able to pursue reparation for those indirect costs, but not have a priority for reparation over the direct victim.

Even within the category of secondary victims, there can be considerable differences, owing to the differences in the causes of their

---

[29] *See* Chapter Three.

injuries. For example, a business that is burglarized may be unable to pay creditors. Those creditors are secondary victims. However, so are the family and friends of the owner of the business, or of the employee who was in the store when the burglary took place, whose indirect injury is due to their relationship with the primary victim and not to the financial or other harm caused to that victim. In addition to those who suffer indirect financial loss because of a crime and those who suffer because someone with whom they have a close relationship has been a victim, there may be a third kind of secondary victim: society at large. We must think carefully before including society as a victim entitled to reparation, because the nature of "harm" to society—and thus the amount and method of reparation—is often vague. In some instances, judges have assigned monetary restitution as reparation to the direct victim of a crime, and community service as a gesture toward making amends to the community. Alan Harland and Cathryn Rosen have made an excellent case for differentiating direct victims from society at large and, therefore, for treating restitution differently from community service:

> [U]nlike victim restitution that is based upon (and limited by) a case-by-case determination of victim injuries, the "harms" on which the offender's community service liability is predicated are far less specific, and the metric against which the amount of service owed is assessed tends to be no less arbitrary than the amount of a fine, probation, incarceration, or any other penal rather than compensatory sanction . . . [I]t is perhaps not unreasonable to question whether community service has any claim at all to be part of the presumptive norm of restitution, and to ask why it is useful to continue to treat the two sanctions as merely different examples of a uniform concept.[30]

While this does not necessarily preclude the use of community service as a form of reparative sanction, it does require that we clarify the nature and extent of the harm done to society at large, as well as the most appropriate means for the offender to repair that harm.

2. *How do we quantify the harm that should be repaired?*

The most direct way to quantify the harm caused by a criminal act is to identify the specific harms and then establish the costs of remedying those harms (to the extent they can be remedied). But the simplicity of this approach begins to evaporate on close reflection. First, not all harms, such as the loss of a treasured memento or heir-

---

[30] Alan T. Harland and Cathryn J. Rosen, "Impediments to the Recovery of Restitution by Crime Victims," *Violence and Victims: Special Issue on Social Science and Victim Policy* 5(2) (1990): 127, 132.

loom, can be remedied. Second, not all harms can be converted with precision into financial amounts. A person who is anxious and unable to sleep after a crime may take time away from work and undergo therapy. The lost wages and costs of therapy can be easily calculated, but the financial value of "anxiety" or "lost sleep" is more elusive. Third, minute, case-by-case evaluation of the value of harms raises the possibility of delay and inefficiency in the criminal court process and of disparate treatment of offenders leading to a tangled mass of litigation and appeals. Finally, while we have argued that harm to society-at-large is one of the bases for retaining criminal law, we have also argued that in general society should not be considered a victim with a reparative interest.

While it may be difficult or impossible to quantify the direct and indirect costs related to a particular crime with absolute accuracy, it may be possible to approximate those costs. Andrew von Hirsch has suggested that harms could be ranked by the extent to which they reduce the victims' standard of living.[31] (He is speaking of typical costs and typical standards of living, not the actual costs and standards of living involved in a particular crime.[32]) While it is not clear whether he includes primary and secondary victims in making this calculation, there seems to be no reason not to do so. This would permit courts in a formal process, or mediators in an informal one, to make use of rationally developed approximations of the harm caused by particular offenders.

A similar approach could be taken in relating reparative sentences to levels of harm. While Harland and Rosen are right that such a system is more arbitrary than case-by-case restitution, it is certainly less arbitrary than current, entirely punitive sanctions. Criteria must be established and applied uniformly throughout the entire sentencing structure within a jurisdiction.[33]

While it is not feasible nor (perhaps) desirable to attach monetary values to every conceivable type of harm, a serious effort to grapple with the issue is necessary. Otherwise, types and amounts of reparation may be simply arbitrary and no different in nature from the abstract "fine," except for who receives the money. If victims are to be paid back, and if offenders are to see their reparation as linked

---

[31] von Hirsch, *supra* note 26, at 29-33.

[32] Ibid., 32.

[33] Great Britain did this several years ago by devising guidelines for restitution. Ironically, they look a great deal like the Anglo-Saxon King Ethelbert's restitution schedules promulgated 1,400 years ago:
Under guidelines sent to the country's 27,710 magistrates, attackers can be forced . . . to compensate their victims by the punch. Sample penalties: $84 for a simple graze, $168 for a black eye, $1,428 for a broken nose, $2,940 for a fractured jaw, and as much as $13,440 for a serious facial scar. Said Home Office Minister John Patten: "I am very anxious that the victims get a better deal." ("World News: Socking It to the Bad Guys," *Time,* 3 Oct. 1988, 43.)
Two things should be noted about the modern British approach: it restricts compensable harms to direct victims and it uses rough equivalencies for the amount of restitution to be ordered.

to the specific harm done, then restitution, like community service, should be as closely related to the particular injury as possible.

3. How do we avoid unwarranted disparity?

This leads directly into the question of disparity—whether particular offenders or victims will receive orders for restitution that are not comparable to those given to other offenders or victims. Disparity can happen in several ways.

First, if each offender is sentenced according to the type of offense alone, the restitution order may fail to reflect the actual harm caused because similar offenders committing similar crimes can bring about dramatically different injuries. Consider two burglaries in which a vase is stolen: if one is from a five-and-ten-cent store while the other is an authentic Ming, treating the offenders alike because their actions were similar would have a disparate effect on the two victims.

Second, if each offender is sentenced only according to the actual harm caused, then similar illegal conduct can result in dramatically different sentences. In the preceding example, the offender who stole the Ming vase could take years to repay the victim, while replacing the dime-store vase would be a matter of days or hours. Both victims and offenders would therefore receive significantly different treatment.

Finally, differing circumstances on the part of victims and offenders may lead to a disparate effect even when the offense and the financial loss are the same. Wealthy offenders may be able to complete their sentences simply by writing a check, while impoverished offenders may have to work long and hard to satisfy the judgment. Similarly, wealthy victims may have far less trouble recovering from crime than those who are without adequate financial resources.

Of course, not all disparity is wrong, nor is it possible to avoid it entirely. However, justice requires that victims and offenders be treated consistently—and that, to the extent possible, outcomes do not fall inequitably because of social, economic or political reasons.

Andrew von Hirsch has suggested an approach that may be useful here. In considering the use of intermediate sanctions, and the resulting substitution of sanctions of equivalent punitiveness under a desert system, he has proposed the development of units of comparable severity—in his words, "equivalent penal bite."[34] This would permit ranking of sanctions according to their severity, which would in turn allow judges to impose different sentences on different

---

[34] von Hirsch, *supra* note 26, 59.

offenders without violating the principle of parity. Therefore, a "day-fine sentence of so many days' earnings might be replaced by an equivalent stint of community service."[35] The determination of penal bite would be made by considering the extent to which a sanction typically interfered with the quality of life of an offender undergoing that sanction.

The advantage of permitting substitution of equivalent sanctions is that while each inflicts an equivalent penal bite, some may be more suited for achieving subsidiary purposes than others. For example, a higher risk posed by one offender would not justify a more severe penalty than that given another, but it could justify a different form of penalty.[36] Penal bite is not the only consideration in developing a range of sanctions; so is something that von Hirsch calls "acceptable penal content."[37] The issue here is to eliminate degrading punishments—those that dehumanize the recipient (such as torture or brainwashing), or force them to undergo demeaning rituals (such as boot camps), or involve compulsory attitudinizing (such as requiring offenders to attach bumper stickers to their cars).[38] A sanction with acceptable penal content, then, is one in which punitive and preventive ends are achieved without demeaning the recipient.[39] It is also one that can be administered without resorting to "grossly humiliating" enforcement mechanisms.[40] Finally, it should intrude as little as possible on third parties (such as family members when the offender's sentence includes the requirement of home visits).[41]

Von Hirsch's argument can inform the earlier discussion on balancing multiple goals. Should the emphasis be on *consistency* in dealing with offenders' actions or on victims' *harms*? This question calls for organization of the goals of fairness and redress: fairness determines the amount of the sanction, and redress determines its method. Therefore, in a restorative justice system, guidelines outlining minimum and maximum amounts of restitution might be established for particular offenses. These would be related to typical losses of primary and secondary victims. If an agreement were not reached through negotiation, victims would present evidence of their actual losses to the sentencing judge, who would then set an amount within the pertinent range.[42] If the actual loss were less than the min-

---

35 Ibid.

36 Ibid., 60.

37 Ibid., 63.

38 Ibid., 84.

39 Ibid.

40 Ibid., 86.

41 Ibid., 87.

42 "[G]iving offenders opportunities to demonstrate a willingness to accept responsibility for their offences is not incompatible with treating like cases alike and assuring that sentences arrived at reflect in appropriate ways the gravity of the offences committed." Wesley Cragg, *The Practice of Punishment: Towards a Theory of Restorative Justice* (New York: Routledge, 1992), 216.

imum established, the victim would receive only the actual loss, and the balance would be set aside into a victim compensation fund for those victims whose loss exceeded the range.

A similar approach might help address the issue of economic imbalance between otherwise comparable offenders. The Swedish "day fine" approach, which bases the sanction on the offender's daily wages, multiplied by a figure that represents the seriousness of the offense, could be adopted here as well.[43] Under this approach, one offender may actually be ordered to pay less than the indicated amount of restitution, with the balance made up from a compensation fund; another offender may be required to pay far more, with the excess going into that fund.

Objection 4: Government and Community Will Not Be Able to Share Responsibility for Public Safety in the Way Anticipated by Restorative Justice Theory

Under restorative justice theory, civil government and the community cooperate in enabling the victim and offender to resolve the crime successfully and in building safe communities. Is this kind of cooperation feasible? Two concerns have been raised in this connection.

First, can community-based programs be linked with agencies of the criminal justice system without losing their restorative values? This concern has been sparked by the experience of some reconciliation and mediation programs in the United States and England, which started with visionary objectives and then found those goals being redirected by a much larger criminal justice system with its own—and different—vision. For example, a reconciliation program may begin to be measured by the *number* of offenders it diverts from prison, rather than by the peacemaking results of the mediation.[44]

Howard Zehr, a pioneer in reconciliation program development, has suggested three reasons that dependence on the criminal justice system can distort the vision of such programs: the criminal justice system's interests are retributive not restorative; its orientation is

[43] Martin Wright, *Making Good: Prisons, Punishment, and Beyond* (London: Burnett Books, 1982), 87-88.

[44] Howard Zehr, *Changing Lenses: A New Focus for Crime and Justice* (Scottsdale, PA: Herald Press, 1990): 233-234.

with the offender not the victim; and its inclination when challenged is self-preservation.[45] Added to these could be the observation that the procedures of traditional criminal justice systems are coercive, which tends to mitigate against reconciliation or mediation.[46]

A second concern is that community-government collaboration will result in expanded state controls. This is the well-known problem of net-widening, and it happens in subtle ways.[47] Suppose, for example, that in order to develop credibility, a community-based diversion program agrees to accept referrals of minor offenses from the local court. The court may respond by referring cases that are so minor they would have been dismissed otherwise. If offenders who fail to comply with the reconciliation agreement are then brought back before the judge and sentenced to jail or prison, the unintended effect of this arrangement, which was designed to be an *alternative* to prison, may actually be that more offenders are locked up.[48]

In a democracy, government does not exist apart from society; it is part of society, with specific powers and interests. This observation suggests that community-government cooperation must be fluid and dynamic because society is fluid and dynamic. Moreover, it permits us to draw certain conclusions about what can make the cooperation effective. First, such an undertaking requires that both parties share the same overarching goal, and not just *any* goal. It is likely even now that government and community share the common goal of security. If the mutual goal is restoration of *both* the victim as well as community safety, then a significant political and public education campaign lies ahead. This is true in the community as well as in the governmental sphere.

Second, influence flows both ways. Thus, community programs themselves have affected both the structure and goals of the criminal justice system. Peter Kratcoski has outlined a pattern of evolving volunteer activity in criminal justice. At the outset, private groups set up

---

[45] Dependence on the criminal justice system is one of three forces that Zehr argues can lead to distortion of vision, the other two of which are nongovernmental. The first is what Zehr calls the "dynamics of institutionalization." These dynamics include the need for easily collected administrative measurements to justify the organization's existence, the tendency for programs to take on the values of their funding sources, differences between the goals of leaders and those of their staffs, and the difficulty of building "prophetic and visioning functions" into the organization's structure. The second is the design and operation of the program. If goal conflicts are not identified and resolved early on, they carry the potential of diverting the organization from a visionary mission. A succession of seemingly small policy decisions may change the long-range direction of the organization. Ibid., 233-235.

[46] Cragg, *supra* note 42, at 199.

[47] *See, e.g.,* Robert Coates and John Gehm, "An Empirical Assessment," in Martin Wright and Burt Galaway, eds., *Mediation and Criminal Justice* (Newbury Park, CA: Sage Publications, 1989): 258-260.

[48] *See, e.g.,* Christa Pelikan, "Conflict Resolution between Victims and Offenders in Austria and in the Federal Republic of Germany," in Frances Heidensohn and Martin Farrell, eds., *Crime in Europe* (London: Routledge, 1991), 151, 164-165. Pelikan describes a pilot program in which prosecutors were granted discretionary authority to divert juvenile offenders into a mediation program, as well as the steps taken to avoid such net-widening problems.

new programs. These programs then receive governmental assistance when the need for services outstrips existing private resources. At some point, however, the government begins to underwrite the program fully, using volunteers to fill in gaps.[49] An example is the probation system, which grew out of a volunteer program initiated by John Augustus in 1842. Eventually the program was absorbed into the criminal justice system, but with a continuing mission to help offenders.[50]

Third, although government and community must seek the same overarching goal, they also play different roles not only in responding to individual offenders and victims, but also in establishing community safety. Both of these objectives must be pursued with equal vigor. While the obstacles to accomplishing this collaboration are daunting, we can be encouraged by reports from Japan. According to John Haley, criminal justice in that nation operates on two tracks. One is similar to the formal criminal justice system found in Western nations.

> Paralleling the formal process, however, is a second track to which there is no Western analogue. A pattern of confession, repentance and absolution dominates each stage of law enforcement in Japan. The players in the process include not only the authorities in new roles but also the offender and the victim. From the initial police interrogation to the final judicial hearing on sentencing, the vast majority of those accused of criminal offenses confess, display repentance, negotiate for their victims' pardon and submit to the mercy of the authorities. In return they are treated with extraordinary leniency; they gain at least the prospect of absolution by being dropped from the formal process altogether.[51]

To illustrate this leniency, Haley notes that prosecutors proceed in only about 5 percent of all prosecutable cases. The vast majority are handled in uncontested summary proceedings in which the maximum penalty is a fine of $1,000 – $1,350. By the time cases have reached this point, the offender has demonstrated remorse, paid restitution and secured the victim's pardon. Haley concludes:

> In this respect the West, not Japan, should be considered remarkable. The moral imperative of forgiveness as a

---

[49] Peter C. Kratcoski, "Volunteers in Corrections: Do They Make a Meaningful Contribution," *Fed. Probation* 46(2) (1982): 30.

[50] A report several years ago from the Missouri Probation and Parole Department stated that it viewed its mission as helping the community determine its goals for offenders under supervision, and then helping it achieve them. Steve German, "Knowledge Is Not Enough: Addressing Client Needs in Probation and Parole," *Community Corrections* (Laurel Lakes, MD: American Correctional Association, 1981), 15, 17.

[51] John O. Haley, "Confession, Repentance and Absolution," in Martin Wright and Burt Galaway, eds., *Mediation in Criminal Justice* (London: Sage Publications, 1989), 195 (citation omitted).

> response to repentance is surely as much a part of the
> Judeo-Christian heritage as the East Asian tradition. . . .
> Whatever the reason, unlike Japan, Western societies failed
> to develop institutional props for implementing such
> moral commands. Instead the legal institutions and
> processes of Western law both reflect and reinforce societal
> demands for retribution and revenge.[52]

For a pattern like Japan's to develop in Western justice systems, victims and offenders (as well as the formal criminal justice system) will need to work together. But what if they fail to interact in the cooperative and voluntary way Haley describes? Clearly they cannot be forced to participate in community-based, informal mechanisms leading to outcomes like remorse, pardon and reconciliation. Although government is authorized to use force to secure participation in the criminal justice system, these outcomes depend on personal commitments, not force.

Current criminal justice procedures are highly coercive for both victims and offenders. They are built on the reasonable assumption that not all defendants will willingly participate in the trial process or voluntarily complete their sentences. They are also predicated on the assumption that not all *victims* will cooperate in the prosecution of their offenders; unwilling victims may have to be subpoenaed to testify at trial.

Restorative justice, with its emphasis on full and early participation of the parties in addressing the injuries caused by crime, places a premium on *voluntary* involvement. For offenders, this demonstrates a willingness to assume responsibility for their actions. For victims, it reduces the likelihood that they will be victimized a second time by the formal or informal responses to crime. When such involvement is not forthcoming, however, what should happen? How this question is answered depends to a certain extent on whether the uncooperative party is the victim or the offender.

An uncooperative offender will need to have sufficient coercion applied to ensure participation in the criminal justice system. However, it should be the least amount of coercion necessary, and voluntary assumption of responsibility should be encouraged. Of course, there is no such thing as completely "voluntary" action in a coercive environment (as when an offender agrees to restitution during a victim-offender reconciliation meeting conducted before sentencing). Nonetheless, assumption of responsibility by the offender should be encouraged by the process.

---

[52] Ibid., 204. Other observers have written about the distinctive role of apology and settlement in how the Japanese respond to crime. *See, e.g.,* Daniel H. Foote, "The Benevolent Paternalism of Japanese Criminal Justice," *Cal. L. Rev.* 80 (1992): 13; Hiroshi Wagatsuma and Arthur Rosett, "The Implication of Apology: Law and Culture in Japan and the United States," *Law & Soc'y Rev.* 20 (1986): 461.

Victims may also choose whether to participate in the process. If they choose not to, they should be permitted to waive any rights they may have to pursue restitution as a part of the criminal case. The offender should then be required to make compensation payments to the victim compensation fund. However, there may be situations in which the actual and potential injuries to the community may necessitate the victim's involvement in order to secure conviction. Under such circumstances, the government should have the authority (as it does today) to subpoena the victim as a witness. Yet even this should be done in a context that will be as protective and supportive as possible, in order that the victim's participation, though coerced, will still contribute to a measure of restoration.

Conclusion

Several objections are raised to the prospect of adopting a restorative vision of justice. Examining them helps make clear the ways in which a restorative vision is different from current practice, but also suggests values and elements that must be incorporated in restorative programs. In concluding this chapter, we would like to review some of the propositions about restorative programs that emerge from this analysis.

First, it is clear that criminal law plays an important role in a total societal response to crime. Because the criminal law makes explicit the kinds of behavior that society rejects as harmful, criminal law should be judged by its demonstrable contribution to reducing socially intolerable behavior. One way in which it can do this is by restraining and helping to resolve retributive anger that arises when citizens are harmed by others. All programs should be tested according to whether they contribute to the overarching goal of the reintegration into safe communities of victims and offenders who have resolved their conflicts. Within this overarching goal, individual sentences should be designed to achieve resolution of the conflict that is represented by the crime, limited by the demonstrable demands of public safety.

Second, restitution and other reparative sanctions should be linked as concretely as possible to the direct harm that was caused to the victim. Furthermore, direct victims should receive reparation before secondary victims, the community and the government. In determining reparative sanctions, the courts must balance the reparative goal with the limiting goals of human dignity and public safety.

Third, crime control and criminal justice are not the exclusive province of civil government; government and the community must play complementary, cooperative roles in promoting safety. The social controls imposed by government should interfere as little as possible with the restoration of victims, offenders and their communities. Because voluntary participation by the victim and offender should be encouraged, government's coercive powers should be exercised only when necessary, and in ways that foster offender responsibility and victim involvement as much as possible.

Part Two

The Venture Toward Restorative Justice

Chapter Five

Encounter

At the end of his epic poem *The Iliad,*[1] Homer recounts an extraordinary midnight meeting between Achilles, the greatest of Greek
warriors, and Priam, king of Troy. For 10 years the Greeks have
besieged Troy, and many warriors on both sides have died. Two
recent deaths have particular importance to these two men. Achilles
is mourning the death of his companion Patroclus, killed by Hector,
Priam's son and the leader of the Trojan forces. Priam in turn grieves
for Hector, killed by Achilles in battle as retaliation for the death of
Patroclus. Achilles has denied burial to Hector's body, choosing
instead to disgrace it by dragging it around the city of Troy at the
back of his chariot and by leaving it exposed to the sun and vulnerable to dogs and scavenger birds. The gods have protected Hector's
body from decay and from being torn apart by animals, waiting for
Achilles' anger to subside and for him to return the body to Troy for
proper burial. But Achilles' grief and anger do not dissipate, even
after Patroclus' funeral and the daily humiliations of Hector's body.
Finally, the gods order him to return the body and they bring Priam
to Achilles' tent under cover of darkness and their protection to
negotiate the release of the body.

The two bitter enemies meet for the first time. Each considers
himself to be the victim of a great loss, and they weep together as
they remember their dead loved ones. Priam appeals to Achilles by
reminding him of his own father who would long to have Achilles'
body returned were he the one who had been killed. Stirred by pity,

---

[1]   Homer, *The Iliad,* Martin Hammond, trans. (Penguin Books, 1987).

Achilles agrees to return the body, and further agrees to a cease-fire for 12 days while Troy mourns the death of its hero.

In his description of this remarkable meeting, Homer paints a complete picture that depicts sharp emotions (grief, pity, anger, fear, admiration and guilt), carefully chosen words, an awareness of non-verbal communication, and symbols of hospitality and respect. Achilles washes and covers Hector's battered body, afraid that Priam's natural resentment at its degrading treatment would provoke his own explosive anger. They eat together and as they talk with and observe one another, each comes to a reluctant admiration for the other's strength and wisdom. Achilles prepares a bed for Priam and promises protection on his return trip to Troy.

War resumes at the conclusion of Hector's funeral. Within days both Achilles and Priam are dead; Achilles is killed in battle before the walls of Troy and Priam in the following days when Troy is finally defeated. But interestingly, Homer did not include those events in *The Iliad*. Instead, he concludes with this dramatic meeting and a brief account of Hector's funeral. His theme, the dreadful consequences of Achilles' anger to both Greeks and Trojans,[2] is completed as he describes the two men's encounter.

Encounter is one of the pillars of a restorative approach to crime. It is greatly restricted in conventional criminal justice proceedings by rules of evidence, practical considerations and the dominance of professional attorneys who speak on behalf of their clients.[3] It is further restricted by the exclusion of persons with an interest in the crime, notably primary and secondary victims. Even defendants are silent pawns in the courtroom, often failing to even comprehend what is taking place because of the arcane language and procedures used.[4]

---

[2] "Sing, goddess, of the anger of Achilleus [sic], son of Peleus, the accursed anger which brought uncounted anguish on the Achaians and hurled down to Hades many mighty souls of heroes, making their bodies the prey to dogs and the birds' feasting: and this was the working of Zeus' will. Sing from the time of the first quarrel which divided Atreus' son, the lord of men, and the godlike Achilleus [sic]." Ibid., 51.

[3] Gilles Launay and Peter Murray, "Victim/Offender Groups," in Martin Wright and Burt Galaway, eds., *Mediation and Criminal Justice: Victims, Offenders, and Community* (Newbury Park, CA: Sage Publications, 1989), 113.

[4] One of us (Van Ness) is an attorney who practiced criminal law for a time. On one occasion, he was contacted by the family of an indigent client awaiting trial in the county jail; he agreed to represent him. The next court date, simply a status hearing in which the judge would determine whether the case was ready to go to trial, was the following day. During that hearing, he informed the judge that he would be representing the client, that he had not yet received a transcript of the preliminary hearing from the prosecutor, but that the other discovery had been made available that morning. The prosecutor indicated that the transcript would be available in two weeks. Following local custom, Van Ness stated that notwithstanding that delay, the defense was answering ready for trial and demanding trial under the Speedy Trial Act. The judge continued the case for another 30 days, but (again following local custom) did not mark the case ready for trial. The next hearing would be another status hearing.

When Van Ness spoke with his client after the hearing, it became clear that he had no idea what had taken place. He had heard his previous lawyer, a public defender, demand trial at the last court appearance, and had therefore assumed that the trial would commence that day. Van Ness explained that the demand for a trial simply triggered the Speedy Trial Act which provided that if he were not tried within 120 days he would be released. The demand for trial was made solely to protect his right to a speedy trial and not because we were in fact prepared to go to trial. That was not the only point of confusion: the defendant (understandably, since no one had ever explained it) had no idea what discovery was, or why it was important. He remembered the preliminary hearing as a court appear-

The right of accused offenders to confront their accusers in court is a well-established international human right. In recent years, some jurisdictions have increased the possibilities for victims of crime to express themselves in, or at least to listen to, court proceedings. For example, some victims are now permitted to remain in the courtroom to hear testimony about their cases, even though they may themselves be witnesses. Some jurisdictions have given victims the right to address the sentencer (generally the judge) about the impact of the crime on their lives. These innovations may be beneficial for victims, and they may have some indirect impact on the attitudes of offenders, but they—like the defendant's right of confrontation—are necessarily limited by the adversarial and judicial dimensions of courtroom proceedings, and by the definition of crime as an offense against government.

In this chapter we will consider programs that have emerged since the 1970s that permit parties to crime to encounter one another outside of the courtroom. This appears to be remarkably beneficial for victims and offenders alike. We will describe three such programs (victim-offender reconciliation programs, family group conferencing and victim-offender panels), discuss the elements they share and those which distinguish them, and consider strategic and programmatic issues to be considered as their use is expanded.

Victim-Offender Reconciliation Programs

Victim-offender reconciliation programs (VORPs) are a relatively recent avenue for pursuing reparation and reconciliation. In these programs, victims and offenders are given the opportunity to meet together with the assistance of a trained mediator to begin to resolve the conflict and to construct their own approach to achieving justice.[5] Unlike the formal criminal justice system, which removes both the victim and offender from proactive roles, these programs seek to empower the participants to resolve their conflict on their own "in an atmosphere of structured informality."[6] Unlike arbitration, in which a third party hears both sides and makes a judgment, the VORP process relies on the victim and offender to resolve the dispute together. No specific outcome is imposed by the mediator; the

---

ance in which something more than usual happened, but at the time he had thought it was the trial and had been surprised that the public defender representing him had not permitted him to testify. He was shocked to learn that the case would not be going to trial even on the next court date, and was dismayed to learn that it would probably not be tried until the 120-day period was nearly over.

[5]   Martin Wright and Burt Galaway, eds., *Mediation and Criminal Justice: Victims, Offenders, and Community* (Newbury Park, CA: Sage Publications, 1989).

[6]   Ibid., 2.

goal is to empower participants, promote dialogue and encourage mutual problem solving.

Some have expressed concern about using the term "reconciliation" in the name and description of the program. For some, the word is unnecessarily value-laden, and could be replaced by the word "mediation."[7] For others, particularly in the victim rights movement, the term is offensive because it implies that there is a duty on the part of victims to reconcile with their offenders. For this reason the programs are sometimes referred to as victim-offender "dialogue."[8] One dictionary defines reconciliation as "the renewal of amicable relations between two persons who had been at enmity or variance; usually implying forgiveness of injuries on one or both sides."[9] Such a definition limits reconciliation to those relationships that (1) started out friendly, (2) became hostile as a result of injuries, (3) are restored to their original state, (4) in a process that includes forgiveness by the wronged party or parties. Often one or more of those elements are absent when victims and offenders meet. For instance, many crimes involve victims and offenders who were strangers to one another before the offense, many victims and offenders who complete the VORP process do not become friends, and apology and forgiveness after a relatively brief meeting can be offered in only a limited way. Is it accurate, then, to describe this process as "reconciliation"?

An answer to that question may depend on whether the word "reconciliation" in the name "victim-offender reconciliation programs" refers to the *outcome* or a *process*. Sometimes it has been used to describe the former (VORP has an "ultimate objective . . . of healing and reconciliation"),[10] and at other times to the latter (the "primary goal of victim offender mediation and reconciliation programs is to provide a conflict resolution process which is perceived as fair by both the victim and the offender").[11] This lack of clarity has sometimes resulted in an apparent inconsistency between the rhetoric of the movement, the design of programs and the standards used to evaluate them. In an attempt to address this confusion, some proponents have distinguished the two by referring to the desired *outcome* as "reconciliation" and to the *process* as "mediation."[12] We will follow that convention and speak of the *mediation process* used to pursue a vision of *reconciliation*. We speak of these as reconcilia-

---

[7] Thomas Trenczek, "A Review and Assessment of Victim-Offender Reconciliation Programming in West Germany," in Burt Galaway and Joe Hudson, eds., *Criminal Justice, Restitution, and Reconciliation,* (Monsey, NY: Criminal Justice Press, 1990), 122 n.1.

[8] American Bar Association Resolution.

[9] *Black's Law Dictionary,* 4th ed.

[10] Martin Wright, *Justice For Victims and Offenders* (Philadelphia: Open University Press, 1991), 113.

[11] Mark Umbreit, "Mediation of Victim Offender Conflict," *Mo. J. Disp. Resol.* (Fall 1988): 85, 87.

[12] Howard Zehr, *Changing Lenses: A New Focus for Crime and Justice* (Scottsdale, PA: Herald Press, 1990), 159.

tion programs, instead of mediation programs, to underscore the existence of an opportunity for reconciliation each time victims and offenders meet.

While there is a basic structure to the VORP process,[13] reconciliation does not lend itself to an assembly-line approach. As Howard Zehr has written, "Mediation must be dynamic, taking into account the participants and empowering them to work in their own ways."[14] But, clearly, the meeting between the victim and offender lies at its heart. These meetings give victims and offenders the opportunity to pursue three basic objectives: to identify the injustice, to make things right and to consider future actions.[15]

Identifying the injustice begins as both parties talk about what happened. They are each given an opportunity to describe the crime and its impact from their own perspective, and to hear the other party's version of the events. Some practitioners have called this "telling their stories."[16] It is during this stage that the parties put together a common understanding of what happened and talk about how it made them feel. Both have an opportunity to ask questions of the other, the victim can speak about the personal dimensions of the victimization and loss, and the offender has a chance to express remorse.[17]

Discussion of how to make things right—to restore equity—can come after the facts are known and responsibility understood. The purpose of this stage is to identify the nature and extent of the victim's loss and to explore how the offender might begin to repair the harm caused by the criminal act.[18] This agreement is typically reduced to writing and specifies the amount of financial restitution, in-kind services or other reparation to which the parties have agreed.[19]

Considering the future, the third stage of the meeting, is a natural outgrowth of the other two. It is here that agreements are made concerning restitution schedules, follow-up meetings and monitoring procedures, for example. Furthermore, because the victim and offender have had the opportunity to present themselves as multidimensional persons, meetings frequently include discussions about the offender's plans to make a better future by addressing drug or

---

[13] Descriptions of the VORP process may be found in Zehr, *supra* note 12, at 160-163; Robert Coates and John Gehm, "An Empirical Assessment," in Martin Wright and Burt Galaway, eds., *Mediation and Criminal Justice* (Newbury Park, CA: Sage Publications, 1989): 251-256; and Howard Zehr, "The VORP Book: An Organizational and Operations Manual" which is available from PACT, Inc., 254 S. Morgan Blvd., Valparaiso, IN 46383.

[14] Howard Zehr, "VORP Dangers," *Accord: A Mennonite Central Committee Canada Publication for Victim Offender Ministries* 8(3) (1989): 13.

[15] In the VORP of the Central Valley program in California, director Ron Claassen has helped develop mediator training that presents the basic components as they are discussed here. We are indebted to Claassen and this program for much of this section.

[16] Zehr, *supra* note 12, at 161.

[17] Coates and Gehm, *supra* note 13, at 254.

[18] Ibid.

[19] Zehr, *supra* note 12, at 161.

alcohol problems, resisting negative family or peer pressures, devoting time to productive activities such as work, hobbies or community assistance, and so on.[20]

Results from these programs suggest that they are beneficial for many victims and offenders.[21] Victims are able to confront the offender, express their feelings, ask questions and have a direct role in determining the sentence.[22] Offenders are given an opportunity to take responsibility for their actions and make amends to the victim. Often offenders have not understood the effect their actions had on their victims,[23] and the process gives them greater insight into the harm they caused as well as an opportunity to repair the damage. Both victim and offender are confronted with the other as a *person* rather than a faceless antagonistic force, permitting them to gain a greater understanding of the crime, of the other person's circumstances and of what it will take to make things right. Several studies have concluded that victims and offenders who go through the mediation process are more likely to feel justice has been done than are those who simply progressed through the criminal justice system.[24] Other studies have found higher rates of completed restitution and reduced future criminal activity by the offender.[25]

---

[20] According to Ron Claassen, the VORP of the Central Valley has revised its victim-offender contract so that all three of the components are reflected in it. The victim and offender agree that they have satisfactorily reviewed the crime itself and their feelings about it; they confirm their plan to restore some equity; and they commit themselves to seeing the plan through. Both parties then put their signature to this contract agreement.

[21] Mark Umbreit et al., *Victim Meets Offender: The Impact of Restorative Justice and Mediation* (Monsey, NY: Criminal Justice Press, 1994), 20:
> [V]ictims who were referred to the VORP and who participated in a mediation session with their offender were twice as likely to have experienced fairness (80%) regarding the manner in which the criminal justice system dealt with their case than victims who were referred to the VORP but who chose not to enter mediation (38%).

[22] The ability to help formulate the outcome addresses a major consequence of crime for victims—powerlessness. The crime itself is an experience of powerlessness (the victim was unable to stop the perpetrator), the criminal justice system's monopoly on initiating and prosecuting cases constitutes a second experience of loss of control, and even those who help the victim may prolong the sense of loss of control by taking charge of their recovery. Morton Bard and Dawn Sangrey, *The Crime Victim's Book*, 2d ed. (Seacaucus, NJ: Citadel Press, 1986) provides much information about victimization and its results, with information about both effective and damaging "help."

[23] In a 1989 letter to Daniel Van Ness, a member of the Victim Offender Reconciliation Group (VORG) at the California Medical Facility-South (Vacaville) wrote the following:
> The face of the victim, as a real, live, breathing human being with feelings, fears, hopes, ambitions, needs and problems, needs to be presented to the offender, and the long-term, profoundly negative impact of a crime against a person must be taught. The offender needs to be made aware that the harmful effects of a crime extend far beyond the crime itself, not only for the victim, but the victim's friends and family as well. Many offenders may not care, but many will, and I can tell you, beyond all hesitation, very few offenders have ever given this much thought. (David B. Smith, "Restorative Justice-Theory: An Offender's Response," (letter, December 28, 1989): 5.)

[24] *See* Chapter Six, "Quality of Justice Impact: Client Satisfaction and Perceptions of Fairness" in Umbreit et al., *supra* note 21.

[25] Mark S. Umbreit and Mike Niemeyer, "Victim Offender Mediation: From the Margins Toward the Mainstream," *Perspectives* (Summer 1996): 28, 29

Family Group Conferencing

Family group conferencing (FGC) emerged in 1989 in New Zealand, was replicated and adapted in Australia, and is now being used in the United States and Europe. This relatively new program actually has ancient roots—the New Zealand model was adapted from the "whanau conference" practiced by the Maori people.[26] It differs from VORPs in that it includes not only the victim and offender but their families or support group as well. The arresting police officer, in some instances the attorney for the offender, and other community representatives may be present as well.[27] The conference was developed for use with juveniles, although conferences involving adult offenders (referred to as community group conferences) have been successfully attempted.[28]

A typical conference might have 12 people in attendance, although conferences have been conducted with substantially more participants.[29] The conference follows a scripted process. Once the coordinator has explained the procedure, the offenders begin telling their side of the story. They are followed by the victims, who describe their experience, express their feelings and direct questions (if they have them) to the offenders. The victims' families and friends may speak as well if they wish. The offenders' families and friends are then given the opportunity to speak.

Following this phase, the coordinator directs the conference into a discussion of what should be done to repair the injuries caused by the crime. The victims, their families and their friends have an opportunity to state their expectations, and the offenders and their families and friends respond. Negotiation continues until all participants in the conference agree to a plan, which is then recorded.

Although FGCs are relatively new, several evaluation studies show promising results. Victim satisfaction with the conferences is very high, consistently around 90 percent.[30] Restitution agreements have been reached in 95 percent of the cases,[31] and restitution pay-

---

[26] Fred McElrea, "Justice in the Community: The New Zealand Experience," in Jonathan Burnside and Nicola Baker, eds., *Relational Justice: Repairing the Breach* (Winchester, UK: Waterside Press, 1994), 98.

[27] *See also* Ted Wachtel, "Family Group Conferencing: Restorative Justice In Practice," *Juvenile Justice Update* 1(4) (1995): 1, 14.

[28] McElrea, *supra* note 26, at 99-100.

[29] *See* Wachtel, *supra* note 27, recounting a conference with 30 participants. The following description is based on his article.

[30] D.B. Moore and T.A. O'Connell, "Family Conferencing in Wagga Wagga: A Communitarian Model of Justice," in Christine Alder and Joy Wundersitz, eds., *Family Conferencing and Juvenile Justice: The Way Forward or Misplaced Optimism?* (Canberra: Australian Institute of Criminology, 1994), 71.

[31] David Moore, "Evaluating Family Group Conferences," in David Biles and Sandra McKillop, eds., *Criminal Justice Planning and Coordination: Proceedings of a Conference Held 19-21 April 1993, Canberra* (1994), 222.

ments have been completed without police follow-up in more than 90 percent of those cases.[32] Repeat criminal behavior appears to be between one-third[33] and one-half[34] of what would normally be expected. A research team that conducted extensive interviews of a randomly selected sample of participants concluded that offenders had developed empathy for their victims, that many families of offenders reported that their child's behavior had changed after the conference, that the support networks of the offender had been strengthened, and that an improved relationship had developed between a number of the parents and police officers.[35]

Victim-Offender Panels

Not all offenders are caught. Moreover, even when a crime is "solved" by the conviction of the offender, the victim or offender may not wish to meet with the other[36] or there may be logistical problems that hinder such a meeting from taking place.[37] In each of these instances, victim-offender panels may provide willing parties an opportunity for a kind of indirect encounter.

A victim-offender panel (VOP) is made up of a group of victims and a group of offenders who are usually linked by a common *kind* of crime, although the particular crimes of which they were the perpetrators or offenders are not in common. In other words, where VORP and FGC meetings bring together offenders with their victims, VOPs bring together groups of unrelated victims and offenders.[38] The purpose of these meetings is to help victims find resolution and to expose offenders to the damage caused to others by their crime,[39] thereby producing a change in the offender's attitudes and behaviors.[40]

---

[32] Wachtel, *supra* note 27, at 14.

[33] Moore, *supra* note 31, at 222.

[34] Wachtel, *supra* note 27, at 14.

[35] Moore and O'Connell, *supra* note 30, at 69-70.

[36] Umbreit has reported that in one program more than 40 percent of cases referred to a mediation center resulted in no mediation. In 35 percent of those cases, the victim was unwilling to participate; in 24 percent the offender was unwilling to participate; and in 10 percent one of the parties could not be located. Umbreit, et al., *supra* note 21, at 21.

[37] Launay and Murray, *supra* note 3, at 113, 121.

[38] Ibid., 121. *See also* Janice Harris Lord, *Victim Impact Panels: A Creative Sentencing Opportunity* (MADD, 1990), 6.

[39] Launay and Murray, *supra* note 3, at 113.

[40] Dorothy Mercer, Rosanne Lorden and Janice Lord, "Drunken Driving Victim Impact Panels: Victim Outcomes," a paper presented to the American Psychological Association Convention, August 11, 1995, New York City, 4.

VOPs are much more varied in form and content than VORPs and FGCs.[41] A program in England, for example, brings together victims of burglary with youthful offenders who have been convicted of unrelated burglaries. The two groups of four to six persons each meet for three weekly sessions of 90 minutes each. During the meetings there is discussion and role-play involving all of the participants and directed by a facilitator.[42]

In the United States, Mothers Against Drunk Driving (MADD) organizes Victim Impact Panels (or Drunk Driving Impact Panels, if offenders or other nonvictims are included) to expose convicted drunk driving offenders to the harm caused to victims and their survivors. The offenders are typically ordered to attend by a judge or probation officer. The victims are selected by MADD or other victim support groups based on two criteria: whether the experience of telling their story is likely to be more helpful than harmful for the victim, and whether they are able to speak without blaming or accusing offenders.[43] There is a single meeting of 60 to 90 minutes duration, during which the victims speak. Carefully screened offenders may participate as panel members if they have shown remorse, have completed all aspects of their sentence or have agreed that participation will not benefit them in a reduction of their sentence, and a screening committee has determined that the remorse expressed seems genuine and that the offender will be an effective speaker.[44] There is no interaction between the victims on the panel and the offenders in the audience, although if the victims agree, there may be a brief question-and-answer period or informal conversation at the conclusion of their presentations.[45]

Studies suggest that VOPs can be beneficial to the victims and offenders who participate. Victims in the burglary panels reported that they were less angry and anxious as a result of the meetings. Offenders demonstrated a better understanding of the impact of their crime on victims: those who believed that burglary victims were more upset about having a stranger come into their house than they were about losing property increased from 22 percent before the meetings to 57 percent after.[46] Research on drunk driving panels has

[41] For example, Dünkel and Rössner describe a prison-based program in Hameln in which young rapists meet with a group of "voluntary female non-professional therapists," many drawn from the women's movement, to help the offender understand the effect of rape on the life of the victim, and to reduce recidivism by teaching respect for female sexual self-determination. Frieder Dünkel and Dieter Rössner, "Law and Practice of Victim/Offender Agreements," in Martin Wright and Burt Galaway, eds., *Mediation and Criminal Justice: Victims, Offenders and Community* (Newbury Park, CA: Sage Publications, 1989), 152, 167.

[42] Launay and Murray, *supra* note 3, at 113, 119-120, 123.

[43] Lord, *supra* note 38, at 21.

[44] Lord, *supra* note 38, at 7.

[45] Lord, *supra* note 38, at 6.

[46] Launay and Murray, *supra* note 3, at 126-127.

shown a dramatic change in the attitudes of offenders[47] and in the likelihood of recidivism,[48] and it has also shown a significant benefit to the victim participants: 82 percent reported that it had helped in their healing. These results were even more dramatic when the participants were compared with a control group of nonparticipants, and when other variables (such as counseling and elapsed time since the crash) were controlled for: participants manifested a higher sense of well-being, lower anxiety and less anger than nonparticipants.[49]

Elements of Encounter

Several aspects of the meeting between Achilles and Priam seem to have been particularly important to Homer. The first, of course, was that they actually met. This was not the story of shuttle diplomacy, nor of negotiation by proxies. Priam came to Achilles' tent for the *meeting* and the two men talked and ate together. The second is that they spoke personally; they told the story from their own perspective. This admittedly personalized approach has been called *narrative*. They did not attempt to generalize or universalize, but instead spoke with feeling about the particulars of the decade-long conflict that concerned them most. The third is related; they exhibited *emotion* in their communication. They wept as they considered their own losses; they wept as they identified with those of the other. They experienced not only sorrow but anger and fear. Emotion played a significant role in their interaction. A fourth element is *understanding*. They listened as well as spoke, and they listened with understanding, and that helped them acquire a degree of empathy for the other. Fifth, they came to an *agreement* that was particular and achievable. Achilles agreed to turn over Hector's body for burial and in addition agreed to give the Trojans time to conduct Hector's funeral.

These elements are also found in the encounter programs described above. All three involve a meeting between victims and offenders. In VORP and FGC the meetings are between offenders and their own victims; with VOP the meetings are between representative victims and offenders. This means that what takes place

---

[47] In one study, nearly 90 percent of the offenders indicated before attending the panel that they would continue to drink and drive or that they were undecided. After the panel, 90 percent stated that they would not drink and drive again. Lord, *supra* note 38, at 14.

[48] The recidivism of one group over a one year period was 8.8 percent compared to a general recidivism rate of 40-45 percent. Another study found that a control group of offenders who did not attend a victim impact panel had a recidivism rate three times higher than the group that did attend panels. Lord, *supra* note 38, at 14.

[49] Mercer, Lorden and Lord, *supra* note 40, at 10-11.

during the encounter is directed to the other party, in contrast to court proceedings at which the best that will happen is that each party will be able to observe the other's statements to the judge or jury. The face-to-face dimension of the encounter is a foundation for the following elements.

At the meeting, the parties talk to one another; they tell their stories. In their narrative they describe what happened to them and how that has affected them, and how they see the crime and its consequences. This is a subjective rather than objective account and, consequently, it has integrity both to the speaker and to the listener. MADD suggests to victim panelists in drunk driving panels:

> Simply tell your story. . . . After you've given the facts about the crash, talk about how you feel NOW—not yesterday or a week ago or when the crash happened. This will keep your story relevant and poignant and protect you from giving the same presentation over and over again. Speak what is true for you, and you can trust that it will be "right."[50]

Narrative permits the participants to express and address emotion. Crime can produce powerful emotional responses that obstruct the more dispassionate pursuit of justice to which courts aspire. Encounter programs provide a context in which those emotions can be expressed. This can result in healing for both victims and offenders. All three of the encounter programs described above recognize the importance of emotion in training facilitators, preparing participants and establishing ground rules. As a result, crime and its consequences are addressed not only rationally but emotionally as well.

The use of meeting, narrative and emotion leads to understanding. As David Moore has observed about FGC meetings, "in this context of shared emotions, victim and offender achieve a sort of empathy. This may not make the victim feel particularly positive about the offender but it does make the offender seem more normal, less malevolent."[51] Likewise, for offenders, hearing the victims' story not only humanizes their victim but also can change the offenders' attitude about their criminal behavior.

Reaching an understanding such as this establishes a productive foundation for coming to an agreement about what should happen next. Encounter programs seek a resolution that fits the immediate parties rather than focusing on the precedential importance of the decision, which opens up the possibility of a uniquely crafted "win-win" resolution reflecting the circumstances of each. Further, they do

---

[50] Lord, *supra* note 38, at 23.

[51] Moore, *supra* note 31, at 213.

this through a cooperative process rather than an adversarial one, through negotiation that searches for a convergence of the interests of victim and offender by giving them the ability to guide the outcome.

Do these elements—meeting, narrative, emotion, understanding and agreement—yield reconciliation when combined? Not necessarily. Achilles and Priam's meeting did not result in the two men becoming friends, nor did it end the surrounding hostilities. But it did increase their ability to see each other as persons, to respect each other and to identify with the experiences of the other, and it did make it possible for them to arrive at an agreement. In other words, some reconciling had occurred. As Claassen and Zehr have noted:

> Hostility and reconciliation need to be viewed as opposite poles on a continuum. Crime usually involves hostile feelings on the part of both victim and offender. If the needs of victim and offender are not met and if the victim-offender relationship is not addressed, the hostility is likely to remain or worsen. . . . If however, victim and offender needs are addressed, the relationship may be moved toward the reconciliation pole, which in itself is worthwhile.[52]

Strategic Issues

Programs that facilitate encounters between victims and offenders have a number of advantages, as we have seen, but they also raise some important issues that should be considered carefully before implementing or using such programs. This chapter will conclude with a review of several strategic issues of particular importance to policymakers and practitioners:

1. How can these programs be made as noncoercive as possible?

2. Who should be included in the encounter?

3. How well do these programs accommodate pluralism and individualism?

4. What are the limitations of the encounter?

---

[52] Ron Claassen and Howard Zehr, *VORP Organizing: A Foundation in the Church* (Elkhart, IN: Mennonite Central Committee U.S. Office of Criminal Justice, 1989), 5.

Coercion

We have said that one of the attributes of the criminal justice system is that it is coercive: government has the authority to punish offenders against their wishes and to compel others (even victims) to participate in the process of exacting retribution.[53] This coercive power is central to the Anglo-American understanding of the criminal justice system and of the due process rights afforded to those subject to it.[54] Any proposal to incorporate encounter as a response to crime must therefore address the problem of coercion and the protection of the dignity of victims and offenders.

Mediation, on the other hand, has been described as a voluntary process, used by disputants because they want to resolve their dispute and not because they are compelled to do so.[55] Many have also noted that it is difficult to refer to a process as truly voluntary if it exists in the context of the highly coercive criminal justice system.[56] This is particularly so when offenders agree to mediate in hopes of receiving a more lenient sentence than they would have without undergoing the reconciliation process. Does this expectation mean that the encounter program is "coercive"? We suggest that it does not, in and of itself, render the offender's participation involuntary. The existence of alternatives to mediation, even ones that produce results more onerous than those achieved by mediation, does not mean that the offender is coerced into mediating, as long as the alternatives can be defended as just. It is, in fact, only when there are no alternatives to mediation that mediation becomes truly coercive. Those who choose to mediate—victims as well as offenders—do so because they believe that there is an advantage to taking this approach rather than litigating or resorting to other alternatives. Those who feel otherwise will simply allow the criminal justice system to take its course.

Two other kinds of coercion have been mentioned in regard to mediation. The first is the pressure under which some victims may be placed in an effort to secure their participation in mediating the offense. Some have referred to this as a kind of second victimization.[57] In its crudest form, the pressure can be an offer by the offender or his or her representatives to make compensation in return for dropping charges. A mediator may also exert pressure on the victim

---

[53] Cf. Chapter Four, especially the discussion of Objection Four.

[54] *See, e.g.,* Herbert Packer, *The Limits of Criminal Sanction* (Stanford: Stanford University Press, 1968) and Mirjan Damaska, "Evidentiary Barriers to Convction and Two Models of Criminal Procedure: A Comparative Study," *U. Pa. L. Rev.* 121 (1973): 506, 574-577.

[55] This claim is raised about mediation generally (*see, e.g.,* Joel Feinberg, *Harm to Others* (New York: Oxford University Press, 1984, S7-S8) and about victim-offender reconciliation programs in particular (*see, e.g.,* Umbreit, et al., *supra* note 21).

[56] *See, e.g.,* Umbreit, et al., *supra* note 21, at 99-100.

[57] Ibid., 99.

in an attempt to overcome early and natural resistance on the part of a victim to meeting with the offender. As in the case of offenders, victims are coerced into mediation to the extent that inducements or sanctions *other than the natural consequences of litigation* are raised. Threats or bribes by the offender are inappropriate (and illegal); and harassment, even by a well-meaning mediator, is improper as well. However, it is appropriate and important that victims as well as offenders receive complete and accurate information about the alternatives they have for resolving the dispute. Mark Umbreit has suggested the following as a way of approaching crime victims with the option of victim-offender reconciliation:

> Many victims have found it helpful to confront their offender, to let them know what it felt like and to have direct input into developing a restitution agreement. You may or may not find it helpful. If you would like to hear more about the program, you can then make your decision about whether you would like to get involved in it.[58]

Some writers have identified a final problem of coercion in the movement toward informal dispute resolution programs such as victim-offender reconciliation or family group conferencing programs: the possibility that these programs are promoted because they are likely to benefit the ones advocating them. When lawyers and jurists began to suggest that some disputes were better handled outside the law, Jerold S. Auerbach concluded that this was simply an effort by the legal profession to take control of the informal justice movement.[59] When government officials endorse the use of programs such as VORP or FGC, is it merely a "way to introduce a new form of social control that is more pervasive and powerful than formal law"?[60] The coercion these writers see is subtle; what appears to be voluntary is in fact compelled; what seems to be the path of liberty for a victim or offender in fact turns out to be "a new form of social control." This problem is substantially reduced when the institution offering mediation has no coercive powers, which is another reason for our interest in community-based programs.

Parties Involved

The VORP process typically involves a mediator as well as the crime victim and offender. Sometimes the victim or offender asks to have parents or friends present, or even (on rare occasions) to be rep-

---

[58] Umbreit, *supra* note 11, at 89.

[59] Jerold S. Auerbach, *Justice Without Law?* (New York: Oxford University Press, 1983).

[60] David M. Trubek, "Turning Away From Law?," *Mich. L. Rev.* 82 (1984): 824, 830.

resented by a surrogate, and in some programs the community may be formally represented through designated participants. Usually the process includes only the individuals directly involved. When there are multiple victims, each victim has the opportunity to participate, and there will be as many VORP processes as there are victims. The family group conference, on the other hand, intentionally includes family and friends of the parties as well as community representatives. When there are multiple victims and offenders, they and their families may be included in a single process. [61]

The Facilitator

The facilitator is responsible for approaching the victim and offender about the possibility of an encounter and for guiding the actual meeting. Although many programs rely on volunteer facilitators, in the case of serious or violent crimes in which a greater level of therapeutic expertise is needed, professional mediators may be used instead.[62] A critical part of the mediator's function is to prepare the way for the actual meeting. Once the intake procedures have been handled by program staff and the case is assigned to a facilitator, a careful process of preparation begins in which the facilitator explains the purpose and process of the particular encounter program to the individual parties to see whether they are willing to meet. The facilitator's approach will vary from case to case, depending on individual participants and their needs. The facilitator must always be especially sensitive to the victim's needs and the timing of the victim's recovery process—particularly when the crime was serious or violent. The facilitator should be trained to handle the complex emotional issues experienced by victims, and to be familiar with local mental health and social service resources to which clients may be referred. The facilitator is not a judge or arbitrator, impartially deciding which party has the best argument and then imposing a ruling. Nor is the facilitator an advocate for either the victim or offender in helping them achieve their goals for the reconciliation process.

---

[61] Wachtel, *supra* note 27.

[62] For a discussion of mediation in cases of violent crime, *see* Mark Umbreit, "Violent Offenders and Their Victims," in Martin Wright and Burt Galaway, eds., *Mediation and Criminal Justice: Victims, Offenders and Community* (Newbury Park, CA: Sage Publications, 1989). In addition, *see* Walter Bera, "Victim-Sensitive Offender Therapy with a Systemic and Attributional Analysis," in James Yokley, ed., *The Use of Victim Offender Communication in the Treatment of Sexual Abuse* (Orwell, VT: Safer Society Press, 1990). Bera has developed a therapeutic approach to some of the issues between sex offenders and their victims. However, unlike the typical VORP approach, the offender (after careful groundwork has been laid) initially communicates to the victim through a letter of apology. Sometimes this is eventually followed by a face-to-face meeting, but in many cases the victim and offender do not meet. Gustafson and Smidstra have compiled a report on the feasibility of victim-offender reconciliation in cases of serious crime, using interviews with both inmates and victims. Overall, the results were positive. *See* David L. Gustafson and Henk Smidstra, "Victim Offender Reconciliation in Serious Crime," a report on the feasibility study undertaken for the Ministry of the Solicitor General (Canada) by Fraser Community Justice Initiatives Association, Langley, B.C. (May 1989).

The facilitator is not the voice of the community, pressing an offender to show remorse and a victim to speak words of forgiveness. Instead, the facilitator is a "neutral third party who arranges and directs the encounter. His or her function is to regulate and facilitate communication, not to represent one side or to impose a solution."[63] Consequently, the facilitator works to develop and maintain an atmosphere of cooperation and constructive interaction.

The Victim

The encounter process emphasizes voluntary participation by victims and offenders. Consequently, facilitators must be careful not to move from outlining the potential advantages of encounter to pressuring the victim to do something they really would prefer not to do. Mark Umbreit's caution about VORPs applies as well to other forms of encounter:

> While crime victims are encouraged to consider the possible benefits of mediation, they must not be coerced into participating. To do so, even with the best of intentions, would be to revictimize them.[64]

Victims who choose to participate in VORP and FGC are given the opportunity to ask questions of the offender, express their feelings about what occurred and suggest ways the offender can begin to make things right.[65] According to research assessing several programs in the Midwest, in entering the VORP process victims' three most important goals were to (1) recover some losses, (2) help offenders stay out of trouble, and (3) have a real part in the criminal justice process.[66] However, once they had participated in the reconciliation meeting these goals changed.

> [Victims] were most satisfied with (a) the opportunity to meet the offender and thereby obtain a better understanding of the crime and the offender's situation; (b) the opportunity to receive restitution for loss; (c) the expression of remorse on the part of the offender; (d) the care and concern of the mediator. Even though the primary motivation for participation was restitution, the most satisfying aspect of the experience was meeting the offender.[67]

---

[63] Howard Zehr and Earl Sears, *Mediating the Victim-Offender Conflict* (Elkhart, IN: Mennonite Central Committee U.S. Office of Criminal Justice, 1980), 7.

[64] Umbreit, *supra* note 21, at 8.

[65] Zehr calls these elements *facts*, *feelings* and *agreements*. Zehr, *supra* note 12, at 161.

[66] *See* Coates and Gehm, *supra* note 13, at 251-263.

[67] Ibid., 254.

A subsequent study found that 80 percent of victims who had participated in a VORP meeting reported that they had "experienced fairness," compared with fewer than 40 percent of victims who had chosen not to enter the program.[68] "Fairness" was defined by these victims as the right to participate directly in the process,[69] as rehabilitation for the offender,[70] as compensation for the victim,[71] as punishment of the offender[72] and as the offender's expression of remorse.[73] As noted above,[74] initial studies of family group conferences indicate that there is a similar degree of victim satisfaction with that form of encounter as well.

Although the facilitator is trained not to side with either the victim or offender, the process recognizes that the victim generally stands in a different moral position than the offender, having been wronged as opposed to causing the harm.[75] A key way in which this happens is that offenders participate only if they have accepted responsibility for the harm that was done. The encounter process itself will also address this issue by engaging the parties directly in conversation about it. For example, a number of programs ask the victims and offenders to identify the injustice involved in the crime, giving them the opportunity to examine the moral implications of the offender's actions.

The Offender

The encounter process puts offenders "in the uncomfortable position of having to face the person they violated. They are given the . . . opportunity to display a more human dimension to their character and to even express remorse in a very personal fashion."[76] In this way, offenders are made active participants in the process, deciding if and how they will begin to make things right with their victims. While this participation is officially voluntary, the very fact

---

[68] Mark S. Umbreit, "The Meaning of Fairness to Burglary Victims," in Burt Galaway and Joe Hudson, eds., *Criminal Justice, Restitution, and Reconciliation* (Monsey, NY: Criminal Justice Press, 1990), 47.

[69] Ibid., 50.

[70] Ibid., 51.

[71] Ibid.

[72] Ibid., 52.

[73] Ibid.

[74] *See supra* notes 26-35 and accompanying text.

[75] Of course, in some cases it is more complicated to determine who was culpable, as the crime itself took place in the context of a larger, longer-lasting conflict in which both parties have been aggressors. An advantage to mediation as opposed to criminal proceedings is that these complexities can be acknowledged and addressed. *See, e.g.,* Deborah Gatske Goolsby, "Using Mediation in Cases of Simple Rape," *Wash. & Lee L. Rev.* 47 (1990): 1183.

[76] Umbreit, *supra* note 11, at 9-10.

that many are affiliated with the criminal justice system introduces a significant element of coercion.[77] Offenders themselves may not view their participation as voluntary; Coates and Gehm found that given the alternatives facing them, most offenders participated in VORP because they felt they had no choice.[78] While a certain degree of incentive is probably appropriate, the risk that facilitators and victims run is that the offender will issue an insincere apology. Furthermore, genuine acceptance of responsibility can be an indication of a change of heart in the offender, and such acceptance may take some time.[79] Consequently, encounter programs should encourage the *voluntary* acceptance of responsibility by the offender.

According to Coates and Gehm,[80] offenders' reasons for agreeing to participate in the VORP process included avoiding harsher punishment, getting beyond the crime and its consequences, and making things right. After completing the process, however, they reported that their criteria for satisfaction with VORP had changed.

> [O]ffenders were most satisfied with: (a) meeting the victim and discovering the victim was willing to listen to him or her; (b) staying out of jail and in some instances not getting a record; (c) the opportunity to work out a realistic schedule for paying back the victim to "make things right." Strikingly, what offenders disliked most was, also, meeting the victim. This reflects the tension between, on the one hand, the stress experienced in preparation for meeting the victim, and, on the other hand, the relief of having taken steps "to make things right."[81]

Early studies of family group conferences suggest similar results. It is reasonable for offenders to experience this tension because of what they have done. Allowing the offender and victim to address what happened in a nonjudicial context gives the offender freedom to repair some of the damage he or she caused by the crime, and thus gain a better moral footing in the situation.

Support Persons

The presence or absence of support persons is the significant difference between VORPs and family group conferences. In the former,

---

[77] "When offenders are ordered by the court, via probation, or are diverted from prosecution if they complete the program, a rather significant amount of state coercion is exercised" Ibid., 8.

[78] Coates and Gehm, *supra* note 13, at 252.

[79] *See* Wright, *supra* note 10, at 95.

[80] Coates and Gehm, *supra* note 13, at 253.

[81] Ibid., at 254.

support groups are usually not included; in the latter they are. Even in traditional VORP programs, victims or offenders sometimes want to bring parents, friends or other support persons with them to the meetings. This may be allowed, or even encouraged, if the party is young or for other reasons needs assistance and the other party is willing, but the role of these support persons is not to participate in the meeting, nor to act as advocates or spokespersons for the party who invited them.[82] The purpose of the VORP meeting is to bring together a victim and offender to deal directly with the crime in a context of reduced coercion and intimidation. If a support person can help create such an environment, the programs permit their participation.

Individualism and Pluralism

The American criminal justice system emphasizes protection of the rights of individuals and distrust of official power.[83] These policy choices have resulted in the "legalism" of that system, what Karl Llewellyn called an "arm's length" system of criminal law.

> The net can perhaps be sloganized as an "arm's length" system of criminal law. The main features are familiar. An offender is viewed in first instance not as a person, not as a member of a going team whose attitude or action is bothering the team's smooth working and who therefore needs straightening out. Instead, he is viewed as a person quite outside, whom the officials are to take hold of only if they can pin upon him some specific act.[84]

The adversarial system exhibits an approach to crime that is significantly different from the more relational encounter. As Llewellyn pointed out, this system resulted from policy choices, and those choices reflected the high value Americans give to individualism.[85] We live in a society that celebrates pluralism, in communities that are culturally complex, with people who are increasingly mobile. As a result, when crime rates rise, we have nowhere to turn for relief but to the coercive powers of the criminal justice system, a system that we officially mistrust. Jerold S. Auerbach has noted that this arm's-

---

[82] In fact, they are typically seated apart from the participants, to reinforce their secondary role.

[83] For a comparison of the Anglo-American and Continental approaches, *see* Damaska, *supra* note 54, at 506.

[84] Karl N. Llewellyn, *Jurisprudence: Realism in Theory and Practice* (Chicago: University of Chicago Press, 1962), 444-445.

[85] Ibid.

length, impersonal vision of justice can produce a reflexive longing for a simpler approach, one that will actually usher in a more communal society:

> It is chimerical to believe that mediation or arbitration can now accomplish what law seems powerless to achieve. The American deification of individual rights requires an accessible legal system for their protection. Understandably, diminished faith in its capacities will encourage the yearning for alternatives. But the rhetoric of "community" and "justice" should not be permitted to conceal the deterioration of community life and the unraveling of substantive notions of justice that has accompanied its demise. There is every reason why the values that historically are associated with informal justice should remain compelling: especially the preference for trust, harmony, and reciprocity within a communal setting. These are not, however, the values that American society encourages or sustains; in their absence there is no effective alternative to legal institutions.[86]

It is possible to agree with Auerbach's point that institutions of justice (formal and informal) are reflections of the values of the community without accepting his conclusion that until those values are communitarian there "is no effective alternative to legal institutions." The institutions we develop and maintain for dealing with conflict not only reflect our values, but help shape them. By defining crime as lawbreaking, for example, the criminal justice system helps shape our expectations of who should be involved in the process, what the goals of that process are and what outcomes we should anticipate. The problem with this limited view is that it does not capture *all* the things we value. As noted earlier, victims and offenders are motivated to participate in encounter meetings for a variety of reasons, some of which (e.g., getting restitution or staying out of jail) could have been pursued through the criminal justice system. Other goals (e.g., helping the offender or making things right with the victim), however, could not have been. Even more revealing are the findings that suggest that *after* encounter meetings both victims and offenders report that their priorities have changed: what they valued most was the ability to address relational goals; self-interest goals had become secondary, although still important.[87]

---

[86] Auerbach, *supra* note 59, at 145.

[87] Umbreit et al., *supra* note 21. *See also* Mark S. Umbreit, "Restorative Justice: What Works?," paper prepared for International Community Corrections Association Research Conference, September 15-18, 1996.

In other words, the availability of a more relational approach to justice helped shape the values of the participants. Howard Zehr has reflected on VORP cases in which the victim and offender started out hostile and at the conclusion of the process were still hostile: "Yet the nature of their hostility had changed. No longer were they mad at an abstraction, at a stereotype of a victim or offender. They were now mad at a concrete person. Even that represents some improvement."[88] The stereotypic picture each had of the other was shattered, and both the victim and the offender had at least come to see the other as a person.

Individualism and pluralism certainly increase the difficulty of fashioning informal settlements. On the other hand, crime presents a point of crisis in the lives of individuals and communities that can draw people from different backgrounds together to design a restorative response. The process of discovering together what justice means in their particular crimes can help victims and offenders to understand more fully what they value, as well as to see the extent to which they share those values with the other party. The likelihood that this will happen is increased substantially when the staff and facilitators reflect the racial, ethnic and gender diversity of the community, and are trained to appropriately facilitate communication between victims and offenders who also reflect that diversity.[89]

Limitations

Encounter programs are relatively new, and from the outset many people have assumed that their use would be limited to relatively simple cases involving the least serious offenses. However, some programs have experimented with approaches that have successfully applied the methodology of a face-to-face victim-offender meeting to more serious and violent crimes.[90] Consequently, while there are certainly limitations to how victim-offender encounter *as currently practiced* can be used, it must be noted that those may reflect only our incomplete knowledge about the potential of this approach. Innovation, if done with an awareness of the limitations of current approaches, may help us develop more effective and less limited strategies.

Because victim-offender encounter depends on communication between the two parties, it is naturally limited to those cases in

---

[88] Zehr, *supra* note 12, at 188.

[89] The American Bar Association has recommended that victim-offender mediation programs meet a series of requirements, one of which is that "[m]ediators are selected from a cross-section of the community to ensure that they reflect the diversity of their community in terms of race, ethnicity, and gender and that there is accurate and meaningful communication and understanding by all parties."

[90] *See, e.g.,* Umbreit, *supra* note 62, at 99.

which both the victim and offender are interested in, and capable of, listening and communicating with the other. Psychological or emotional circumstances may hinder the ability of one or the other party to such a degree that encounter should not be attempted. Language, culture and background present obstacles as well, and it is important that those be appropriately addressed and overcome.[91]

Second, victim-offender encounter is predicated on the assumption that the offender is indeed the offender. When an accused individual does not admit culpability, VORP, FGC and VOP are not appropriate or effective means of assigning it. Thus, encounter meetings begin with an agreement that each is indeed the victim or offender and then proceed from there.[92]

Third, the process of preparing victims and offenders for their meetings can be lengthy, and sometimes cannot be accelerated to meet the time constraints of the criminal justice system. Consequently, their readiness may come at a much later date than is required to meet speedy trial provisions of the constitution, with the result that the meeting is far less likely to influence the sentence the offender receives. This is particularly true when the victim is recovering from a violent or serious offense.[93]

Finally, victim-offender encounters such as VORP or FGC cannot take place when the victim or offender is unavailable because of death, incarceration, distance or unwillingness to participate. Victim-offender panels, on the other hand, are not confronted with this limitation because they involve the use of surrogates—other victims or offenders—for a more generalized, yet helpful, conversation about crime and its aftermath.

Conclusion

Victim-offender encounter programs offer a context in which the parties to crime have an opportunity to face one another. The formal criminal justice system polarizes the parties and limits their contact, reduces the conflict to a simple binary choice of guilty/not guilty and

[91] Mark Umbreit, "Victim Offender Mediation in Urban/Multi-Cultural Settings," April 1986 (manuscript in the author's possession).

[92] But Braithwaite has noted that there are different ways in which an offender may admit culpability. One is to admit guilt to a crime. Another is to "decline to deny" guilt. A third is to accept a level of civil liability. There may be other ways in which this can be done, and it is worth considering the advantages and disadvantages. Our point, and Braithwaite's, is that encounters are not typically (or best) used to determine guilt when a defendant claims to be innocent. John Braithwaite, "Thinking Harder About Democratising Social Control," in Christine Alder and Joy Wundersitz, eds., *Family Conferencing and Juvenile Justice: The Way Forward or Misplaced Optimism?* (Canberra: Australian Institute of Criminology, 1994).

[93] Umbreit, *supra* note 62, at 109-112.

deems irrelevant any information related to the conflict and the individuals that does not directly prove or disprove the legal elements of the crime charged. An encounter, on the other hand, offers victims and offenders the chance to decide what *they* consider relevant to a discussion of the crime, tends to humanize each of them to one another and permits them substantial creativity in constructing a response that deals not only with the injustice that occurred but with the futures of both parties as well. In this discussion of victim-offender encounter programs, we have identified several elements that are key to their success.

First, the encounter process is designed to empower participants, promote dialogue and (in the cases of VORP and FGC) encourage mutual problem solving. Consequently, prudential or conceptual changes that limit their ability to do any of these should be examined very carefully to determine whether other, more effective approaches might be tried.

Second, the primary goal of these programs is to offer the opportunity for encounter of victims and offenders. While systemic pressures from various parts of the criminal justice system may attempt to move the programs to adopt new goals (such as diversion of offenders from prison), these pressures should be addressed so as not to lose sight of the overall goal. Programs should have clear missions and related goals and objectives that guide planning, operations and evaluation. Program evaluation plays a very important role in helping program administrators and funders determine whether the program is remaining focused on its mission, and whether its activities are effectively accomplishing that mission.

Third, the encounter process requires both the victim and the offender to participate voluntarily. The victim's readiness may not coincide with the pace of the criminal justice system (particularly in the case of violent or otherwise serious offenses), and program administrators will need to handle this tension with sensitivity to avoid creating a climate of coercion. Offenders who are approached to participate in encounter may hope that their willingness to do so will help get them a more lenient sentence. However, the more voluntary the party's participation, the more likely it is that reconciliation and healing will take place. Consequently, program administrators will encourage the offender's voluntary acceptance of responsibility.

Fourth, encounter programs are most effective when they are motivated equally by concern for victims and offenders, and not allied with the interests of one or the other. This is important for program administrators to consider in adopting program goals, and in considering how to incorporate the concerns and interests of persons responsible for the local criminal justice system. A program that has been funded to divert offenders from prison, for example, will design its screening policies and procedures carefully to identify offenders who might be prison-bound, but once the case has proceeded past the screening stage it will proceed impartially.

Finally, encounter programs must be designed to meet the needs of the victims and offenders who will participate in them. Consequently, training, facilitator selection, policies and procedures related to contact with the victim and offender as well as to how to conduct the meetings will vary from program to program. In particular, violent and more serious cases require more intense, longer and more professional intervention and support than do most nonviolent or less serious cases.

Chapter Six

Reparation

Reparation is a restorative way for the justice system to respond to the harm done to victims. Webster defines *reparation* as "the act of making amends, offering expiation, or giving satisfaction for a wrong or injury; something done or given as amends or satisfaction."[1] A reparative sanction such as restitution,[2] then, is one that requires the offender to recompense the victim for the harm sustained. Restitution is made by returning or replacing property,[3] by monetary payment[4] or by performing direct services for the victim.

---

[1] *Webster's New Collegiate Dictionary.* Although *restitution* is a more commonly used term, it is only one of several means of "repairing" the harm. Reparation involves any means by which a victim's harm or injuries resulting from crime are made good. Restitution is an offender's monetary or other repayment for damages sustained by a victim of the offender's crime.

[2] In some countries the term *compensation* is used instead of restitution. *See, e.g.,* Lucia Zedner, "Victims," in Mike Maguire, Rod Morgan and Robert Reiner, eds., *The Oxford Handbook of Criminology* (New York: Oxford University Press, 1994), 1237, 1239. However, we will use that term more narrowly to refer to payments made by the government or by another party unrelated to the offender, in an amount typically based on the nature and extent of the harm. Compensation was first proposed in modern times by a British Magistrate, Margery Fry, who argued that because government has assumed responsibility for public order and forbidden private citizens from arming themselves in self-defense, crime represents government's failure to protect the victim. She proposed that compensation would be one way of making amends. (Margery Fry, "Justice For Victims," *London Observer,* 7 July 1957). Few governments have been willing to recognize victim compensation as an obligation they owe to victims, but many have implemented victim compensation schemes. This chapter will focus on restitution and other reparative sanctions that require the offender to assume responsibility for the injury resulting from the crime, rather than on obligations the government assumes as a result of the breakdown of order.

[3] Alan Harland's survey of restitution statutes and the court opinions interpreting them led him to conclude that this is the narrowest application of the term used by legislators, and that it is typically referred to as *restoration.* (Alan T. Harland, "Monetary Remedies for the Victims of Crime: Assessing the Role of the Criminal Courts," *UCLA L. Rev.* 30 (1982): 52, 61.

[4] Harland found disagreement over whether the monetary payment should be based on the fruits of the offense or the loss or damage caused by the offense. The Supreme Court of Oregon, for example, held:

As we saw in Part I, there is ample evidence that reparation was an important part of criminal justice in the past. Even after the shift in thinking that led to the offender becoming the passive recipient of sanctions imposed by criminal courts, calls for reparative sanctions continued to be raised. In his 1516 book *Utopia*, Sir Thomas More proposed that convicts be sentenced to work on public works for pay in order to have funds from which to reimburse their victims. The eighteenth-century philosopher Jeremy Bentham argued for mandatory restitution in money or in-kind services in all property crimes. In the latter part of the nineteenth century, a succession of reformers proposed to international penal conferences that restitution be revived. Such calls continued into the twentieth century. In some instances, these were based on the principle of fairness to victims; in others, on the beneficial effects to the offender.[5] It was not until the 1980s, however, that restitution became firmly established in the United States.[6] It is, however, a sanction of secondary importance to other more traditional sanctions in the criminal justice system.[7]

Who Should Receive Reparation?

Alan Harland's survey of restitution statutes found substantial ambiguity concerning who was eligible to receive restitution.[8] Some legislative schemes specified particular classes of victims, such as the elderly or physically disabled, whom courts were to favor in imposing restitution orders.[9] Others specified types of victims who were ineligible for restitution, such as accomplices in the crime.[10] Still others used the enigmatic term "aggrieved parties."[11] Harland noted that appellate courts have had to decide whether the public is entitled to restitution of the costs of prosecution,[12] whether insurers or other third parties are eligible to recover their losses[13] and whether

---

We construe the term "restitution" to mean the return of a sum of money, an object, or the value of an object which a defendant wrongfully obtained in the course of committing the crime. "Reparation" is a somewhat broader term which has been defined as a "repairing or being repaired; restoration to good condition." This construction would embrace medical expenses, wages actually (not prospectively) lost, and reimbursement for easily measurable property damage. (State v. Stalheim, 275 Or. 683, 687-88, 552 P.2d 829, 832 (1976), as cited in Harland, *supra* note 3, at 63 n.69).

[5] Bruce Jacob, "The Concept of Restitution: An Historical Overview," in Joe Hudson and Burt Galaway, eds., *Restitution in Criminal Justice* (Lexington, MA: D.C. Heath and Company, 1975), 47-51.

[6] Andrew Karmen, *Crime Victims: An Introduction to Victimology*, 2d ed. (Pacific Grove, CA: Brooks/Cole Publishing Company, 1990), 282.

[7] Ibid.

[8] Harland, *supra* note 3, at 78-80.

[9] Ibid., 78.

[10] Ibid.

[11] Ibid.

[12] Florida courts decided that it was; California courts have disagreed. Ibid.

[13] In a federal case the surety on a fiduciary bond was held eligible, in cases in New York and Oregon the insurer was held not eligible. Ibid., 79.

survivors of victims who died as a result of the crime are eligible for recovery of related expenses.[14]

If we imagine a series of concentric circles around each crime, the direct victim—the one against whom the crime was perpetrated—would be in the center circle. The remaining categories of victims could be placed in the remaining circles, with secondary victims such as homicide survivors in the second circle, the local community in which the crime took place in the third, those who have suffered indirect injuries, such as insurers or employers in the next, and the general public in the last (see Figure 6.1). Must a reparative criminal sanction include all the victims in each of these circles? Can it do so? The claim to reparation loses intensity and credibility as the harm involved becomes less concrete, but it does not follow that those claims must be ignored or minimized; after all, criminal laws express the public's censure of behavior that violates the *common* weal. Even more, criminal laws and the institutions of the criminal justice system encourage a public expectation of safety and security that is violated when crime occurs.

Figure 6.1

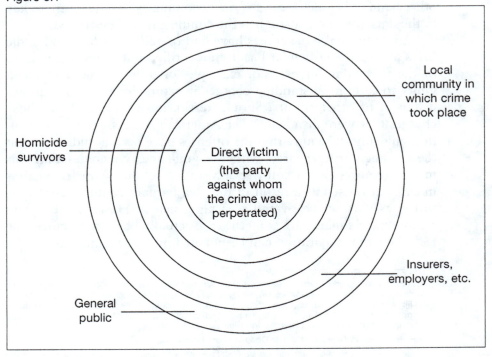

___

[14] Most states have concluded that they are. Ibid., 80.

We suggest, as a general principle, that those who have suffered *direct and specific* injuries receive compensation in criminal proceedings.[15] Therefore, the more indirect or general the injuries, the less obligation there would be for a judge to order restitution. For practical reasons, it may be useful for legislatures to establish categories of victims and injuries that are eligible for restitution so that the decision need not be made on a case-by-case basis, but such categories should reflect the principle of directness and specificity.[16] This will be particularly important in considering the role of community service orders, which require the offender to serve a specified number of hours performing unpaid labor. These have sometimes been described as a form of reparation for harm done to the community, but without first defining the exact harm done to the community, it is unlikely that this will be anything more than a rhetorical and imprecise phrase, with the resulting sentence having less to do with reparation than with enhanced punishment. For example, if a burglar who destroyed a school's computer equipment is sentenced to "community" service picking up highway trash, how can this be described as reparative? It is not at all clear who is being compensated (is it the highway department? taxpayers in general? the people who use the highway?) or how they were injured in a direct and specific way by the crime. On the other hand, it is much clearer if the "community" service were to key in the data that were lost when the equipment was destroyed.

An additional issue courts have had to address is how to handle cases in which an offender has been identified but is never convicted of the particular offense. For example, offenders sometimes plead guilty to certain outstanding charges in return for the prosecution's dismissal of other counts. Should restitution be ordered for those charges that were dismissed? The American Bar Association restitution guidelines[17] require that the offenses have been adjudicated, but the commentary prepared with the guidelines concludes that this merely requires that a court review and sanction the order; victims in cases dismissed as a result of the plea bargain could receive restitution as part of the overall plea agreement.[18] However, the more remote the claimants are from the case actually being prosecuted, the less likely that reparation can be pursued in the criminal case.[19]

---

[15] This recommendation follows the reasoning of the American Bar Association Criminal Justice Section in its commentary on the *Guidelines Governing Restitution to Victims of Criminal Conduct* (1988), 6: [I]t is contemplated that damages that are not directly related to the criminal conduct of the defendant will not be considered. Damages which are not easily quantified, e.g., pain and suffering, mental anguish and loss of consortium, are excluded.

[16] *See* discussion of Objection Three in Chapter Four of this book.

[17] American Bar Association Criminal Justice Section in its commentary on the *Guidelines Governing Restitution to Victims of Criminal Conduct* (including commentary on the guidelines) (1988).

[18] Ibid., 8.

[19] "Part of the rationale for the limited merging of the criminal and civil courts permitted by the restitution procedure is that the parties to both actions are the same and are thus before the court with what also may prove to be the only realistic opportunity to resolve all issues between them." American Bar Association, "Comment to Guideline 1.2" Ibid.

Should Reparation Reflect the Seriousness of the Offense or of the Injury?

Some actions are more detrimental to public order than others. Relative seriousness is not necessarily reflected in the physical damage that results. For example, an aborted attempt to break into a building may result in a broken window, but so might a failed assassination attempt; in such a case, replacing broken glass is not the only issue that must be addressed. The gravity of attempted murder is not adequately addressed by a restitution order. This is reflected in the charges that will be brought in each case as well as in the sentences imposed. Standards of lawful conduct must be reinforced by considering the seriousness and nature of the offense as well as the nature of harm suffered by the victim and the community in which it occurred.[20]

Andrew Klein describes how courts across the United States have used these considerations to design many sentences that are primarily nonincarcerative for a wide range of serious, even violent, offenses. If such sentences included restitution, they would address the harm done to the victim while confirming the unacceptability of the behavior.[21] For example, according to the U.S. Department of Justice, the median loss from household burglary in 1993 was $200.[22] Would straight reparation sufficiently address the seriousness of burglary? What if a standard minimum amount of, say, $500 per offense was expected of offenders convicted of household burglary? The victim's loss would be the first claim on that amount, and any excess would go to a crime victims' compensation fund. If the victim's losses were greater than $500, then the full amount of the loss would be considered in the sentence. Aggravating or mitigating circumstances in the offense, the offender, the victim and/or the locale would influence the sentence in terms of reparative and punitive amounts, as well as incapacitative and rehabilitative conditions.

We argued in Part I that multiple goals can be pursued to advance the restorative justice purpose of restoring into safe communities victims and offenders who have resolved their conflicts. There we suggested that considerations of fairness (that is, what is a

---

[20] These are not, of course, the only considerations in sentencing. As we will suggest, the offender's risk of future criminality and potential for dangerousness must also be considered, as well as the offender's ability to make reparation. Further, it may be appropriate for the court to consider local standards as well. None of these factors may be excluded from the sentencing decision but they must be balanced in a principled way.

[21] Andrew R. Klein, *Alternative Sentencing: A Practitioner's Guide* (Cincinnati: Anderson Publishing Co., 1988).

[22] Craig Perkins et al., *Criminal Victimization in the United States, 1993* (Bureau of Justice Statistics, U.S. Department of Justice, May 1996).

fair sentence for this offense?) could determine the amount of a sanction, while redress (that is, what will it take to make good the victim's loss?) could determine the method of the sanction. When the resulting financial penalty is more or less than the actual loss of the victim, a victim compensation fund could be used to receive the excess penalty or to make up for the uncompensated loss. However they are designed, sanctions should emphasize redress of the harm to victims. The risk and needs of offenders, as well as the seriousness of offenses, should be addressed in ways that do not defeat this primary purpose.

For Which Injuries Should Reparation Be Provided?

The government has a legitimate interest in curtailing individual liberty in order to prevent behavior that causes or presents a risk of serious harm to persons or society. If avoiding harms is one of the justifications for making and enforcing laws that prohibit criminal behavior, then it follows that harm should be addressed in the establishment of penalties or sanctions.[23] But what kinds of harm can properly be redressed through criminal sanctions? Harm falls into several general categories: property loss, damage or destruction; physical and psychological injury; and death. These involve medical and rehabilitative costs, lost wages and out-of-pocket expenses. Crimes often result in less direct damage as well, such as rising fear in a neighborhood that was once considered safe, or a growing general sense of lawlessness. Restitution alone may be insufficient to address these kinds of harm. However, opportunities to "unmask" the fear and anger through open discussion and positive action can help a neighborhood or community overcome the effects of victimization.[24]

In the late 1980s, the Criminal Justice Section of the American Bar Association examined the legal boundaries and precedents related to restitution, concluding that since the purpose of restitution is to reimburse the victim, there is "no reason to place unreasonable limitations upon the type of damages recoverable." It left much latitude to courts, with the exception that courts should not consider damages that are not directly related to the criminal conduct of the

---

[23] *See* Joel Feinberg, *Harm to Others* (New York: Oxford University Press, 1984), 31. "The criminal law system is the primary instrumentality for preventing people from intentionally or recklessly harming one another."

[24] This happened in Genesee County, New York, where a community was shocked and outraged by a serious sniping incident. There are also examples of neighborhoods that have organized against drug dealing. Reparation by convicted offenders may be an important part of the healing, as in Genesee County, but it must take place in a context where the community itself takes positive action.

defendant or damages that are not easily quantified (such as pain and suffering).[25] These should be pursued in civil proceedings.

We suggest that a guiding principle for reparation be that insofar as possible, the most significant harm suffered should be the first to be redressed through reparative sentencing. For example, if a victim misses two weeks of work due to hospitalization for injuries sustained from a robbery, the hospitalization and injury expenses may be the most significant harm. The lost wages should be reimbursed as well, but as a subcategory of the most serious harm suffered by the victim.

Is Reparation Feasible?

Few offenders have the income or resources at hand to repay their victims. This discourages many victims or prosecutors from requesting restitution orders. Studies have shown, however, that restitution could be utilized more often if courts and correctional authorities were committed to restitution as a sentencing priority.[26] For example, offenders could be put to work to provide the means to repay their victims. If needed, offenders could be given extra time by the court to complete their restitutionary obligations, without necessarily continuing other conditions of community correctional supervision beyond the normal sentence. In some cases, when a victim's need for redress is immediate and the victim cannot or will not wait for the offender to pay, a reparative option could be to compensate the victim from a central fund (as discussed above), with the offender later reimbursing the fund.

In some jurisdictions, compensation funds are established using monies paid by offenders for whom no direct victim needed payment and by excess funds when sentences exceeded the reparation due the victim. Victims who cannot recover damages from their offenders can be repaid from the fund. Forfeiture laws can be applied so that seized assets are used to support compensation funds or assist communities ravaged by crime. The important thing is that offenders make reparation and victims receive redress—directly when possible, indirectly when necessary.

---

[25] American Bar Association, *Guidelines Governing Restitution to Victims of Criminal Conduct* (including commentary on the guidelines) (1988), 5-6. The federal Victim and Witness Protection Act of 1982 states that the court must not be unduly burdened or the proceeding unduly broadened by including a restitution action in a criminal case.

[26] *See* Barbara E. Smith, Robert C. Davis and Susan Hillenbrand, *Improving Enforcement of Court-Ordered Restitution: Executive Summary* (A Study of the American Bar Association Criminal Justice Section Victim Witness Project, 1989).

Some have advocated the use of community service in cases where offenders are financially unable to pay restitution. As previously discussed, the problem with this concept is that the service is often arbitrarily assigned and bears no relation (either for the offender or the victim) to the harm caused by the offense. If community service is a reparative option acceptable to the victim and the court (due to the victim's preference or the offender's circumstances), it should be as closely related as possible to the harm. Preferably the circumstances preventing the offender from payment should be positively addressed so that monetary restitution is feasible over time.

A commitment to reparation involves a commitment to making it feasible. Impediments to reparation can be overcome by committed government and community agencies working together.[27] Currently, an offender's inability to pay is often simply accepted, and the victim's hope of redress set aside. The government, local businesses, vocational educators and others can cooperate to address the reasons why an offender has no means. When rehabilitative interventions are needed, human services agencies could also be involved. The community setting provides a potential network of services and opportunities that can help make reparation work.[28]

How Can Courts Manage the Risk of Community-Based Sentences?

Our criminal justice system seeks to uphold the integrity of law by meting out punishment to those offenders it apprehends; they are punished because they broke the law. As we have seen, though, crime is more than lawbreaking; it also causes injuries to victims, the community and even to offenders.[29] A response to crime that does nothing about those injuries, or that seeks to repair the wounds of only one of the parties, will also fall short of restorative justice. An example of the latter is the rehabilitation movement of the nineteenth century. Its most notorious edifice, the prison, was originally conceived as a place of repentance and rehabilitation for offenders. While prisons are now generally acknowledged to be a failure at that purpose,

---

[27] Examples of such commitment are the Quincy, Massachusetts, Earn-It Program, and Genesee Justice in Genesee County, New York.

[28] We recognize that there are many issues involved here, including social and structural injustices. We do not intend to minimize these. They must be addressed if justice is to be advanced. Criminal justice is just one piece of the whole cloth of justice, and its "solutions" are limited. Just enabling an offender to make payments to his or her victim will not ameliorate the root social problems. However, if, for example, making reparation feasible would provide skills and experience that would enhance an offender's future employability, it might be one step in the right direction.

[29] As explained in Part One. More will be said in Chapter Seven as well.

the institution lives on as a place in which to punish offenders and incapacitate dangerous criminals.[30] While it is intuitively obvious that imprisonment is one way to incapacitate, it is less obvious why prison should be the punishment of choice for offenders who do not pose the kind of risk that necessitates 24-hour incarceration. Community-based sanctions such as probation, electronic monitoring and day reporting centers are principally justified on the pragmatic ground of cost-effectiveness, suggesting that were sufficient funds available even those offenders would be locked up.

Seventy percent of the people convicted of felony crimes are sentenced to jail or prison.[31] Why this attraction to incarceration? Why does America use this expensive, limited resource so extensively? We suspect that in part it is a force of habit, as prison sentences have become the standard against which all other punishments are measured. In part it is because the offenders who do require close incapacitation often commit the kind of crimes most people fear—sudden, unprovoked, violent attacks by a stranger. Prisons are therefore equated with protection from serious crimes. In part it is because prison is a symbol of exclusion from society. Prisoners are physically removed from the community, and that isolation symbolizes their status as "outlaws"—those who have placed themselves outside the law and thus beyond the pale of "decent" society. This symbol is effective only as long as crime is viewed solely as lawbreaking, and not as injury to others as well. When we understand all the injuries crime causes, then the criminal is not simply an outlaw but also someone who has now incurred obligations to make good the harm that resulted from the crime. Current justifications for both prison and probation (punitive and pragmatic considerations), although important, fail to address a basic injustice of crime—the harm suffered by *victims*. A restorative perspective forces us to pursue public safety, offender accountability *and* the needs of crime victims.

A significant percentage of current prisoners could be serving community-based sentences instead of prison without significantly increasing public risk. Nearly 20 percent of the people sent to state

---

[30] Traditionally, the purposes of punishment have been given as deterrence, incapacitation, rehabilitation and retribution. With a loss of confidence in the ability of prison programs to rehabilitate, increased attention has been paid to the other three justifications in the last two decades. The just deserts movement emerged during that time, advocating proportionate punishment rather than utilitarian goals such as rehabilitation or deterrence. (*See, e.g.,* Andrew von Hirsch, *Doing Justice: The Choice of Punishments* (New York: Hill and Wang, 1976). Rising crime and fear of crime since the 1960s have heavily politicized the topic, and the "wars on crime" launched by various administrations have emphasized the need to incapacitate repeat and violent offenders by imprisonment. This has been supported by criminological theory that emphasizes the cause of crime as wrong individual choices, without as much regard for the context or reasons for those choices. *See* Chapter Eight, "Conservative Criminology: Revitalizing Individualistic Theory," in J. Robert Lilly, Francis T. Cullen and Richard A. Ball, *Criminological Theory: Context and Consequences*, 2d ed. (Thousand Oaks, CA: Sage Publications, 1995).

[31] John Irwin and James Austin, *It's About Time: America's Imprisonment Binge* (New York: Oxford University Press, 1994), 24.

and federal prisons each year are guilty of only a technical violation of parole.[32] Nearly 50 percent of the people admitted to prison were convicted of nonviolent crimes (property crimes, drug offenses or public order crimes).[33] Even when they are given sentences that include reparation to their victims, it is difficult for offenders to fulfill those obligations while in prison (although we will later suggest a strategy for increasing the likelihood that at least some prisoners can make reparation). In recent years, a range of community-based sanctions with varying levels of restrictions and supervision has been devised by governmental officials attempting to cope with overcrowded jails and prisons.[34] Such sanctions can require and enable many offenders to make reparation to their victims, and at the same time provide adequate supervision to safeguard the community. By shifting to consider such sanctions as normative (and not merely as "alternatives to prison"), the criminal justice process could maximize the likelihood of timely reparation to victims, while effectively managing the potential risk to public safety. To do so would require commitment and investment in effective community-based programs as valid in themselves and not simply as cost-cutting measures ("cheaper than prison").[35]

An emphasis on reparation in community-based sanction programs must be accompanied by careful attention to public safety. This involves at least two issues: how to *assess* an offender's risk of further criminality and potential dangerousness, and how to *manage* that offender's potential dangerousness while in the community. In this discussion, we refer to *risks* and *stakes* as factors in determining offenders' levels of dangerousness and need for correctional control. By *risk* we mean the likelihood that an offender will commit another offense; *stakes* is a calculation of the gravity of the potential recidivism.[36] Because any undue deprivation of liberty is not only destructive and counterproductive but also makes reparation virtually impossible, the use of incarceration should be limited to otherwise unmanageable offenders to prevent endangering the public.

---

[32] According to various federal reports, 28 percent of the people admitted to prison in 1990 were sent for parole violations; two-thirds of those were for technical violations (like missing appointments with the parole officer or testing positive for drug use) and only one-third had their parole violated for committing new crimes. Irwin and Austin, *supra* note 31, at 23.

[33] Ibid.

[34] A community-based sanction is one in which offenders' obligations to their victims and courts are served while remaining in a community setting rather than in a prison facility. Examples of community-based sanctions are probation, intensive probation, restitution centers and specialized supervision programs such as treatment-oriented programs for drunk drivers, and the like.

[35] Good community corrections costs money and we should be honest about that. We currently spend about $200 per year per probationer for supervision. It is no wonder that recidivism rates are so high. Effective treatment programs cost at least $12,000 to $14,000 per year. Those resources will be forthcoming only if the public believes the programs are both effective and punitive. Joan Petersilia, "A Crime Control Rationale for Reinvesting in Community Corrections," *The Prison Journal* 75(4) (1995): 490.

[36] Don M. Gottfredson and Stephen D. Gottfredson, "Stakes and Risks in the Prediction of Violent Criminal Behavior," *Violence and Victims: Special Issue on the Prediction of Violent Criminal Behavior* 3(4) (1988): 247-262. Weiner summarizes their use of the terms:

In current correctional parlance, *intermediate sanctions* refers to community-based programs for specifically targeted offenders who fall on the correctional continuum somewhere between simple probation and incarceration in jail or prison.[37] It is already the case that huge numbers of offenders are being supervised in the community—and not just because there is a shortage of prison space. The majority of offenders are sentenced to probation because it is acknowledged by the courts that prison is too extreme a remedy. We argue that it is too extreme for all but truly unmanageable offenders and those who have committed truly heinous crimes.

Assessing Risks

Risks of future criminality must be identified so that sanctions can be designed to manage them and offenders can be sentenced properly. Risk assessment or prediction is a specialized area in criminal justice research. Various methods have emerged and become standard tools in correctional decisionmaking.

Predicting Dangerousness

A survey of the literature on risk assessment stresses how difficult it is to make categorical statements about which offenders should be called "dangerous." Risk assessment methods simply identify *categories* of offenders, not specific individuals. In assigning offenders to risk groups, assessment methods tend to "overclassify" offenders, overestimating an offender's likelihood of recidivating.[38] No one wants to take responsibility when an offender who was predicted to be safe in the community commits a new crime, so the prediction tables are designed to minimize the likelihood of such mistakes. The result is that a much larger number of offenders are "overclassified" and thus kept under needlessly restrictive control.

To the issue of the probable risk of repeated violent behavior, [Gottfredson and Gottfredson] explicitly add the idea of predictive 'stakes,' i.e., the seriousness or degree of social harm of the behavior. . . . Risk is the statistical probability of a violent reinvolvement; stakes is the degree of harm or loss (whether physical, social, economic or emotional) should the predicted behavior recur. In order to weigh the relative costs of implementing alternative decisions that are to be made on the basis of predication instruments, risks and stakes need to be taken jointly into account. (Neil A. Weiner, "Editorial," *Violence and Victims: Special Issue on the Prediction of Violent Criminal Behavior* 3(4) (1988): 243-246.)

[37] In practice, "alternatives" designed to divert prison-bound offenders often tend to fill up with less serious offenders who would probably not have gone to prison anyway. This so-called net-widening is only partly due to the public's (and public officials') legitimate concern for safety. It also springs from the long-standing belief that prison is the normative and appropriate response to crime.

[38] Clear discusses the procedural, ethical and policy issues involved at some length. According to his definition, a false positive is an incorrect prediction that an offender will recidivate. A false negative is an incorrect prediction that the offender will *not* recidivate. Todd Clear, "Statistical Prediction in Corrections," *Research in Corrections* 1(1) (1988): 1 ff.

The cost of this approach has been demonstrated to be grossly disproportional to its benefits.[39]

While risk prediction is not an exact science, and while it does involve some serious issues, we agree with Marc Miller and Norval Morris that the choice is not between systematic prediction or no prediction. Prediction screening is constantly done by judges, prosecutors, corrections officials, parole boards, and so on. The choice, then, is between implicit, intuitive prediction and explicit, statistical prediction.[40] Recognizing this, one may be aware of the pitfalls inherent in both, and then seek to use the most equitable and objective approach possible. After the predictive process is complete, the results should be evaluated considering the individual involved. Reliance on a score or grid to the exclusion of individual factors increases the propensity toward error in the prediction system.[41]

Considering Stakes as Well as Risks

Gottfredson and Gottfredson have explored the limitations inherent in risk prediction from a policy perspective.[42] They propose three considerations necessary for a rational strategy: (1) the likelihood of new offenses (risk); (2) the nature of the harm expected if new offenses are committed (stakes); and (3) the calculated seriousness of the combination of risks and stakes.

Judges usually evaluate risks and stakes, at least in an intuitive way. A frequent petty shoplifter may have a high risk of re-offending, but the stakes involved are relatively minor. The community and judge are likely to treat this person as a minor offender—a public nuisance but not a danger. But even if a murderer's risk of killing again is extremely low, the stakes involved should that happen are very high indeed. So although the person is not likely to murder again (and thus presents a low risk), the stakes are high enough that the community and judge will treat this person as a serious offender.[43]

---

[39] Ibid.

[40] "The choice facing the criminal justice system is not whether explicit, statistical predictions of dangerousness should be used at all; rather the choice is between using explicit predictions, whether statistical, clinical, or intuitive, and using implicit, intuitive predictions. . . . By viewing the problems as a choice between statistical predictions and implicit predictions, judges and legislatures can squarely face the ethical and practical problems raised by the use of explicit predictions of dangerousness in the criminal justice system." Marc Miller and Norval Morris, "Predictions of Dangerousness: An Argument for Limited Use," *Violence and Victims: Special Issue on the Prediction of Interpersonal Criminal Violence* 3(4) (1988): 271.

[41] Clear, *supra* note 38, illustrates the point. "By nature, traditional risk instruments do not take into account unusual events, nor can they easily be designed to consider special circumstances. For example, it makes little sense to classify as high-risk an armed robber who was shot and made quadriplegic during his last holdup, just because he scores as high-risk on the instrument."

[42] Gottfredson and Gottfredson, *supra* note 36.

[43] Stakes are not just a matter of community safety; they are highly charged politically. Judges and corrections officials bear responsibility for the disposition of offenders, and policymakers at many levels are held responsible for the outcomes of the criminal justice system. An obvious example is the 1988 presidential race, in which Michael Dukakis was held responsible for the release and subsequent violence of a single offender—Willie Horton. The stakes for Dukakis were extremely high. So public officials are naturally reluctant about nonprison sentences for even serious nonviolent offenders.

Community safety is best served by local programs that balance considerations of risks and stakes. In selecting a target population of "nondangerous offenders," local officials would be wise to evaluate the categories of offenders currently sent to prison. Although this is not an exact, empirical process, the evaluation should disclose the reasons such offenders are sentenced to incarceration in that jurisdiction, and how community-based sanctions might be structured to address those underlying concerns.

One might devise a grid containing quadrants based on the risk and stakes represented by each offender (see Figure 6.2).

Figure 6.2

I. High Risk High Stakes	II. Low Risk High Stakes
III. High Risk Low Stakes	IV. Low Risk Low Stakes

In current practice, offenders categorized in Quadrant IV (low risk/low stakes) are often the target for probation (although it also appears that many such offenders are currently in some prison or jail). Those in the Quadrant I (high risk/high stakes)—a relatively small number of people—are clearly the group for whom incarceration is necessary. The other two quadrants provide the target population for the range of community-based intermediate sanctions (such as intensive supervision, shock probation, electronic monitoring and day reporting centers) that could include reparation as a major component. To meet legitimate concerns for managing high-risk offenders, it is imperative that community-based reparative sanctions be designed and given sufficient resources to establish and maintain supervision components that will manage the risks and stakes involved. Although well-designed community-based sanctions are currently available, they are often used in a way that tends to add controls to regular probationers, thereby missing their intended targets—offenders who pose higher risks or stakes. Courts and correctional departments must be willing and able to apply these sanctions to nondangerous offenders convicted of serious crimes.

Managing Risks and Stakes

The key to the effective management of risks and stakes is to construct a range of sentencing options along a continuum from least restrictive to most restrictive.[44] An offender's particular risk can thus be addressed by corresponding restrictions and/or requirements. Similarly, the offender's particular areas of need (such as substance abuse) may be addressed. Rehabilitative elements combined with necessary restrictive and reparative components can result in a community-based sentence that will reduce the offender's risk of serious re-offending and provide several kinds of accountability to reduce the stakes. In short, offenders' risk and the level of stakes can be effectively managed if the commitment to do so is present. The real challenge is for the system to assume that commitment. Genesee County, New York, offers an example of this. The sheriff's office coordinates with the judiciary and the prosecutor as well as with community volunteers in an innovative program called Genesee Justice. It supervises serious offenders in the community through stringent, carefully managed programs that have won public acceptance.[45]

No criminal sanction can guarantee that an offender will never re-offend, but research suggests that even serious offenders under community supervision commit fewer new crimes than comparable offenders released from prison.[46] Furthermore, if as a result of conditions of supervision, an offender who does commit a repeat offense commits a less serious crime, the sanction has at least reduced the *stakes* of new crime. Parsimony dictates that an offender should not be burdened any more than necessary to achieve the reparative goal and adequately manage his or her risk. *Reparation* is the focus of the sanction (the determining goal, as discussed earlier), while risks and stakes help dictate the structure of the sanction. The extent to which the offender must be deprived of liberty should be judged by the combination of risk and stakes. If deprivation of liberty is not necessary to manage the risk and stakes, it should not be imposed. Tough enhancements to community supervision are available when needed to manage tough cases, but they should not be added on unnecessarily when they are not warranted by risks and stakes analysis.

---

[44] The National Institute of Corrections, Community Corrections Division, has developed a stair-step diagram showing "Sanctioning Options by Levels of Supervision." It moves from fines up to day fines, probation, house arrest, intensive supervision and residential supervision to prison. Then it moves back down from prison to residential and intensive supervision to parole, community service and finally restitution. (Other steps are in the diagram, but space does not permit the inclusion of them all.) The concept is that offenders can move up or down according to their risk and level of compliance. Corrections should not be locked into viewing offenders as either probationers or prisoners.

[45] For more information, contact Dennis Wittman, Genesee County Sheriff's Department, County Building 1, Batavia, NY 14020 (Phone: 716-344-2550).

[46] "After finding that recidivism among prisoners was higher than that of a matched group of probationers (53% of prisoners charged with new crimes versus 38% of probationers), Rand researchers concluded that as long as imprisonment is assumed to be the only means of incapacitating high risk felons, the system will not get the greatest return possible in public safety from the resources available for corrections" (Klein, *supra* note 21, at 281).

Evaluation and Other Ongoing Issues

Good ideas can falter in implementation due to defective foundations, changing circumstances or loss of the original intent.[47] It is not sufficient simply to set up a community-based program of sanctions. The program must also be evaluated periodically to determine whether it is accomplishing what was intended, whether it is succeeding or failing, and why. Reparation should be documented and tracked to ensure equitable sentencing and to monitor compliance, enforcement and disbursement. Community-based sanction programs should be evaluated regularly to increase the likelihood that they will be reparative in structure and outcome.

Even well-structured programs face obstacles to the actual delivery of restitution. Restitution sentences involve several phases: judicial order; collection and disbursement of funds and/or goods *or* work service placement and supervision; and enforcement (including consequences for noncompliance). All of these phases are now hampered by the lack of specific information on restitution orders and how they are carried out. As Harland and Rosen have shown in their discussion of the various "impediments" to the reparative intent of restitution, lack of information is a critical problem.[48] Inadequate or inaccessible information makes it difficult to analyze whether reparation is being applied in practice. Are judges giving out reparative sentences? Are the sanctions being used equitably? Are offenders complying? Are victims receiving satisfactory reparation? Data to answer such questions are critical to establishing the use of reparation as a fair and prevalent sentencing component.

Some have expressed the concern that a criminal justice system focused on reparation would virtually grind to a halt. We believe that this need not be so. We agree with the American Bar Association that civil claims should not be brought into the criminal justice process unduly. We recognize that there is a right and proper role for the civil courts, and that many reparative needs should still be handled there. We also recognize that victims rightly desire reparation as soon as possible after their losses or harms occur, and that offenders are constitutionally guaranteed the right to a speedy trial. In the

---

[47] As Joan Petersilia, *Expanding Options for Criminal Sentencing* (Santa Monica, CA: The Rand Corporation, 1987), 8 observed, "The evolution and performance of community-based programs invite close scrutiny, because these programs represent a critical, and potentially far-reaching, experiment in U.S. sentencing policy. While they promise much, they could cause serious problems if left unmonitored."

[48] Alan T. Harland and Cathryn J. Rosen, "Impediments to the Recovery of Restitution by Crime Victims," *Violence and Victims: Special Issue on Social Science and Victimology* 5(2) (1990) discuss the practical impediments that prevent restitution from being used in sentencing, even though it is a tremendously popular concept. The lack of empirical data is one such major impediment.

interest of all concerned, the criminal justice system should not be made excessively slow or more inefficient by the addition of reparation. Yet this is not an excuse for laying aside the reparative goal.

Meaningful Work in Prisons

Once incarcerated, most offenders have virtually no means of making restitution or paying family support. This is why nondangerous offenders should serve their sentences in the community where they may have a better opportunity to redress the harm caused by their crime. But what about those offenders for whom the risks and stakes are so high that they must be incarcerated? We suggest that prisons become a place in which prisoners are encouraged to engage in *meaningful* work.

Meaningful work for prisoners benefits all involved: prisoners, victims, the community and the government. Prisoners gain job training, an alternative to the draining idleness of prison life, and an opportunity to repay their victims and support their families. Victims receive restitution from offenders. Employers have access to a flexible and relatively low-cost workforce. The community gains through reduced costs of incarceration and the possibility that some prisoners will become constructive citizens. Correctional institutions recover some of their costs from deductions in prisoners' wages and are able to keep prisoners productively occupied.[49] Meaningful work for prisoners, then, meets several goals of restorative justice. Prisoners have an opportunity to gain skills and make amends; victims are compensated; the community gains the useful service of inmates; and the government benefits through more manageable institutions.

---

[49] Prison administrators testify to the benefits of prison work programs. According to the director of Nebraska's state prison industry, "Inmate attitudes change after they become involved [with work]. As their feelings of self-worth and accomplishment are developed, they tend to become better citizens" (Don Lincoln of Cornhusker State Industries in a letter, August 1, 1990). Working can prepare prisoners for reentering the community and it can prevent some of the frustration that comes from idleness. For example, when Minnesota had 85 percent of its prison population working, it had—not coincidentally—one of the lowest rates of prison violence in the country (John Boal, "Helping Prison Work," *American Way*, 7 Jan. 1986, 38).

Georgia prison officials found that a work program brought about a "remarkable transformation in the inmates' attitudes, both about themselves and their environment." Over a five-year period, correctional officers witnessed something "they never dreamed would happen in the lives of mentally handicapped and retarded inmates." As a result of work, "self-esteem and self-worth have increased and individual perspectives have been changed. They take pride in what they accomplish." Dr. Jane Hall says that, "the work program we have here is the most significant impact we've made in these people's lives" (Michael Ankerich, "GDC's MH/MR Work Program Transforms Inmates' Attitudes," Georgia Department of Corrections *Newsbriefs* 11 July 1990, 6).

History of Prison Labor Programs[50]

Inmate labor has a long history in the United States. When the Quakers established the first penitentiary in the 1790s, they intended it to provide solitude so that inmates would reflect upon their errors and reform their ways. Work opportunities were necessarily limited to cottage industries that could be maintained by one person alone. As officials realized that the work of inmate laborers could cover many of their costs, new models of prisons were developed based not on isolation and reflection, but on silence and congregate labor. The first prison factory was established at Auburn, New York, in 1824, and by the end of the nineteenth century, prison industries flourished.

Unregulated use of prison labor led to abuses of the inmates, while opposition from businesses and labor unions increased because of the unfair competition presented by the minimal wages (if any) paid to inmates. With the collapse of the economy in 1929, opposition to prison industries strengthened. Beginning with the Hawes-Cooper Act in 1929, Congress began restricting the sale of prison-made goods across state lines. The effect of these laws was to limit prison-made goods to state-use, public-sector markets. These efforts coincided with the rise of the correctional model of rehabilitation, according to which inmates were expected to attend counseling services, educational programming and vocational training, but not necessarily to work.

In 1967, President Johnson's Commission Task Force Report on Corrections marked a watershed for prison industries. The report downplayed the importance of the medical/correctional model and emphasized a work-based approach to reintegrating inmates into society.[51] The rapid growth of the prison population in the 1970s, along with the increase in inmate idleness and violence, further fueled this reevaluation of prison industries, as prison officials began to see prison industries as a way to keep inmates busy and to generate revenue for the state.

The growing emphasis on inmate work paved the way for the private sector to become once again involved in prison industries. In 1979, Congress removed certain federal restrictions on the interstate sale of prisoner-made goods in order to encourage the development of private-sector prison industries. This legislation, known as the Percy Amendment, set forth the following minimum conditions for interstate shipment of prisoner-made goods: (1) inmates working in private-sector prison industries must be paid at a rate not less than that paid for work of similar nature in the locality; (2) prior to the

---

[50] The information in this draws heavily from George Sexton et. al., *Developing Private Sector Prison Industries: From Concept to Start Up* (National Institute of Justice, U.S. Department of Justice, 1991).

[51] Dan Pilcher, "State Correctional Industries: Choosing Goals, Accepting Tradeoffs," *National Conference of State Legislatures* (June 1989): 2.

initiation of a project, local union organizations must be consulted; and (3) the employment of inmates must not result in the displacement of employed workers outside prison, must not occur in occupations in which there is a surplus of labor in the locality and must not impair existing contracts for service.[52]

Since 1979, Congress and the states have passed further legislation removing additional restrictions on the development of private-sector prison industries. In 1990, Congress authorized expanding interstate sale of goods made in prison from 20 test sites to all 50 states. In that same year, California voters passed a referendum to remove the constitutional prohibition against the use of inmate labor for any private entity. This public support for private-sector prison industries was impressive because most initiatives on the ballot failed that year.

Meaningful Work

The National Institute of Justice (NIJ) has defined jail (or prison) industry as follows: (1) it uses inmate labor; (2) to create a product or provide a service; (3) that has value to a public or private client and for which; (4) the inmates receive compensation, whether it be pay, privileges or other benefits.[53] We find this definition to be helpful, but prefer to narrow it somewhat by adding criteria for determining whether those industries provide *meaningful* work. We suggest that the following four factors distinguish meaningful work from other forms of prison industry. Each corresponds to one of the four parties addressed by restorative justice: offender, victim, community and government.

1. Meaningful work fosters training in the work ethic. While there are a number of ways that work programs can help foster the work ethic, one is to compensate inmates for their labor, preferably at market wages. Paying prisoners market wages is advantageous for several reasons. First, this assures adequate income so that prisoners can pay restitution, family support, fines and some incarceration costs to the state. Second, paying market wages forces prison industries to operate under the same standards and pressures of other businesses, giving inmates the kind of training they need once they are released. Third, it reduces opposition from private-sector businesses and

[52] Barbara J. Auerbach, *Work in American Prisons: The Private Sector Gets Involved*, National Institute of Justice: Issues and Practices (National Institute of Justice, U.S. Department of Justice, 1988), 10-11.

[53] Rod Miller, George E. Sexton and Victor J. Jacobsen, *Making Jails Productive* (National Institute of Justice Report # 223, January/February 1991), 2-5.

unions that oppose prison industries that do not pay comparable wages, on the ground of unfair competition.[54] Paying wages comparable to those outside the prison reduces this opposition.

2. Meaningful work fosters payment of restitution. The primary benefit to victims in prison industries is the restitution they may receive; if offenders are able to work for decent wages, they have an opportunity to make amends, both financial and symbolic, to their victims. Of course, this potential is dependent upon whether the court has ordered restitution. In those cases in which the court has done so, prison industries should be *required* to provide some mechanism for the payment of restitution. We suggest that prison industries include a mandatory restitution mechanism for those inmates who have been ordered to pay restitution. Victims also have an interest in prison industries paying offenders market wages. For offenders to repay victims—and contribute to the cost of their incarceration and provide family support—they must earn decent wages. Inmates should be able to divert some of their wages to their victims and their victims' families—something not all prison industries guarantee. Prison industries are perhaps the only way that prisoners can earn enough money to pay restitution.

3. Meaningful work fosters development of a productive workforce. The development of a productive prison workforce benefits the community in many ways. First, the community gains the products or services that inmates as workers can provide. Further, when inmates are able to provide some family support while incarcerated, the burden of that support does not rest completely with the taxpayers. Finally, it offers a flexible, entry-level workforce to U.S. companies that have had increasing difficulty finding such workers.

4. Meaningful work fosters well-managed correctional institutions by reducing costs and prisoner idleness. The government and correctional institutions in particular benefit from prison industries through reduced costs. Inmates pay taxes on their earnings and usually are required to contribute a portion of their earnings to the state for room and board. Prison industries help to reduce idleness in employed inmates, which makes institutions easier to manage.

---

[54] This issue of prison industries competing with private sector businesses is complex. While paying market wages to inmates benefits the employee and puts the prison industry on an equal footing with other companies, the costs of doing business in prison are often higher than outside the prison walls. Prison industries must cope with a very high turnover rate, the interruptions of prison regimen and inspections during the business day, and, in the case of state-use industries, a limited market for its products. While some prison industries have succeeded paying open market wages, others have developed innovative understandings of what is a market wage for prisoners.

Conclusion

A restorative system is more concerned with repairing harm than with punishment that ignores the need and obligation to make reparation. It also attempts to reduce the likelihood of future harms, and this means that incarceration must be used to restrain exceptionally dangerous individuals. In either event, however, the criminal justice process should maximize the likelihood of timely reparation to victims, while effectively managing the potential risk to public safety.

Sanctions should first redress the harm to victims. The risk and needs of offenders as well as the seriousness of offenses can be addressed in ways that do not defeat this primary purpose. Furthermore, the most direct victims should be considered for redress first, and the most significant harms suffered should be the first to be redressed. Therefore, if complete deprivation of liberty is not necessary to manage the risk and stakes, it should not be imposed. This is because a commitment to reparation involves a commitment to making it feasible.

To meet the legitimate need to manage high-risk offenders, reparative sanctions must be designed and given sufficient resources to establish and maintain supervision components that will cope with the risk involved. Regular evaluation of these programs will increase the likelihood that they will be reparative in structure and outcome. Finally, a restorative system will strive to develop and maximize the use of reparative sanctions while guarding victims' and offenders' interests in an efficient and timely disposition of their cases.

Incarceration need not be the standard against which all punishments are measured. In a restorative system, reparation rather than incarceration provides that gauge. If reparation for the harm done to victims is returned to its central place in the sentencing process, programs will do more than divert nondangerous offenders from prison; they will ensure that offenders make reparation to victims.

Chapter Seven

Reintegration

It may seem strange to discuss reintegration of victims and offenders in the same chapter. Their needs are different and their moral positions, vis-à-vis the crime, are different as well. Nevertheless, victims and offenders often share one common problem: stigmatization.[1] Each is treated as an outcast by the community; each finds that many around them are threatened by them: victimization makes nonvictims feel more vulnerable ("if it happened to her, it could happen to me");[2] identifying offenders creates anger and fear ("if he did

---

[1] "Since most victims are stigmatized by family, friends, and the public, who often blame the victim for his or her own plight, so that they do not have to confront the fact that it could happen to them, victims learn to hide their status, not to speak of what occurred, not to share their feelings. These actions increase a sense of shame and rejection, compounding the victim trauma response." Susan E. Salasin, "Introduction: A Blow of Redirection," in Shelley Neiderbach, *Invisible Wounds: Crime Victims Speak* (New York: Harrington Park Press, 1986), 3.

"The general society has always held convicts in some contempt, but in earlier decades there was a greater willingness to forget their past and, once they had served their time, 'give them another chance.' In the 1960s, there was a large outpouring of sympathy for convicts, and substantial progress was made in reducing the barriers blocking ex-convicts' reemersion into conventional society. For a short period, ex-prisoners were folk heroes and many strutted around, loudly proclaiming and capitalizing on their ex-convict status. This period ended by the late 1970s, and once again the convict and ex-convict became a widely hated and feared pariah. In recent years, whenever an ex-convict is in the news, the media usually focus negatively on that status. Politicians harp on criminal acts committed by released prisoners. Legislators and policy makers, usually with dramatic public display, have passed laws or established policies against hiring ex-convicts for a growing number of jobs. Consequently, most prisoners are acutely aware that they are among society's leading pariahs, and this awareness has greatly increased their alienation from conventional society." John Irwin and James Austin, *It's About Time: America's Imprisonment Binge* (New York: Oxford University Press, 1994), 84.

[2] "Victim-blaming is a very common occurrence in the aftermath of a personal crime. It provides a readymade answer to the question 'Why me?' It's a cruel answer, and it is almost always unwarranted by the facts, but it can be terribly seductive. Practically everyone has been exposed to enough popularized psychology to know about concepts such as unconscious motivation. Under the influence of their need to attribute, both victims and their loved ones are ripe to decide that the victim has

it once, he could do it again"). So without equating their experiences at all, we would like to focus on one common experience that victims and offenders share—stigmatization—and how the community might offer a solution. First, though, it is important to understand what issues and injuries victims and offenders carry with them as they begin the process of reintegration.

Victims

Crime victims are widely diverse in demographics, prior history of victimization and personal stability preceding victimization. According to Dean Kilpatrick, "most studies show that victims' demographic characteristics such as gender, race, and age have little (if any) impact on crime related psychological trauma."[3] However, prior victimization (especially in cases involving violence or crimes against the person) does increase the incidence of serious trauma for victims. Post-Traumatic Stress Disorder (PTSD) and depression are among the symptoms identified for such victims. Even in cases in which serious psychological trauma is not necessarily likely, victims frequently experience a crisis reaction for which some form of intervention is indicated.[4] Arlene Bowers Andrews offers the following description of victims in crisis:

> Persons in crisis tend to be emotionally aroused and highly anxious; often they are weepy. Occasionally they will act extremely controlled and noncommunicative as a way of coping with high anxiety, but most often they will express despair, grief, embarrassment, and anger. Their thoughts are disorganized, leading to trouble in relating ideas, events, and actions. They may overlook important details, or may jump form one idea to another, making communication hard to follow. They may confuse fears and wishes

---

been somehow unwittingly responsible for his or her own injury. Victims who accept the blame may be further violated by their confusion and guilt as they struggle to uncover the alleged unconscious impulses that made them arrange for the crime to happen." Morton Bard and Dawn Sangrey, *The Crime Victim's Book*, 2d ed. (Secaucus, NJ: Citadel Press, 1986), 65.

[3] Dean G. Kilpatrick, "The Mental Health Impact of Crime: Fundamentals in Counseling and Advocacy," in materials for the *1996 National Victim Assistance Academy* sponsored by the U.S. Department of Justice Office for Victims of Crime. *See also* Arthur J. Lurigio and Patricia J. Resick, "Healing The Psychological Wounds of Criminal Victimization: Predicting Postcrime Distress and Recovery," in Arthur J. Lurigio, Wesley G. Skogan and Robert C. Davis, eds., *Victims of Crime: Problems, Policies, and Programs* (Newbury Park, CA: Sage Publications, 1990); B.M. Atkeson et al., "Victims of Rape: Repeated Assessment of Depressive Symptoms," *Journal of Consulting and Clinical Psychology* 50 (1982): 96-102.

[4] Anne Seymour, Christine Edmunds and Jane N. Burnley, "Crisis Intervention," in materials prepared for the *1996 National Victim Assistance Academy* sponsored by the U.S. Department of Justice Office for Victims of Crime.

with reality. Persons in crisis may not be able to perform routine behaviors such as basic grooming. They may avoid eye contact, and may mumble. Some persons may act impulsively. People in crisis have reported feelings of fatigue as well as appetite and sleep disruptions. They are socially vulnerable, which means that a helper can have significant influence, but so can people with exploitive motives. People in crisis act in ways similar to people with certain forms of chronic mental illness, but it must be emphasized that the crisis state is time limited, usually lasting no more than a few days to six weeks.[5]

For a victim in crisis, the isolation and disorientation may be limited by time, as Andrews indicates. A source of support and understanding, as well as practical links to available resources, can mitigate the intensity of the crisis as well as its duration, and in so doing lessen the damage to relationships, employability and other factors related to the victim's long-term readjustment.[6] For a victim experiencing psychological trauma, crisis intervention should involve referral to mental health resources in order that the trauma may be assessed and appropriately treated. For example, PTSD and depression are often associated with violent crime victimization, and there is evidence that many crime victims do not spontaneously recover without treatment.[7]

Beyond the crisis or trauma resulting from the crime itself, there is also a negative self-identity that sometimes occurs for victims. Morton Bard and Dawn Sangrey have devoted a chapter of *The Crime Victim's Book* to "The Mark: Feelings of Guilt and Shame." They quote a robbery victim:

> I just hate to think of myself as a victim. It's like when I lost my job—I hadn't done anything wrong, but it was so embarrassing to have to tell people that I had lost my job. And when this happened, I felt the same way. It was like a guilty secret. I didn't want to talk about it.[8]

Furthermore, Bard and Sangrey point out that crime victims are commonly viewed as having failed in some way to protect them-

---

5   Arlene B. Andrews, "Crisis and Recovery Services for Family Violence Survivors," in Arthur J. Lurigio, Wesley G. Skogan and Robert C. Davis, eds., *Victims of Crime: Problems, Policies, and Programs* (Newbury Park, CA: Sage Publications, 1990).

6   "Crisis helpers must essentially be empathic, able to listen actively, able to focus the [victim's] immediate problem and . . . knowledgeable about community resources. The goals . . . are to help the [victim] feel supported and able to cope and to link the [victim] with resources for longer-term support." Ibid., 217.

7   H.S. Resnick et al., "Prevalence of Civilian Trauma and PTSD in a Representative National Sample of Women," *Journal of Clinical and Consulting Psychology* 61/6 (1993).

8   Morton Bard and Dawn Sangrey, *The Crime Victim's Book*, 2d ed. (Secaucus, NJ: Citadel Press, 1986).

selves. Often criminal justice procedures reinforce this negative view—that somehow the victim is responsible for the occurrence of the crime. This stigma may have long-term, unexpected negative results in a victim's life. Once the immediate crisis has passed, victims are left with an ongoing battle to preserve their sense of self-control and dignity.

Reintegration for victims, then, focuses first on crisis intervention and help with the stress resulting from the crime, and then on ongoing support as life is resumed in the new "normal" patterns, while coping with the resurgence of crisis symptoms from time to time. A stabilizing family or community in which the victim feels secure and cared for offers the victim an environment in which to work out the feelings and fears following victimization, and in which to redefine and redirect his or her life.

Offenders

Offenders are responsible for their lives and choices. Their perpetration of crime must be faced honestly, including recognition of the effects of that crime on others—the victim, the offender's family and the community. Nonetheless, offenders face personal, societal and spiritual obstacles when it comes to reintegration after being sanctioned. As the recidivism rate for prisoners indicates, far too few individuals establish themselves in productive, crime-free lives following their prison sentence. Although not all offenders face the same issues as transitioning ex-prisoners, it is certainly true that huge numbers of offenders are coming out of prisons daily. They tend to represent the most stigmatized offenders, and those perhaps most in need of reintegration.

Research shows that prisoners generally harbor an assortment of needs upon release from incarceration. Released prisoners often meet immediate discrimination by society, and such categorical discrimination can be compounded for ethnic minorities.[9] Furthermore, they often do not connect with or have access to resources for overcoming obstacles. Moreover, many released prisoners are not aware of either public or private agencies upon which they can call for help; few of those who are aware actually seek help.[10] One of the most dif-

9   Sherry Stripling, "A Life of Opening Doors, Hearts—Herb Smith Helped Former Prisoners Through Respect," *Seattle Times*, 7 Nov. 1991, E1.

10 Harvey L. McMurray, "High Risk Parolees in Transition from Institution to Community Life," *Journal of Offender Rehabilitation* 19 (1993): 159.

ficult challenges an ex-prisoner encounters is finding employment.[11] A large percentage of ex-offenders also report that they lack start-up money for food and clothes, reliable transportation, suitable shelter, adequate education, psychological counseling, drug treatment, societal acceptance or approval, and positive role models.[12] Other difficulties include peer pressure, low self-esteem, unrealistic expectations, an excessive or deficient sense of sin and guilt, fear of failure, distrust of others, hopelessness and the lure of addictive behaviors.

According to one study, more than one-half of all inmates would have to rely on somebody else for support and a place to live when discharged.[13] Ex-prisoners who live alone or with their parents generally have more problems than those who live with their spouses and children.[14] Even intact marriages, however, often experience serious marital discord in the post-prison home environment, or an absence of warmth, trust and support. Offenders may have weak prosocial skills that hinder their relationships with family as well as with friends, neighbors and employers. The experiences of many former prisoners have fostered inappropriate relationships, antisocial values and ethical insensitivity, destructive habits and an inability to make decisions or plan ahead.

These issues are exacerbated for prisoners by the specific effects of being held in an institution, where most decisions—both important and trivial—are made for the prisoner. The regimen inside prison walls, which produces the so-called "institutionalized mentality," can make even simple matters on the outside paralyzing to the ex-offender. Matters such as paying an electric bill, replacing an empty jar of coffee or choosing among various brands at the supermarket are overwhelming, let alone more complex matters like holding down a job or forming a healthy relationship with a significant other.[15] The expecta-

[11] Carl Robins, "Finding Jobs for Former Offenders," *Corrections Today,* Aug. 1993, 140; and Clay Robison, "Jobs for Ex-Offenders a Crime Issue, Too," *Houston Chronicle,* 17 July 1994, 2. We must admit doubts have been raised about the assumption that unemployment is a major cause of recidivism (*see* citations by Dennis B. Anderson, Randall E. Schumacker and Sara L. Anderson, "Releasee Characteristics and Parole Success," *Journal of Offender Rehabilitation* 17 (1991): 136). Contrast, however, the affirmation that a good job furnishes an excellent support system (Howard L. Skolnik and John Slansky, "A First Step in Helping Inmates Get Good Jobs after Release," *Corrections Today,* Aug. 1991, 92).

[12] Hartzel L. Black, Pam G. Turner and James A. Williams, "There Is Life after Prison: Successful Community Reintegration Programs Reduce Recidivism in Illinois," *Common Ground,* Spring 1993, 51; and Harvey L. McMurray, "High Risk Parolees in Transition from Institution to Community Life," *Journal of Offender Rehabilitation* 19 (1993): 154.

[13] Bill Kole, "Freed Convicts Say They Don't Even Get Lunch Money," *Los Angeles Times,* 14 Feb. 1993, A12.

[14] Creasie F. Hairston, "Family Ties During Imprisonment: Important to Whom and for What?" *Journal of Sociology and Social Welfare* 18 (1991): 99.

[15] Ingrid Peritz, "On the Outside, Lifers Struggle to Pick Up the Pieces," *Montreal Gazette,* 14 March 1993, A1; Carla Rivera, "Guiding Ex-Offenders Back into Society," *Los Angeles Times,* 11 Dec. 1991, B2; and Joe Maxwell, "Getting Out, Staying Out," *Christianity Today,* 22 July 1991, 36.

tion that offenders can emerge as law-abiding citizens ready to assume a responsible place in the community—even if the community were prepared to accept them as such—is in fact fanciful. Offenders are isolated from the community by their own problems and issues, as well as by a public that is distrustful and cynical about them.

In summary, victims and offenders both experience alienation that is often the result of emotional distress, family tension, physical dislocation, loneliness and stigmatization. For victims, the sense of isolation is an additional injury stemming from the crime. It is also experienced as an injustice by offenders who have "paid their debt to society" but find that they are still excluded from their communities.

Reintegration

When we speak of reintegration we mean re-entry into community life as a whole, contributing, productive person. This means more than simply tolerating the person's presence in the community. Reintegration requires relationships characterized by respect, commitment and intolerance for—but understanding of—deviant or irrational behavior. This requires action on the community's part, but also on the part of the offender and/or victim involved. The work of John Braithwaite on what he calls "reintegrative shaming" will help us understand why that is.

Although Braithwaite's work focuses on how to respond to offenders, we think that many of his observations on the factors that support reintegration apply to victims as well. In *Crime, Shame and Reintegration,*[16] Braithwaite argued that there is a correlation between low crime rates and the high social power of shaming. Cultures and historical eras that have experienced low rates of crime are characterized by social structures in which *reintegrative* shaming (which Braithwaite contrasted with disintegrative shaming, or stigmatization) plays a central role.[17] He argued that internal control is more effective than external control in restraining crime, that internal control—the conscience—is *acquired,* usually during childhood, and that families are better able to build consciences in their children when their society is characterized by reintegrative shaming.[18]

The shaming part is fairly straightforward: people who are shamed feel personal remorse for what they have done as well as the disapproval of significant people around them. What keeps reinte-

---

[16] John Braithwaite, *Crime, Shame and Reintegration* (New York: Cambridge University Press, 1989).

[17] Ibid., 84-85.

[18] Ibid., 71-75.

grative shaming from becoming disintegrative (stigmatizating) is that it is "followed by gestures of reacceptance" from those who did the shaming. Stigmatization, on the other hand, creates a "class of outcasts," people whose "master status trait" is that they are criminals (or, we suggest, crime victims).[19] In other words, the external controls that must exist in a society can be imposed in one of two ways: through reintegrative shaming or through what he calls "punishment" (by which he means infliction of pain in order to deter):[20]

> [S]haming has a great advantage over formal punishment. Shaming is more pregnant with symbolic content than punishment. Punishment is a denial of confidence in the morality of the offender by reducing norm compliance to a crude cost-benefit calculation; shaming can be a reaffirmation of the morality of the offender by expressing personal disappointment that the offender should do something so out of character, and, if the shaming is reintegrative, by expressing personal satisfaction in seeing the character of the offender restored. Punishment erects barriers between the offender and punisher through transforming the relationship into one of power assertion and injury; shaming produces a greater interconnectedness between the parties, albeit a painful one, an interconnectedness which can produce the repulsion of stigmatization or the establishment of a potentially more positive relationship following reintegration. Punishment is often shameful and shaming usually punishes. But whereas punishment gets its symbolic content only from its denunciatory association with shaming, shaming is pure symbolic content.[21]

This model illuminates a number of problems with current criminal justice administration. Occasionally, we do not shame the offenders; in fact, the people who are significant to them may not even know that they have gotten into trouble, or may feel that prison is simply an unfortunate consequence of some more important rite of passage. Too often, we shame the *victim*, who has done nothing to deserve it. For both victims and offenders, a more critical problem is our failure to reintegrate them into the community. Here Braithwaite meant more than help with re-entry (although that may be needed); he meant permitting the offender to rejoin the community

---

[19] Ibid., 55. In a subsequent article, Braithwaite summarized the distinction in this way: "Stigmatization is shaming which creates outcasts, where 'criminal' becomes a master status trait that drives out all other identities, shaming where bonds of respect for the offender are not sustained. Reintegrative shaming, in contrast, is disapproval dispensed within an ongoing relationship with the offender based on respect, shaming which focuses on the evil of the deed rather than on the offender as an irremediably evil person, where degradation ceremonies are followed by ceremonies to decertify deviance, where forgiveness, apology, and repentance are culturally important." John Braithwaite, "Shame and Modernity," *Brit. J. of Crim.* 33 (1993): 1.

[20] Braithwaite, *supra* note 16, at 69-71

[21] Ibid., 72-73.

as a full member, instead of being cast out or being permitted to stay on a provisional basis. Reintegration requires that we view ourselves (and others) as a complex mixture of good and evil, injuries and strengths, and that while we resist and disparage the evil and compensate for our weaknesses, we also recognize and welcome the good and utilize our strengths. He noted that Japanese culture values apology as a gesture in which people divide themselves into good and bad parts with the good part renouncing the bad. This not only helps build community peace, but also aids in the development and maintenance of community norms.[22] The community then forgives and readmits the good self, not the bad.

Reintegrative shaming is most effective when the shaming is done by someone important to the offender—someone with whom the offender is *interdependent*, meaning that they have attachments to each other that are strong enough that they invoke mutual obligations to one another.[23] It is also most effective in a society that is *communitarian*, by which Braithwaite means a society with dense networks of interdependencies and with strong devotion to the mutual obligations created by those interdependencies.[24] Such a society need not be homogeneous, as long as it is one in which mutually dependent relationships flourish and are valued. It works less well in highly individualistic and urbanized societies in which shaming (or punishment) is done by an impersonal state.[25] This last qualification has led critics of Braithwaite to conclude that although his theory may be interesting, it is by definition irrelevant to individualistic, urbanized Western societies. For example, Robert Weisberg makes this dismissal:

> [L]ike some earlier liberal criminologists, such as those touting subcultures and differential association, Braithwaite is circular in that he leaves us working backward to imagine transforming American culture into something that can fulfill this daunting task. Indeed, like those earlier sociologists, he seems to ignore the key question he raises—how, if at all, can culture be changed. Without such a theory, the theory of reintegrative shaming, though offering sophisticated analysis and powerful aspiration, runs the risk, if read as a reform agenda, of sounding like another chastening reminder that we have not achieved the social homogeneity of the Japanese.[26]

---

[22] Ibid., 64-65 and 74-75.

[23] Ibid., 85.

[24] Ibid.

[25] Ibid., 86.

[26] Robert Weisberg, "Criminal Law, Criminology, and the Small World of Legal Scholars," *U. Colo. L. Rev.* 63 (1992): 521, 556.

Braithwaite's response to this challenge has been two-fold. First, he has argued that Western history over the last 700 years shows an *increase*, not a decrease, in the use of shaming accompanied by a drop in crime rates. It was not until the latter half of the twentieth century that shaming ceased to be used because of its humiliating and stigmatizing nature, and it is during that period (since the 1960s) that crime rates have risen.[27] In other words, modernity is not necessarily antithetical to shaming, nor is high crime a necessary by-product of modernity.

His second point was that urbanization creates interdependencies that connect fragments of the personality, not the whole person. Therefore, urbanization does not lead inexorably to a loss of potency of reintegrative shaming; in fact, the proliferation of roles may make us more susceptible to shame:

> We all experience the minor embarrassment of coming into contact with others who know us in different roles—the former Sunday School teacher from whom we purchase condoms in a pharmacy, the appointment with a doctor married to a colleague at work, the inhibition we feel at enjoying an intimate meal with our spouse in a restaurant when some of our students are seated at the adjoining table.[28]

So while segmentation may make it possible for us to play multiple roles before multiple audiences, when our wrongdoing in one of those roles becomes public to the other audiences, the potential for shame is much greater. Interviews with white-collar offenders showed that public exposure made it impossible to continue to play to different audiences; children, fellow churchgoers and acquaintances were suddenly confronted with the offender's most corrupt business decisions.[29] The result may be stigmatization, either by others who cut off their relationships with the offender, or by the offender in a kind of self-stigmatization in which the offender chooses to focus on one role and cut off interdependencies that existed in other roles.[30] In other words, the potential for stigmatization and for reintegrative shaming remains even in urbanized societies.

Braithwaite insists that his theory is relevant even though culture has changed. Although reintegrative shaming works best in communitarian and nonurban societies, it can work in individualistic and urbanized ones as well. It is not necessary to turn back the clock to the 1950s. He may be right; what is needed is more research in the ways in which shaming (both reintegrative and stigmatizing) takes

---

[27] Braithwaite, *supra* note 16, at 2, 6 and 10.

[28] Ibid., 14.

[29] Ibid., 14-15.

[30] Ibid., 15.

place in our culture. This does not minimize the challenge raised by Weisberg: we live in a culture in which individuals look out for themselves, in which even families are disintegrating and in which external controls are replacing what are apparently declining internal controls. As we noted earlier, community safety is achieved through a combination of two factors: the order imposed through force by government and the peace (harmony) that exists in the community. Both must be present in some amount, but the less peace there is the more force will be required to preserve order.[31] A culture that assigns less value to harmony than to self-expression will find itself relying more on imposed order for safety.[32]

While reintegrative shaming is an intriguing and helpful theory, and one that is certainly consistent with a restorative approach to offenders, we discuss it in this chapter not because of what it suggests about shaming, but because of what it teaches about reintegration. For reintegration to take place, the relationship between the one being reintegrated—whether victim or offender—and the reintegrating community must be characterized by at least three traits: (1) mutual respect for one another, (2) mutual commitment to one another, and (3) intolerance for—but understanding of—deviant behavior. One other characteristic should be added when the person being reintegrated has been an offender: repentance/forgiveness.[33]

Reintegrating Communities

Braithwaite's work has been criticized for the admission that reintegrative shaming does not work as well in urbanized and individualistic societies. Much of the discussion on this has focused on the lack of potency of *shaming* in such cultures (although Braithwaite has argued that the self-segmentation in such societies can make shaming even more potent than in rural, communitarian soci-

---

[31] Cf., Part I of this book, especially Chapter Three.

[32] Lawrence Friedman concludes his exhaustive *Crime and Punishment in American History* with this observation: "In my view, the 'crime problem' flows largely from changes in the culture itself; it is part of us, our evil twin, our shadow; our own society produced it. It has been a central theme of this book that criminal justice systems are organic, rooted in society. Crime is no different. It is part of the American story, the American fabric. Perhaps—just perhaps—the siege of crime may be the price we pay for a brash, self-loving, relatively free and open society. . . . For this reason, I fear, we are likely to bump along more or less as we are. The siege of crime and all the misery it brings, both to those who commit it and those who are victimized, is a high price to pay for our liberty. It is a cost that is badly and unfairly distributed. But for now, at least, there may be nothing to do but grit our teeth and pay the price." Lawrence M. Friedman, *Crime and Punishment in American History* (New York: Basic Books, 1993), 464-465.

[33] "[A] combination of shame at and repentance by the offender is a more powerful affirmation of the criminal law than one-sided moralizing. A shaming ceremony followed later by a forgiveness and repentance ceremony more potently builds commitment to the law than a shaming ceremony alone. Nothing has greater symbolic force in community-wide conscience-building than repentance." John Braithwaite, *supra* note 16, at 81.

eties). Perhaps a more difficult challenge has to do with the reduced likelihood of *reintegration* in such societies. If reintegration requires relationships characterized by mutual respect, mutual commitment and intolerance for—but understanding of—deviant behavior, then the problem we face has a great deal to do with the lack of such relationships. It is relatively easy to think of ways to stigmatize offenders even in our individualistic society, and such shaming efforts are being done today.[34] The problem we face is less how to shame than how to reintegrate.

Braithwaite argued that reintegration is done by people who have an existing relationship with those who are alienated. Applying this to our culture requires that we assume that everyone has such relationships, and that the people in those relationships are able and willing to do the work of reintegration. Neither assumption is self-evident, and an individualistic and urbanized culture is not likely to foster such relationships. In seeking to reintegrate victims and offenders, then, where do we look for persons willing to offer the respect, commitment and "understanding intolerance" that is required?

One answer, which has been reasonably successful, is to look among others who have been in a similar situation. Self-help and support groups have developed for both victims and for offenders. Because of shared experiences (including shared alienation from the community), members of these groups find strength in meeting together to talk and encourage one another. Shelley Neiderbach described the effect of victim group counseling sessions in this way:

> The degree of victim isolation cannot be overestimated. Crime victims feel lost not only within themselves but within the human community as well. Therefore, the conversion of the CVCS counseling group into what became a virtual subculture and "intentional family" was swift, predictable, and enthusiastically determined by the participants. This fairly immediate sense of group identity laid the groundwork for the more acute and profound psychological revelations that victims then permitted to surface as the sessions continued.[35]

Neiderbach distinguished such support groups from "most publicly funded victims' services," the object of which is to promote the welfare of the victim "in the service of converting victims to witnesses,

---

[34] Toni Massaro cites three cases as illustrations. In one, a convicted child molester was required, as a condition of his probation, to purchase a four-by-six ad in the local newspaper with his picture and the warning that other child molesters would receive similar treatment. In the second, an Oregon judge requires convicted offenders to apologize for their crimes in newspaper ads that they must buy. In the third, a Nevada judge gives drunk drivers a choice between imprisonment or community service; if they choose the latter they must wear distinctive clothing that identifies them as drunk drivers. Toni Massaro, "Shame, Culture, and American Criminal Law," *Mich. L. Rev.* 89 (1991): 1880, 1881-1882.

[35] Shelley Neiderbach, *Invisible Wounds: Crime Victims Speak* (New York: Harrington Park Press, 1986), 9.

so that prosecution rates can be higher."[36] While such programs may perform important services and may be staffed by highly motivated and compassionate people, Neiderbach's point was that they do not create the kind of relationships necessary to aid in what we have called reintegration. They have a different purpose.

Ex-offenders are also organizing to assist other ex-offenders with the challenges of reintegration. The Network for Life® is organizing groups of ex-offenders in cities across America specifically for this purpose. Affiliated chapters of the Network for Life garner "network" support from businesses, service agencies and churches for the express purpose of "reaching back" and assisting those who are coming out of prison. These groups are service-oriented, rather than simply support-oriented, and their aim is to assist with the very real, practical and personal needs of ex-offenders in a holistic and organized way. The Network for Life is an explicitly Christian organization, although assistance is offered to anyone in need, regardless of their religion or lack of religious faith.

These affinity groups are important as we consider the process of reintegration, because they demonstrate that the significant relationships that are necessary to reintegration do not need to have existed prior to the need to reintegrate. The common struggle to deal with a crisis and to re-establish oneself can provide a basis for such relationships. But there are limitations to affinity groups as well. Support groups for victims or offenders may offer validation to those recovering from their experiences with crime, and may be a source of strength for them as they work to re-enter a community that is significantly different as a result of their experience. For reintegration to be complete, similar relationships must be forged with members of the community, not simply with others who feel alienated from it.

Faith Communities as Reintegrating Communities

For this reason, we propose that faith communities offer the potential to be agents for reintegration—both for victims and offenders. We understand that there are significant obstacles to such an undertaking. Christian churches, for example, have appeared to be better at proclaiming love than demonstrating it: they are fragmented (witness the proliferation of denominations), they are viewed with suspicion by many nonmembers as more interested in wealth than in sacrificial service, and some of their members too often give simple,

---

[36] Ibid.

glib answers to the searching and questioning that follows a crisis. Nevertheless, the church's strong and extensive history of involvement with those in need, its traditions that speak of both the call and the resources to undertake such a task and its presence in every part of the country make it a promising agent for reintegration, as we will demonstrate in the following paragraphs. We have used a variety of Christian faith traditions to illustrate this point, because that is where our research and experience are most extensive. Others with different expertise may be able to test our hypothesis using other faith communities as examples.

History

For two millennia, and in a variety of cultures and nations, many churches have been a reintegrating community for those who are alienated. That has certainly been true in the United States, where the church has been actively involved in issues ranging from the abolition of slavery to the humane treatment of criminals.[37] It was Quakers in Philadelphia who convinced the city to establish what is generally credited as the first penitentiary—a place of penitence—in 1790, as an alternative to cruel corporal punishments. They believed that crime resulted from a negative moral environment, and that the foundation for reformation was to provide a solitary, moral environment. The first nationally recognized prison expert was Louis Dwight, whose work distributing Bibles for the American Bible Society had taken him into jails where he had been shocked into action by the unconscionable conditions he found. He became a leading proponent of what was called the "Auburn System" of corrections, the major alternative to the Pennsylvania approach, which emphasized collective treatment of offenders in religious revival meetings, religious teaching and congregate labor. Since that time, religiously motivated individuals have proposed and implemented new ways of improving the effectiveness of those prisons through rehabilitative programs. Others have pioneered programs to help offenders and victims with the process of reintegration into the community.

It is also true that religious people and institutions have often been all too happy to relegate the responsibility for "law and order," including retributive measures against lawbreakers. The following indictment was leveled by Gerald Austin McHugh in his 1978 book, *Christian Faith and Criminal Justice:*

---

[37] The following illustrations are drawn from Daniel W. Van Ness, "Christians and Prison Reform," in Daniel Reid et al., eds., *Dictionary of Christianity in America* (Downers Grove, IL: InterVarsity Press, 1990), 944-945.

> Throughout its history, the Christian Church in America has endorsed, tacitly approved, or at the very least been shamefully ignorant of the inhumanities of our criminal justice system. Even after the explicitly religious penal models of the penitentiary movement have faded into history, it was (and is) widely assumed that the punishment of criminals is in some way a holy duty. . . . And where Christians have been concerned with justice, it has all too frequently been the selective vengeance we have sanctioned as retribution, as opposed to the all-encompassing righteousness which is known as justice in the bible. It is not at all unusual to hear a Christian minister decry the rising tide of crime and immorality in print or in the pulpit, but it is rare indeed to hear a Christian minister exhorting the faithful to actually dare to love their enemies.[38]

Yet, since McHugh's book was published, a great movement of Christian churches and churchpeople has quietly been reaching out in caring and concern for prisoners, justice and victims. Prison Fellowship Ministries, founded by convicted Watergate conspirator Charles W. Colson following his own term in prison, has become one of the largest, best trained and most pervasive volunteer forces in the country. Through Prison Fellowship, more than 50,000 volunteers go into prisons to build "person bridges" and offer practical programs and Christian spiritual support to prisoners, ex-prisoners and their families. Prison Fellowship is an explicitly Christian organization, but it reaches out to all who are willing to accept its help. Prison Fellowship provides support groups for prisoners' families, seminars to strengthen prisoners' marriages, life skills training for those preparing for release and mentoring through churches as prisoners return to the community. During the Christmas holiday season, Prison Fellowship volunteers deliver gifts to nearly one-half million prisoners' children, gifts that come through the request of—and in the name of—the incarcerated parent.

Through its subsidiary organization, Justice Fellowship, volunteers are organized into citizen task forces in 26 states in order to help analyze states' criminal justice needs and advocate changes or improvements that will make the states' policies and practices more restorative. Another subsidiary organization, Neighbors Who Care, organizes community programs to recruit, train and mobilize church volunteers to serve crime victims. The volunteers assist law enforcement and victim services agencies by offering practical assistance and personal support to victims of crime in the critical hours and days immediately following the crime. Neighbors Who Care has often

---

[38] Gerald A. McHugh, *Christian Faith and Criminal Justice: Toward a Christian Response to Crime and Punishment* (New York: Paulist Press, 1978), 133.

been on the scene when no one else had time—particularly in cases of burglary and other nonviolent crimes that many victim services agencies are not usually staffed to handle.

All of this activity is motivated by the biblically based principle that all persons are created by God and valuable in God's eyes, and that Jesus Christ offers hope, new life and transformation to everyone—no matter who they are or what they have done. Certainly churches have not always been willing to reach beyond their walls to those in need around them, but the examples of Prison Fellowship, Justice Fellowship and Neighbors Who Care show plainly that churches and churchpeople can be a powerful force for help to the hurting.

Tradition

The Judeo-Christian tradition is rife with teachings regarding care for the outcast, relief for those in need and the worth of human beings as created and loved by God. Biblical tradition and stories teach about God's desire that all should be redeemed. While history offers plenty of examples of how Christians have abandoned their responsibility to stand for justice, there are also notable examples of extraordinary courage and commitment to justice. The biblical commandments to love one's neighbor, and even more, to love one's enemy are a compelling reason for churches to rise to their role and responsibility for assisting with reintegration.

The New Testament story of the "Good Samaritan" is a direct lesson in caring for a victim of crime as a person in need. As members of a community, church members can be "Good Samaritans" by offering to assist victims in moving toward physical, emotional and spiritual recovery. Through caring enough to be there and get involved, church members are saying with their actions that the victim is not alone, that caring people are willing to be there with victims through their struggles. As victims deal with the crisis, their anger, hurt, disorientation and isolation may be mitigated through the caring presence of someone whose motivation is simply to help in whatever way the victim needs and wants. In this way, the damaging effects of crime may be limited or at least lessened. Further, some victims may desire to explore the spiritual or theological aspects of what happened to them. This is an area in which church or pastoral interventions may offer a victim something beyond the meeting of practical needs. This is undeniably a difficult and sensitive area, for victims may be angry and vulnerable—and may say or do things that many churches or church members would find distressing or even heretical. However, if properly equipped, we still suggest that churches are a "sleeping giant" for help in reintegration of victims of crime.

We have already mentioned the thousands of church volunteers who are presently involved in reaching out to offenders. Much of this work is going on in prisons and jails, but a great deal of it is also happening within communities. For those who have developed friendships or mentor relationships with prisoners, it is a hard fact of life that many hopeful and determined prisoners fail to make it once they are released. All over the United States and in other countries, churches and church members are stepping forward to help those coming back from prison who are willing to accept help and work hard toward reintegration. Halfway houses, job training and placement efforts, drug and alcohol treatment programs, life skills training and mentoring are all ways church members are getting involved. It seems to be making a verifiable difference for even relatively high-risk ex-prisoners, as will be discussed below.

Presence

There are some 258,000 churches, synagogues and mosques in the United States.[39] They are visible, at least to some extent, in virtually every community. This fact has been recently noted by policymakers who recognize that community-based programs, including faith communities, have potential for delivering social services that may far outstrip government programs in effectiveness. Religious influence—even simple attendance at church, in at least one study—is being shown to mitigate a whole variety of social ills, from drug use, disease and depression to delinquency and crime.[40] This positive association offers hope for reintegration for both victims and offenders, who are each faced with issues (albeit in very different ways) that could benefit from a touch of the "faith factor."[41]

What can faith communities do to assist victims and offenders with reintegration? Again, we come to the notion of *presence*. When victims and offenders feel stigmatized and isolated, a faith community can be a source of positive personal contact and support. Both victims and offenders can benefit from available practical and phys-

---

[39] According to Joseph P. Shapiro, "Can Churches Save America?" *U.S. News and World Report*, 9 Sept. 1996, 49.

[40] *See, e.g.,* T.D. Evans et al., "Religion and Crime Reexamined: The Impact of Religion, Secular Controls, and Social Ecology on Adult Criminality," *Criminology* 33 (1995): 195-217; J. Gartner, D.B. Larson and G.D. Allen, "Religious Commitment and Mental Health: A Review of the Empirical Literature," *Journal of Psychology and Theology* 2 (1991): 1115-1123; E.L. Idler and S.V. Kasl, "Religion, Disability, Depression, and the Timing of Death," *American Journal of Sociology* 97 (1992): 1052-1079. *See also* Chapter Nine, "Who Escapes? The Relation of Churchgoing and Other Background Factors to the Socio-Economic Performance of Black Male Youths from Inner City Tracts," in Richard B. Freeman and Harry J. Holzer, eds., *The Black Youth Employment Crisis* (Chicago: University of Chicago Press, 1986), 353 ff.

[41] This term has been popularized by Dr. David Larson of the National Institute for Healthcare Research, based on several meta-analyses and systematic reviews of the research literature on faith and health. Ibid.

ical assistance, emotional care and support, and spiritual nurturing in a context of trust and concern.

For victims of crime, crisis services can help lessen the duration and severity of the stages of victimization by: (1) helping the victim rebuild a sense of safety and security; (2) allowing the victim to ventilate questions and feelings and validating those feelings; and (3) preparing the victim for what he or she might experience through the crisis.[42] There is no formula for healing. The road to recovery will be different for individual victims, and they must be empowered to work toward it in their own ways.

> . . . [A] "helpful" person who tries to second-guess the victim, imposing what the helper thinks the victim wants, can add to the sense of violation. . . . Really helping a person in trouble requires extraordinary sensitivity and discipline. People who really want to help must focus on the victim, listen carefully for the victim's expression of his or her needs and then respond to that expression—without imposing their own suggestions or judgments or perceptions. The ideal helper is one who is able to create a climate in which victims will be able to ask for and get whatever help they want.[43]

Especially in the impact stage of victimization, victims may need a variety of practical services such as transportation to a hospital or clinic, crime scene cleanup, help with police and insurance forms, calling friends or clergy, help with burial arrangements, and emergency food, clothing, shelter and finances. Some victims may need help navigating the maze of the criminal justice system; someone able to explain the criminal justice process may be helpful. Because prosecutors' offices are often unable to notify victims adequately and directly of the progress of their cases, volunteers can work with these offices to keep victims informed of upcoming hearings.

Victims, especially in the crisis phase, have emotional needs as well as physical or practical ones. Research has consistently shown that the most significant intervention cited by crime victims is that "someone cared about me."[44] In all stages of victimization, just having another person at hand can be important. A primary role of the caregiver is to be a friend to the victim. Since victims frequently feel a loss of dignity and control, compassionate care can help restore a sense of worth and self-respect. While victims may not be in a posi-

---

[42] This is expanded upon in Anne Seymour, Christine Edmunds and Jane N. Burnley, "Crisis Intervention," in materials prepared for the *1996 National Victim Assistance Academy* sponsored by the U.S. Department of Justice Office for Victims of Crime.

[43] Bard and Sangrey, *supra* note 8, at 38.

[44] A.R. Denton, "Victims of Violent Crime," in David G. Benner, ed., *Baker Encyclopedia of Psychology* (Grand Rapids, MI: Baker Book House, 1985).

tion to hear attempts to answer their cries of anger and distress, the freedom to express these feelings in a supportive context is deeply needed.

For offenders, basic personal and practical assistance in the critical weeks and months of initial transition to the community can be the key to beating the recidivism odds. Based on research and experience, it is possible to somewhat arbitrarily define the re-entry or transition process as generally having several phases: pre-release/release (0–60 days); orientation (60–120 days); direction (4–8 months); settlement (9–18 months); and growth (18–36 months).[45] In the first four months after release, there are often short-term, practical needs that are urgent. These include the very basics: money, food, clothes, housing and transportation. However, because of the effects of incarceration (and previous life experiences, in many cases), most prisoners are disoriented and disorganized about what to do to meet these basic, practical needs. Furthermore, because these phases are highly stressful for the transitioning prisoner, the danger of drug/alcohol abuse and personal conflict is especially high during the first four months or so. So there is also a significant need for a coach, advisor or mentor during this period to help with orientation, encouragement and follow-through. In order to deal most effectively with this crisis period, practical planning can help the person in transition see beyond the immediate needs to a strategy that will diminish the crisis mode, build confidence and promote independence. In the following months and years, though crisis times do occur, needs have more to do with sustaining a stable residence and job, developing and maintaining healthy relationships with family and friends, setting and meeting personal goals and reorienting life patterns. The kinds and intensity of these needs will vary among individuals, based largely upon the support systems they already may have in place.

Government programs are limited in their ability to help victims and offenders with faith issues, but faith-based programs are free to explore such issues if the person desires it.[46] By providing practical

---

[45] Prison Fellowship Ministries (PFM) research reports, 1993 and 1994. PFM's Research and Development Department conducted a literature review and research project in 1993-94. The research included surveys received from about 1,000 repeat prisoners and 95 ex-prisoners, as well as interviews with 10 outside programs and service agencies that specifically work with ex-prisoners. Prison Fellowship also manages several different aftercare programs, and the directors of those programs were interviewed for input on this breakdown of the general re-entry process.

[46] Funding sources can have a significant impact on a program. Government funding entails certain restrictions on religious activities—particularly if they involve one specific faith perspective. Church-based programs must recognize this, and determine how to avoid unwanted compromises. However, the present climate offers new potential for faith-based organizations to receive funding, even from the government, for social services activities, despite their religious context. This will undoubtedly be challenged, but a prime example is federal legislation that was signed into law in August 1996. The *Personal Responsibility and Work Opportunity Reconciliation Act of 1996, Section 104,* provides that states are allowed "to contract with religious organizations on the same basis as any other nongovernmental provider without impairing the religious character of such organizations, and without diminishing the religious freedom of beneficiaries of assistance funded under such program."

assistance and opportunities to discuss spiritual and emotional issues in a supportive context, programs can assist victims and offenders in moving beyond their alienation to greater emotional, physical and spiritual health. Of course, offenders and victims come from diverse ethnic, religious and cultural backgrounds. They may have varying cultural assumptions about managing anger, grief and stress. They may be deeply involved in other religions or may be hostile to religion. Programs offering a spiritual component must be sensitive to this and able to help the victim or offender gain the most from their own tradition and support network.

One of the only truly church-based victim assistance organizations in the United States, Neighbors Who Care® (NWC), has wrestled with this important issue. The program is explicitly Christian, but does not approach victims regarding religion directly. Trained NWC volunteers offer to help a victim connect with his or her own spiritual leader, counselor, family member or other support person. The volunteers readily assist the victim with this connection, if he or she wishes. If not, the volunteers simply ask whether the victim would like to speak with a minister or receive contact from a church. If not, that is the end of it. After all services are provided, the victim receives a letter of encouragement from the local NWC program, which explains in very matter-of-fact language, "why we care." The response to this communication, since it follows (rather than precedes) a concrete expression of caring and concern, has been overwhelmingly positive, according to NWC's president, Lisa Barnes.[47]

With regard to offenders, in addition to what the research literature describes about the practical and social issues that complicate the re-entry process, there is also a spiritual dimension to both the problems and resources of ex-offenders. This dimension is evident in the reverberating effects of child abuse and violence, and the chokeholds of addictions and depression. Temptations to take short cuts or escape routes rather than dealing honestly or effectively with problems and obstacles reflect more than just bad habits; they are also spiritual snares. Twelve-step programs have recognized this fact for years. There is also a negative spiritual dimension to the dehumanizing societal structures that feed anger and snuff opportunities, that quench hope and mock faith. So those in transition can need spiritual resources and strengths—as well as practical and emotional ones—in order to discern between truth and lies about themselves, their circumstance and the choices before them. They need spiritual reinforcement to help them stand against prejudice and malice. Spiritual nurturing and a supportive faith community are beneficial for transitioning offenders, personal growth and maturation as members

---

[47] For further information, contact Neighbors Who Care, P.O. Box 16079, Washington, DC 20041 (Phone: 703/904-7311).

of families and society. Faith communities are able to give offenders a place to learn, grow and gain strength in an atmosphere of both accountability and support. One example is a demonstration project in Detroit, Michigan, called Detroit Transition of Prisoners® (TOP). Detroit TOP's start-up and first four years were funded by a grant from the W.K. Kellogg Foundation in conjunction with Prison Fellowship Ministries.[48] TOP is a church-based, nonresidential aftercare program. Its purpose is to help selected prisoners overcome personal, economic and societal barriers in order to lead productive, crimefree lives following their return to Detroit. TOP engages and equips community churches and volunteers to encourage, assist and strengthen accountability for ex-prisoners. TOP also works to leverage the assistance of the business community, social service agencies and other local resources on behalf of participants and their families. TOP has a small staff, but much of the program's work is done through the more than 25 local churches who have allied themselves with TOP in a commitment to assist transitioning prisoners and their families. The churches are TOP's primary client, in that TOP staff focus on equipping, training and assisting the churches (pastors, lay leaders and members who serve as mentors) to handle the needs and issues involved in ongoing assistance to ex-prisoners. In this way, TOP is increasing the churches' capacity to assist in offenders' reintegration, even apart from their involvement in the TOP program.

Upon admission into TOP, participants undergo a thorough assessment that identifies their risk of recidivism and their areas of particular risk and need. Based on this information, TOP's case manager works with each participant to establish a specific transition plan. TOP participants "graduate" from the program once they successfully meet their program goals—up to two years following release into the community. Each participant is matched with a trained mentor who acts as a resource person and advisor, and who also helps keep the participant accountable to his or her transition plan. Each mentor-participant match is rooted in a church that has an expressed commitment to the TOP participant, offering a base of Christian love and nurturing in a community of believers to the participant and his or her family (if possible). In its fourth year of operation, TOP has a recidivism rate of just 9 percent. This may be compared to an anticipated recidivism rate of 50 percent for TOP participants, based on their risk scores (using the LSI-R[49]) when they

---

[48] For more information, contact Detroit TOP, P.O. Box 44196, Detroit, MI 48224-0196 (Phone 313/875-3883). The first four years of TOP were evaluated by the Center for Social Research, Thomas P. O'Connor, president.

[49] The Level of Service Inventory–Revised (LSI-R) is a risk and needs assessment designed to help predict prisoners' post-release risk of recidivism and to help target services to areas of relevant need in order to reduce the risk. D.A. Andrews and James L. Bonta, *Level of Service Inventory–Revised* (North Tonawanda, NY: Multi-Health Systems, Inc., 1995). *Also see* D.A. Andrews and James L. Bonta, *The Psychology of Criminal Conduct* (Cincinnati: Anderson Publishing Co., 1994).

enter the program. According to evaluation by the Center for Social Research, TOP participants' risk scores drop significantly during their time in TOP—which corresponds with the low actual recidivism rates in TOP.

Conclusion

We have shown that both victims and offenders wrestle with stigmatization and other issues as they face their futures, and we have suggested that faith communities are a pervasive potential resource in communities. Whether it is churches, faith communities or secular agencies that provide the services, the important point is that for restoration to occur, victims and offenders need to find wholeness and establish themselves in the community as participating members. To do so, each has barriers to overcome, and it is part of the community's role to take some responsibility for assisting with the needed reintegration. It is not sufficient simply to see that a victim is paid back—although that is a very important goal. The victim's other harms also need to be addressed within the context of a caring community. It is not enough simply to hold offenders accountable for the harms they have created—although that is also a very important goal. The offender then must be offered a real opportunity to gain a full place in the community. In each case, both victim and offender will frequently need attention and assistance from the community in order for reintegration to occur.

Chapter Eight

Participation

Crime is often a personal and painful experience with devastating consequences. The great majority of crimes involve at least two individuals: the perpetrator and the victim who bears the brunt of the harm caused by the crime. Yet the American criminal justice system focuses on the criminal act as lawbreaking—as an offense against the state. Victims who want to recover damages must file separate civil actions. As a result, a conflict exists between the government and the victim over "ownership" of the victimization experience. As Abraham Goldstein has noted, "the victim has been so much separated from the crime against him that the crime is no longer 'his.' . . ."[1]

The victim role is limited to being a *witness* for the prosecution. He or she may file a civil suit to seek damages or other remedies, but the criminal proceeding is designed to serve public goals of incapacitation, rehabilitation, deterrence or retribution. In that proceeding (analytically speaking), the victim is interested only as a *citizen* unless he or she is participating as a witness.

The victim rights movement has challenged this neat division, and appears to assume that the victim has a *party interest* of some sort, although that interest is not always clearly stated (and it is a relatively novel position). This suggests one of two possibilities: the victim rights movement is muddying the waters by injecting confusion into what should be a clear distinction between civil and criminal justice,

---

[1] Abraham S. Goldstein, "Defining the Role of the Victim in Criminal Prosecution," *Miss. L.J.* 52 (September 1982): 518.

or the victim rights movement (and other movements) are harbingers of a new model of criminal justice that is more comprehensive.

While the prosecutor and defendant have a formal role in the criminal justice process, victims have no *standing* to pursue their interests in recovering and/or reducing the likelihood of further damages. One reform to be considered, therefore, is to give them such standing in the criminal justice process, a role that permits them to pursue reparative interests.[2]

Because a restorative approach would modify the aims of criminal justice to include repairing the injuries caused by crime, the *procedures* of the criminal justice system need to be reexamined to more fully incorporate the interests of victims in reparation. A direct way of doing that would be to grant the victim legal standing to argue the primary importance of restitution at sentencing and at any other stage in which that interest may be affected. While this proposal would dramatically alter contemporary American criminal justice procedures, it would certainly not be without precedent in our legal heritage, as we will show. The injustice of victims' exclusion from the process has become a rallying cry of the victim rights movement that has promoted a number of reforms over the last 20 years. Among these are victim compensation funds, mandatory restitution legislation and victim "bills of rights" granting victims the rights of allocution[3] and notification concerning the status of their criminal cases. As helpful as these advances are, they fall short of providing victims with a formal role as active parties in criminal cases. They do, however, mark a willingness to return to the former, more inclusive, view of criminal processes.

It has been argued that practice in the United States is already moving in this direction.[4] Despite the traditional distinction between the punishment of criminal offenders through the criminal law and the compensation of crime victims through civil tort law, as a practical matter the wide acceptance and use of restitution within the criminal justice system has already resulted in the partial merger of

---

[2] Thorvaldson has suggested that such an approach fits a model of victim participation and restitution that he calls the *civil restitution model*, and that he contrasts with the *criminal restitution model* that focuses not on the private interests of the victim but only the public, and that uses restitution only as it meets the "primary justifying aim" of criminal justice, which is the maintenance of public law. Sveinn Thorvaldson, "Restitution and Victim Participation in Sentencing: A Comparison of Two Models," in Burt Galaway and Joe Hudson, eds., *Criminal Justice, Restitution and Reconciliation* (Monsey, NY: Criminal Justice Press, 1990), 23-36.

[3] According to *The Attorney's Victim Assistance Manual*, the right of allocution permits victims to address the court at the sentencing hearing in order to express their views on the crime, the person who committed it, the effect of the crime on the victim and the sentence that should be imposed. The judge is required only to listen to the victim. In other words, the legal right of the victim is entirely procedural—to speak—and not substantive. *The Attorney's Victim Assistance Manual: A Guide to the Legal Issues Confronting Victims of Crime and Victim Service Providers.* Prepared for the Sunny von Bulow National Victim Advocacy Center in cooperation with the Attorney's Victim Assistance Project of the American Bar Association, Criminal Justice Section, 1987.

[4] Josephine Gittler, "Expanding the Role of the Victim in a Criminal Action: An Overview of Issues and Problems," *Pepp. L. Rev.* 11 (1984): 139.

criminal and tort law. As a consequence, the victim can be viewed as having a direct interest of a restitutive nature in the criminal proceeding. To the extent that this is true, greater participation of the victim in criminal proceedings would be consistent with recent trends. It would also be consistent with legal tradition.

The History of Private Prosecution

Even after Henry I succeeded in redefining crime as an offense against the king instead of the victim, the victim was assured a significant procedural role in the criminal process through the mechanism of private prosecution. Indeed, it was not until the nineteenth century, and the rise of public prosecution, that victims can be said to have been fully relegated to their current, passive role as a witness for the prosecution. At the beginning of that century, victims were the dominant force in criminal proceedings, initiating criminal cases, prosecuting them and obtaining financial restitution for their trouble. By the end of the century, the police dominated the investigation of crime, the State's Attorney dominated prosecution and correctional officials dominated the sentencing process.

Between 1815 and 1900 the United States created its modern criminal-justice system. In 1815, key institutions—the police, the prison, probation, parole—did not yet exist in their modern form. By 1900, they were parts of a new apparatus of social control. To be sure, not every state had adopted all of the new institutions by 1900, but the idea of a criminal justice *system* was firmly established. This system involved a set of interrelated bureaucratic agencies performing specialized tasks for the purpose of controlling crime, deviance and disorder.[5] The victim's role was to serve as little more than a witness. There are two strands we must follow to understand how this change came about: the rise of public prosecution and the abolition of magistrate's courts.

English Roots

Both the magistrates' courts and private prosecution had their roots in medieval England. While private prosecution preceded the

---

[5] Samuel Walker, *Popular Justice: A History of American Criminal Justice* (New York: Oxford University Press, 1980), 55.

Norman Conquest,[6] the magistrate's court was a comparative new-comer, established by statute in 1361 but with its roots in the mid-thirteenth century when "keepers of the peace" were first elected.[7] The function of these courts was to screen lesser criminal cases by bringing victims and defendants before it, questioning them about the crime and, if possible, disposing of the matter themselves (or, if not, passing the case on to other courts).[8] In addition to their judicial functions, magistrates also carried on a variety of administrative functions. They supervised labor laws, wage and price regulations, the building of roads and bridges, the operation of markets and liquor control laws.[9] Over time, these administrative burdens increased. One historian, for example, noted the increased amount of time justices in Southwark devoted to operating the county jail during the second half of the eighteenth century.[10]

Politics was never far removed from the magistrate's role. Many found that a judicial commission lent prestige when they ran for other offices in local elections, and political administrations found it beneficial to have supporters appointed to the magistrate's court. Consequently, electoral politics was a factor in the selection and conduct of magistrates.[11] Drawn from the landowner class, magistrates furthermore represented an economic system that was unpopular to significant portions of society.[12] In light of this, it is not surprising that private prosecution was hailed as a limit on the power of the

---

[6] In fact, private prosecution is one of those institutions that have been known since time immemorial. It is more feasible to pinpoint the date at which an alternative to it was first proposed. Sir Thomas Hetherington, the Director of Public Prosecution for England, has been able to do so:

> Researchers from Sheffield University, commissioned by the Royal Commission on Criminal Procedure, reported in 1980 that they had traced the origin of the proposal for a system of public prosecution in England and Wales to Henry VIII. In 1534, the king suggested that "laws are not put into force unless it be by malice or rancour or evil will. Better it were that they had never been made unless they should be put into perfect execution." The execution, he stated, was far from perfect, and to remedy that situation he proposed that "Sergeants of the Common Weal" should act as prosecutors. This proposal, like all those that followed until 1879, was not implemented. (Thomas Hetherington, *Prosecution and the Public Interest* (Old Tappan, NJ: Waterlow/Macmillan, 1989), 4.)

[7] Elizabeth Burney, *Magistrate, Court and Community* (London: Hitchinson, 1979), 46. The 1361 statute provided:

> In every county of England shall be assigned for the keeping of the peace, one lord and with him three or four of the most worthy in the county, with some learned in the law, and they shall have power to restrain the offender . . . and to pursue, arrest, take and chastise them according to their trespass and offence. (Ibid.)

Burney notes one inclusion and one exclusion of interest. *Included* was a requirement that some of the justices of the peace be learned in the law. *Excluded* was the word "trial" between the words "take" and "chastise." Ibid., 47.

[8] J.M. Beattie, *Crime and the Courts in England: 1660-1800* (Princeton, NJ: Princeton University Press, 1986), 36.

[9] Burney, *supra* note 7, at 48-49.

[10] Ibid., 64.

[11] Beattie, *supra* note 8, at 60.

[12] "The justices fell to their lowest point in public esteem during the 50 years up to 1830. As a rule, this was not because of personal failings but because they came to represent a legal and economic system that was harsh, outdated and increasingly resented. The ferocious game laws, frequently broken by starving laborers, were applied by the land-owning justices summarily and fiercely. To this day the image of the magistracy has never quite recovered from this period of blatant exercise of propertied class interest." (Burney, *supra* note 7, at 51.)

crown and landowners. A private prosecutor managed the entire case (from apprehension through trial) as though it were a civil matter. While the private citizen (usually the victim) was required to bear the financial costs of the prosecution, there were also financial incentives for the successful victim, such as recovery of restitution, on occasion with treble damages added.[13] Nineteenth-century supporters of private prosecution, such as Sir James Stephen, applauded it as a highly effective means of upholding the integrity of law.

> [N]o stronger or more effectual guarantee can be provided for the due observance of the law of the land, by all persons under all circumstances, than is given by the power, conceded to every one by the English system, of testing the legality of any conduct of which he disapproves, either on private or on public grounds, by a criminal prosecution. Many such prosecutions, both in our days and in earlier times, have given a legal vent to feelings in every way entitled to respect, and have decided peaceably, and in an authentic manner, many questions of great constitutional importance.[14]

Calls for a Public Prosecutor

During the nineteenth century, British reform advocates such as Jeremy Bentham and Sir Robert Peel began campaigning for the establishment of a public prosecutor, although they did not argue for the abolition of private prosecution. In fact, Bentham argued for a system with both public and private prosecution. Private prosecution alone, he believed, was inadequate for crimes that were essentially public in nature. He opposed public prosecution alone as granting the state a monopoly and hence establishing "an arbitrary dispensing power."[15]

---

[13] Juan Cardenas, "The Crime Victim in the Prosecutorial Process," 9 *Harv. J.L. & Pub. Pol'y* (1986): 359, 360 & 367.

[14] James F. Stephen, *A History of the Criminal Law of England* (London: MacMillan, 1883), 496. Sir James recognized that private prosecution was subject to criticism, particularly if pushed to an extreme.

> It never is pushed to an extreme, however: first, because a jury as soon as the character of such a prosecution as I have suggested was exposed, would be certain to acquit, unless there were some extraordinary reason for sanctioning it; and secondly, because the result of such an acquittal would be an action for malicious prosecution followed by a verdict for exemplary damages. Besides which, the management of a criminal prosecution is so expensive, so unpleasant, and so anxious a business, that no one is likely to undertake it without strong reasons. (Ibid., 495-496.)

We will see in the Philadelphia Magistrate's Courts what some argued was a chronic state of "pushing to an extreme."

[15] Hetherington, *supra* note 6, at 5.

There were other complaints as well: that at times of high crime when so much depended on the deterrent ability of the legal system, it was unwise to rely heavily on the willingness of victims to prosecute; that private prosecution might be ineptly conducted and result in unnecessary acquittals; that it might be motivated by revenge or greed; and that the victim and offender might settle privately.

In 1751, Henry Fielding identified three major causes of a recent increase in crime in London. First, he believed that the poor were becoming increasingly immoral in the face of increased prosperity and business in the city. Second, he thought that the courts were so lenient that they were failing to deter people from turning to crime. Third, and most troubling to Fielding, was the lack of cooperation from victims. Property crime victims were simply not bringing offenders to court, even when they knew who they were and could have them arrested. This reluctance was due in part to the costs and trouble involved, but also by what he thought was "altogether misplaced tenderness that made some men reluctant to see offenders hanged for minor offenses. The weak-kneed responses of victims and the courts were together, he was certain, undermining the deterrent capacities of the law."[16]

Hay and Snyder recite the stages through which a private prosecutor might be required to go in attempting a successful prosecution:

> First, to give evidence to a magistrate (perhaps by first going to a constable, or in order to compel a constable to act on a warrant), thereby being bound, with two others as sureties, in a recognizance (a penal bond) to prosecute. Secondly, to conduct proceedings then and later personally or to engage a solicitor. Third, to interview witnesses and to bring them before the magistrate (or pay the solicitor to do this and most of the following tasks). Fourth, to decide upon the charge, in those many cases where several choices were possible. Fifth, to attend the court clerks (Clerk of Indictments at assizes, Clerk of the Peace at quarter sessions) to draw the indictment, which could take one, two, or even three days' attendance in the nineteenth century, or to send copies of the depositions to counsel for a bespoke rather than off-the-peg job. Sixth, to ensure the attendance of prosecution witnesses at the grand jury hearing (usually the important ones would already be bound in recognizances to do so) in order to have the indictment found "a true bill," suitable for trial. Seventh, to ensure the attendance of witnesses at trial. Eighth, to present the prosecution case in open court, including questioning the accused, or to pay counsel to do so. Ninth, to apply for

---

[16] Beattie, *supra* note 8, at 35.

any rewards or other public moneys that were granted by
the court for the trouble and expense of prosecution, and
to distribute any sums owing to the witnesses, as well as
paying the court costs and any fees incurred for solicitor or
barrister. Finally, in cases where a conviction was obtained,
to intervene further if a pardon was sought by the convict
or his friends. Some prosecutors, sharing or shamed into
the belief that a sentence was too harsh, joined petitions
for mercy in the knowledge that their intervention was
given particular notice; others, dismayed that their efforts
might be undone by royal clemency, petitioned for the exe-
cution of the original sentence.[17]

One researcher has concluded that informal settlements were indeed
common, particularly in small communities.[18]

This debate culminated in the passage of the Prosecution of
Offenses Act in 1879, which established the office of the public prosecutor, charged with supervising prosecutions of a limited range of
offenses in which the ordinary form of prosecution was seen as insufficient.[19] The remainder of the cases were left to private prosecutors,
but the overwhelming numbers of those prosecutions (some report
80 percent) were initiated by police officers.[20]

American Colonial Experience

American colonists brought both the magistrate's courts and the
system of private prosecution with them. In fact, these dominated
criminal proceedings up to the Revolution in most colonies.

In North Carolina, justices of the peace were "the most
important law enforcement officer(s) in each county," and
also sat as judges of precinct courts. Over half of the cases
in those courts were dismissed because of the failure of the
private parties to carry through with the process. Justices
were also of central importance in New York, where they
"were, on the whole, an ignorant lot" prone to the abuse
of power. With powers of summary jurisdiction, they han-

---

17. Douglas Hay and Francis Snyder, eds., "Using the Criminal Law, 1750-1850: Policing, Private Prosecution, and the State," *Policing and Prosecution in Britain 1750-1850* (Oxford: Clarendon Press,
1989), 26.

18. "[I]n the small-scale society of the village a prosecution may not have been the most effective way to
deal with petty violence and theft. Demanding an apology and a promise not to repeat the offense,
perhaps with some monetary or other satisfaction, may have been a more natural as well as a more
effective response to such an offense, or perhaps simple revenge, directly taken." (Ibid., 8.)

19. Hetherington, *supra* note 6, at 10-14.

20. Hay and Snyder, *supra* note 17, at 3.

dled the bulk of minor criminal business, and even heard many cases on the General Sessions bench. High dismissal rates were common before these magistrates, especially in New York City. . . . Even in those places which have become known for their early rejection of private prosecution or acceptance of the public prosecutor, justices and private citizens played leading roles at least well into the eighteenth century. In pre-Revolutionary Massachusetts, most criminal cases were commenced by the state in name only; they "were in reality contests between subjects rather than contests between government and subject." Justices had wide-ranging jurisdiction over criminal matters in eighteenth-century Connecticut; the early establishment of county public prosecutors in Virginia was a direct response to the power of private citizens to abort prosecutions.[21]

As in England, many victims chose to settle informally with the offender rather than go to the trouble and cost of initiating criminal proceedings. In part, this was due to widespread distrust of lawyers—a perspective expressed forcefully by John Dudley, a farmer turned judge who once charged a jury:

> They talk about law—why, gentlement [sic], it is not law we want, but justice. They want to govern us by the common law of England; trust me for it, common sense is a much safer guide for us. . . . A clear head and an honest heart are wuth [sic] more than all the law of the lawyers. . . . It's our business to do justice between the parties; not by any quirks of the law out of Coke or Blackstone—books that I never read and never will—but by common sense and common honesty between man and men.[22]

However, the English colonists were joined by immigrants from civil law countries with an entirely different system of prosecution from that practiced in England. The Dutch brought the *schout*, and the French the *procureur publique*.[23] As a result, most colonies developed a hybrid system of private and public prosecution, with private action dominating.

---

[21] Allen Steinberg, "From Private Prosecution to Plea Bargaining: Criminal Prosecution, the District Attorney, and American Legal History," *Crime & Delinq.* 30 (1984): 568, 571-572.

[22] Quoted in Richard E. Ellis, *The Jeffersonian Crisis: Courts and Politics in the Young Republic* (New York: Oxford University Press, 1971), 115.

[23] According to Joan Jacoby, there are three significant differences between the *procureur,* the *schout* and the English Attorney General and the modern American prosecutor.
  Whereas the *procureur,* the Attorney General, and the *schout* all were involved in criminal prosecution, none was truly the primary law enforcement official in a specific jurisdiction. All three officers were essentially operatives of a national and centralized authority and drew their power from another official; the American prosecutor is an officer of local government with little or no supervision from other levels of government. The European officials were appointed to office and served at the pleasure of the appointer, whereas the American prosecutor is generally elected and answerable to his constituency. (Joan E. Jacoby, *The American Prosecutor: A Search for Identity* (Lexington, MA: Lexington Books, 1980), 5.)

The Professionalization of Justice

For years, historians assumed that the adoption of public prosecution meant the elimination of private prosecution. Consequently, it has been frequently stated (because of passage of laws providing for public prosecution) that private actions fell into disuse after the Revolution.[24] It was historian Allen Steinberg's research into the magistrate's courts in Philadelphia that shed new light on the operation of a hybrid public-private prosecution process during the nineteenth century. In his book *The Transformation of Criminal Justice: Philadelphia, 1800–1880*,[25] Steinberg makes a convincing case for the dominance of private prosecution until the 1880s (at least in dealing with the largest numbers of prosecutions: those for relatively minor offenses). The reason for this dominance was the popularity of the magistrate courts, operated in Philadelphia by elected officials known as Aldermen who, like their English counterparts, conducted administrative as well as judicial functions.

Although these courts were highly informal in operation, the justices had the power to hold defendants in jail pending trial by a court of record, to dispose of certain minor cases and to require the posting of a peace bond. The Aldermen were for the most part unschooled in the law, and were even willing to create new offenses on the spot if it seemed necessary. Aldermen were frequently resorted to for justice, particularly by the poor.

According to Steinberg,

> Private prosecution gave citizens the power, in practice, to define crime. Because the minor judiciary let them do so, almost anything that annoyed or irritated a person could be treated as a crime, for whatever motives a prosecutor might have. Private prosecutions fell into two broad groups. Some cases were seriously and fully pursued, others only partially pursued. Within both of these groups, some cases were instituted with the honest intention of attaining some measure of justice, others with ulterior or malicious motives. There were substantial numbers of all types of cases. Aldermen provided people with the freedom to police themselves, to determine when the law should be invoked and, often, how far the criminal justice process should continue, even though in an imperfect and sometimes exploitative way.[26]

---

[24] Steinberg, *supra* note 21, at 569.

[25] Allen Steinberg, *The Transformation of Criminal Justice: Philadelphia, 1800-1880* (Chapel Hill: University of North Carolina Press, 1989).

[26] Ibid., 77.

It is the popularity of the magistrate's courts that Steinberg finds intriguing, particularly in light of what appear to twentieth-century lawyers to be significant flaws in how these courts operated. They were crowded, unruly and undignified.[27] Because the Aldermen were "unencumbered" by the law, they were often arbitrary.[28] As noted previously, this sometimes meant that they created new offenses and made them effective retrospectively.[29] Private prosecutors were occasionally motivated by spite; others failed to pursue their cases to completion (sometimes leaving impoverished defendants languishing in jail).[30] Finally, because the Aldermen were paid fees by the litigants for handling their case, there was little incentive for them to refuse a prosecution, and there was ample opportunity for corruption.[31]

Interestingly, even with these flaws, the magistrate's court was popular. Steinberg's theory is that they were a form of popular, local and informal justice. They offered a forum in which disputes could be readily resolved. More important, they offered a forum in which the disputants controlled what happened. While there were regular outcries against the courts' abuses, these were raised by reformers who did not use the courts.

Further, Steinberg argues, the courts served an important law enforcement function. Philadelphia did not have a police department until 1854.[32] Prior to that time it relied on a night watch system with

---

[27] Even during routine proceedings, the behavior of spectators was much like that of theater audiences. After 1860, partly because of the "daily and hourly" chattering of the spectators, it became "impossible, at the best of times, to maintain entire order in the Quarter Sessions." Conversations raged about politics, cases under trial, the weather, "all subjects, no matter how lofty or how insignificant." Try as he might, the crier's efforts to silence the court room were in vain, there being "no timid ones among [the spectators] to quail at his appeal." (Ibid., 22.)

[28] "On a day in 1853, an event occurred that was unusual even for the court of quarter sessions. A man who was accused of assault and battery waited for his case to be called. As he surveyed the courtroom, he recognized several of the faces in the crowd, witnesses to the alleged assault who he assumed were present to testify against him. When the district attorney called the case, the defendant approached the bench but the prosecutor failed to appear. . . . Intimidated by the presence of witnesses, unsure of what was about to happen next, and unaccompanied by counsel, the defendant confessed. Judge Oswald Thompson saw an opportunity to provide everyone with a lesson in how the criminal law ought to operate, and he took it. Portending a position that would be adopted frequently by the bench in years to come, he declared that he was concerned only with the "outrage to the public" not with the "private wrong," and so, despite the absence of the prosecutor, he sentenced the man to six months." (Ibid., 79.)

[29] In one remarkable case a woman prosecuted her husband for "refusing to come to bed and making too much noise, preventing her from sleeping." He was ordered to go to bed when called. Ibid., 48.

[30] "The spatial and social density of life in Philadelphia produced the circumstances in which ordinary people came to depend—and prey—upon one another. All facets of popular life in Philadelphia created the propensity toward litigation: poverty, the stress of bewildering social change, family tensions, ethnic and racial prejudice and rivalry, the boisterousness of the streets and saloons—in short, the everyday affairs of ordinary people living in crowded conditions in, or on the edge of, poverty. The resolution of their quarrels and spats, and their attempts to take advantage of one another or to avenge injustices, took them regularly to court." (Ibid., 17.)

[31] It was the political corruption of the Aldermen that eventually led to the abolition of the office in 1874. Ibid., 196 ff.

[32] Thomas A. Reppetto, *The Blue Parade* (New York: Free Press, 1978), 41. The City had experimented with temporary police arrangements as early as 1833. This was prompted by the bequest of one Stephen Girard, who died in 1831. His will provided a large sum of money to the City to be used to create a "competent police." In 1833, the City enacted an ordinance that established a force of 24 police during the day and 120 at night. An innovation (for the United States, at any rate) was its requirement that advancement in the force be based entirely on merit rather than political connections. John L. Sullivan, *Introduction to Police Science* (New York: McGraw-Hill, 1971), 18.

only limited police coverage during the day,[33] and the patrol was much more passive than proactive. This is why the police force was such an innovation.

According to Roger Lane,

> The new police officers were expected to be professionals in the fullest sense. They would not, like the watch, be confined by custom to watching for fires, fights and other overt disturbances. They would not, like sheriffs and constables, rely largely upon the complaints of the injured. The police would prevent trouble by actively seeking it out on their own, before it had time to reach serious proportions.[34]

Prior to 1854, the initiative in the criminal justice system fell to the private citizen. It was the citizen who filed a complaint with the sheriff or with the magistrate. With the advent of the police force, a new possibility emerged for initiating criminal cases, one which was believed would bring greater efficiency to crime fighting:[35] to require that all cases be initiated by the public prosecutor based on investigative work performed by the police.

Eventually, the development of the public police force (combined with the long-standing complaints about abuses of informality) led to a reorganization of the magistrate courts, which effectively ended private prosecution. The principal reason for this development (the transformation to which Steinberg refers in the title of his book) is that criminal justice had become professionalized. The police and the prison agency were more effective in dealing with lawbreakers than were the victims and community. Salaried magistrates were more likely to administer even-handed justice than were those who were paid for each case they accepted.[36] Nevertheless, Steinberg mourns the demise of the courts and of private prosecution, because in a real sense those courts were "people's courts." While that was ultimately their downfall, it was also their strength.

---

[33] The night watch was a colonial fixture. Many municipalities had required from the earliest days that all able-bodied men over age 16 be available to patrol the town at night. Those who were disabled or were otherwise unable to serve were excused so long as they paid a qualified person to take their place. Over time this exemption was abused, developing an informal and semi-professional police force. Ibid., 17.

[34] Roger Lane, *Policing the City: Boston 1822-1885* (Cambridge: Harvard University Press, 1967), 35.

[35] Crime fighting was a significant concern in nineteenth-century Philadelphia. Not only did the city have its share of routine crime, but it also experienced a dozen major riots between 1834 and 1860. These riots have been attributed to tensions between immigrant and ethnic groups. Walker, *supra* note 5, at 55.

[36] All that was undoubtedly true. In fact, Gerald Caplan, in a review of Steinberg's book, notes:
> Steinberg's description of magisterial practices looks like an indictment to a lawyer. What he describes is not law by any conventional definition. No lawyer would feel comfortable with a judicial system so unstructured, so willing to dispense with rules, definitions, and procedural regularity, without knowing precisely what benefits would result. (Gerald Caplan, "Criminal Justice in the Lower Courts: A Study in Continuity" *Mich. L. Rev.* 89 (1991): 1694, 1703.)

> The central point is that, at bottom, the criminal court was dominated by the very people the criminal law was supposed to control. . . . The ordinary people of Philadelphia extensively used a system that could also be so oppressive to them because its oppressive features were balanced by the peoples' ability to control much of the course of the criminal justice process. Popular initiation and discretion were the distinctive features of private prosecution, rooted in the offices of the minor judiciary where it began, and remained the most important aspect of the process even in the courts of record. Whether it be to intimidate a friend or neighbor, resolve a private dispute, extort money or other favors, prevent a prosecution against oneself, express feelings of outrage and revenge, protect oneself from another, or simply to pursue and attain a measure of legal justice, an enormous number of nineteenth-century Philadelphians used the criminal courts. . . .[37]

Victim and Prosecutor

Some would argue that the prosecutor adequately represents the victim's interest. According to the American Bar Association's "Standards Relating to the Prosecution Function," however, the prosecutor's responsibilities are "to convict the guilty, enforce the rights of the public, and guard the rights of the accused."[38] Victims' interests are not mentioned and could be included (arguably) only within the broad category of "enforcing the rights of the public." If and when the public's interest conflicts with the victim's interest, the victim is clearly not included. This is reflected in the American Bar Association's *Guidelines Governing Restitution to Victims of Criminal Conduct:* "The prosecuting attorney should advocate fully the rights of the victim on the issue of restitution *to the extent* such advocacy would not unduly prolong or complicate the sentencing proceeding, nor create a conflict of interest for the attorney acting as advocate for the government."[39]

Judith Rowland, a former prosecutor, has argued the need for "independent attorney advocates" to represent victims in the criminal justice system.

---

[37] Steinberg, *supra* note 25, at 78.

[38] Gittler, *supra* note 4, at 144.

[39] American Bar Association, *Guidelines Governing Restitution to Victims of Criminal Conduct* (1988), 4 (emphasis added).

> In our legal system, it may be a conflict of interest for one attorney to represent two clients in the same cause of action. A very real possibility is that such a conflict arises when a prosecutor represents both the victim and the state in the same criminal action when the aim of the prosecution is to obtain a conviction for the state.
>
> In whose best interest, for instance, is a "nolo contendere" plea, or the dismissal of counts affecting one or more victims while taking a plea to others? As to the former, the prosecutor will be the first to admit that the people's interest in getting the plea ("nolo" being for the purposes of a criminal proceeding the same as guilty) and not in assisting the victim; in the latter example the risk is great that restitution, insurance, or victim compensation rights may be plea bargained away, lost or compromised.[40]

What the prosecutor thinks is good for the public may be at odds with the victim's interest. This argues for victims being given standing to act independently of the prosecutor at any stage in the criminal justice process when their interests in recovering restitution and securing personal protection are at risk.[41] Each victim would necessarily have the right to private representation for those stages of the criminal justice process that relate to the victim's pursuit of restitution or personal protection. This may actually help the prosecutor: it is obvious that prosecutors rely on victim cooperation to secure convictions. They may benefit, then, if the possibility of securing restitution encourages increased victim participation in the criminal justice process.

In summary, giving victims a formal role in the criminal justice system would result in both an explicit recognition that crime is an offense against the victim and a distinction between the legal interests of the victim and the government.

---

[40] Judith A. Rowland, "Representation of Victims' Interests within the Criminal Justice System," in *The Attorney's Victim Assistance Manual*, 219.

[41] It should be noted that currently in most states victims may hire private attorneys to assist the prosecutor. The case is controlled by the prosecutor, and the private attorney does not represent the victim in the sense we are calling for here. The private attorney is not an advocate for separate, clearly defined legal interests of the victim, but is instead essentially a privately paid member of the prosecution team (*Attorney's Victim Assistance Manual*, 1987). Other states prohibit even this limited role for private attorneys. For example, the Missouri Supreme Court called participation by a private attorney "inherently and fundamentally unfair." Deborah P. Kelly, "How Can We Help the Victim Without Hurting the Defendant?" *Crim. Just.* 2 (1987): 39.

Victim Participation at Various Stages of Criminal Proceedings

In recent years there has been a growing body of literature in American journals on the role of victims in Western European criminal justice systems.[42] This literature yields a wealth of suggested roles for victim participation in the criminal justice system of the United States. Although the stages of the criminal justice process vary from country to country, there is a basic process common to almost all jurisdictions. We will discuss possible formal roles victims and their counsel might play in the following key stages: investigation, bail, trial, plea bargaining, sentencing and postsentencing. In each of these stages there are two basic forms that victim participation might take: (1) consultation with the prosecutor[43] and (2) initiation of action independent of the prosecutor. The first requires direct access to prosecutors, the second to the judge.

Investigation

The decision to prosecute normally rests with the public prosecutor for the reasons that historically gave rise to public prosecution: the need for even-handed and consistent prosecution and the importance of considering public interests over private in initiating criminal actions. The decision to charge a defendant nevertheless affects the future interests of the victim. If there are several potential charges and the prosecutor wants to include one charge (e.g., for a violent crime) but ignore another charge (e.g., theft), the victim has an interest in negotiating with the prosecutor. Because a victim can secure restitution only after the defendant is found guilty, the victim clearly has an interest in what charges are brought against the accused.[44]

European systems offer four basic options for such intervention:[45] (1) the victim may ask the prosecutor to review an adverse decision; (2) the victim may appeal to the decisionmaker's superior

---

[42] *See* Matti Joutsen, "Listening to the Victim: The Victim's Role in European Criminal Justice Systems," *Wayne L. Rev.* 34 (Fall 1987). *See also* Patrick Campbell, "A Comparative Study of Victim Compensation Procedures in France and the United States: A Modest Proposal," *Hastings Int'l & Comp. L. Rev.* 3(2) (1980): 321-348.

[43] In the United States, victims have recently been given certain rights, such as to be informed of proceedings and to consult with the prosecutor at various stages of the process. (e.g., Victim and Witness Protection Act of 1982).

[44] This is particularly true in light of the statistics concerning arrests and convictions. Only one out of three crimes is reported to the police. Of those, only 20 percent result in an arrest. This means that there are only seven arrests for every 100 crimes. However, the attrition does not end here. Nearly one-half of the people arrested have their charges thrown out by the prosecutor. At most, only four out of every 100 crimes results in charges being filed. Charles W. Colson and Daniel W. Van Ness, *Convicted: New Hope for Ending America's Crime Crisis* (Westchester, IL: Crossway Books, 1989).

[45] See Joutsen, *supra* note 42, at 95-124 for a comprehensive review of the various victim intervention practices in European criminal justice systems.

or to an independent board of complaints; (3) the victim may appeal to the court; or (4) the victim may initiate a private prosecution. These methods of victim intervention employ formal administrative procedures, although few European jurisdictions have a formal appeal process.[46] The Office of Crime Victims Ombudsman (OCVO) offers assistance to crime victims who feel that their rights have been violated or who feel that they have been treated unfairly by the criminal justice system or by victim assistance programs. It investigates complaints and acts as a referral and information resource. The OCVO's function could be expanded to include serving as an ombudsman between the victim and the prosecutor. It could also develop a review process to ensure that the prosecutor is addressing the victim's interests.

Arraignment through Presentencing

Decisions regarding bail could also affect the victim's interests. For example, victims may believe that their personal or family safety will be at risk should bail be granted. If so, they could be permitted to present supporting evidence to the judge (independent of the prosecutor) in the interest of limiting future harm at the hands of the defendant. In such a situation, victims could also request a restraining order against a defendant about to be released. It is conceivable that a victim might actually request that the accused be released on bail in order to continue work and increase the likelihood of collecting future restitution.[47]

Plea Bargaining

Victim involvement in the plea agreement stage is essential. The great majority of all cases are resolved by plea agreement. A plea agreement relieves the court and the prosecutor of the burden of a trial. It is typically an agreement among the prosecutor, defense counsel and the accused to plead to reduced charges resulting in a lighter sentence. While statistics on the exact percentage of cases resolved by plea agreement are difficult to find, statistics on the number of cases resolved by guilty plea suggest a general understanding of how many cases are resolved by plea agreement. Of 100 felony

---

[46] These four basic methods of victim intervention are subsumed in one of the guidelines of the Council of Europe's Recommendation, which states, "the victim should have the right to ask for review by a competent authority of a decision not to prosecute, or the right to initiate private proceedings" Ibid., 109.

[47] In France, the bail must be sufficient to cover the costs of the proceedings and damages demanded by the *partie civile*. Campbell, *supra* note 42. Further discussion of the French *partie civile* is included in this chapter.

arrests, 55 are carried forward. Fifty-two (95 percent) of these were disposed of by guilty plea.[48] The victim has an interest in securing a plea that will maximize the potential restitution ordered. The interest of the state in obtaining a quick agreement may be at odds with the victim's interest in restitution.

However, the victim's interests and the prosecutor's interests may very well overlap. The victim's interest in restitution and the state's interest in efficient resolution of the case are not mutually exclusive. It is conceivable that restitution to the victim by the offender could satisfy at least a portion of the government's need for punishment.[49] The payment of restitution also might be part of the bargain to reduce other charges.

Sentencing

A number of studies have indicated that victims are more interested in sentencing than in any other stage of the criminal justice process. Eighty percent of California victims interviewed indicated that the existence of their right to allocution at felony sentencing was important to them.[50] It is at sentencing that the justice system moves from a legal determination of how to characterize the offender's behavior (did it violate the law?) to both the practical and symbolic act of deciding what to do about that lawbreaking. According to one study of burglary victims, three basic components make up victims' understanding of "fairness" when it comes to sentencing: the punishment the offender will be given, the compensation the victim will receive and the rehabilitation services that will be made available to the offender.[51] Giving victims the right to intervene at sentencing to seek reparation, then, addresses at least one of these dimensions and arguably may address the other two as well.

Restitution is often treated as an "add-on" to the real sentence, even though it is mandated in many jurisdictions. For it to be a meaningful sanction, judges must fashion sentences in which all components, including restitution, can be satisfied. For example, a sentence to incarceration may preclude the payment of restitution while a sentence of intensive supervision probation would not. Sentencing should be constructed so as to increase the likelihood of restitution

---

[48] Barbara Boland et al., *The Prosecution of Felony Arrests, 1986* (U.S. Department of Justice, Bureau of Justice Statistics, June 1989).

[49] Campbell, *supra* note 47.

[50] Edwin Villmoare and Virginia V. Neto, *Victim Appearances at Sentencing Hearings under the California Bill of Rights: Executive Summary* (U.S. Department of Justice, National Institute of Justice, March 1987).

[51] Mark Umbreit et al., *Victim Meets Offender: The Impact of Restorative Justice and Mediation* (Monsey, NY: Criminal Justice Press, 1994), 20.

being paid. In other words, restitution should be normative unless there is a compelling, overriding reason.

While it is commonly assumed that offenders cannot provide adequate compensation to their victims, studies have concluded that there are relatively few victimizations that are so costly as to negate the possibility of restitution, even after taking into consideration the extremely low income levels of some defendants.[52] One comparative study of restitution programs found that the average compliance rate is 68 percent, suggesting that more offenders are able to comply than is generally assumed. Moreover, this does not touch on the rate of compliance that might be achieved if restitution were given higher priority by sentencing and correctional authorities.[53]

Postsentencing

Probation and parole violation hearings can affect the recovery of restitution. Victim interest in timely and full recovery is at risk if the offender violates the conditions of probation or parole and is returned to incarceration. The feasibility of restitution recovery from incarcerated offenders is clearly limited. It is not unreasonable, however, to expect offenders released into the community on probation or parole to pay restitution based on realistic payment plans and effectively monitored restitution collection. The Earn-It Program, run by the Quincy (Massachusetts) Court, reports that more than 70 percent of offenders pay their restitution in full.[54] Both probation and parole supervision could be extended on an informal supervisory level until restitution is paid in full. In addition, currently recognized system deficiencies in monitoring and collecting restitution need to be addressed in order to provide a reparative framework of criminal justice.

The Victim as Civil Claimant in Criminal Cases

In considering how victims' restitution claims could be incorporated in the criminal justice process, the role offered the victim in France is noteworthy. Crime victims there can bring a civil action for damages as part of the criminal proceedings, using the *partie civile*[55] procedure. A victim who brings such a civil action thus

---

[52] Gittler, *supra* note 4.

[53] Daniel McGillis, *Crime Victim Restitution: An Analysis of Approaches* (National Institute of Justice, U.S. Department of Justice, December 1986).

[54] Andrew R. Klein, *The Earn-It Story* (published by the author, 1981).

[55] For an extensive discussion on the *partie civile* procedure, *see* Campbell, *supra* note 42.

becomes a party to the related criminal action and can play an active role, through counsel, in asserting a right to civil damages. A significant number of victims seek this relief rather than instituting civil proceedings.[56]

French experience has demonstrated the advantages of this one-court approach. Combining all the actions in one proceeding has been more efficient and has assured that penal and civil decisions will be consistent. For victims, the use of the criminal process has been faster, simpler and cheaper than the civil proceeding. The prosecutor proves the guilt of the offender, so victims are relieved of that obligation.[57]

A separate hearing on the victim's civil claim is held after the criminal charges have been settled. If the accused has been found guilty, the victim must (1) show that the injury he or she suffered was directly caused by the prosecuted acts and (2) prove the amount of the alleged damages to his or her person and property. If the accused has been found not guilty, the victim must show by a preponderance of the evidence that the damages suffered were directly caused by a violation of the Civil Code and were the result of the facts adjudicated at the preceding trial.[58]

Issues

As previously discussed, victims rights advocates have achieved much over the past 20 years. Support for certain victim rights legislation has come from a broad range of groups—for example, feminists have joined with law-and-order groups to work for rape victim law reform, and the American Civil Liberties Union joined with the National Organization for Victim Assistance to support the Victim and Witness Protection Act of 1982.[59] These efforts have demonstrated that change is possible, but we are proposing more comprehensive changes to expand victim involvement in the criminal justice process. Although several important issues are raised by these proposed changes, we believe that further involvement for victims is not only a matter of basic fairness and justice; it is also practical. Let us examine some of the issues that our proposals must address.

---

[56]   Gittler, *supra* note 4.

[57]   Joutsen, *supra* note 42.

[58]   Campbell, *supra* note 42.

[59]   Kelly, *supra* note 41.

1. Will granting victims a formal role in the criminal justice system cause more delay?

Some argue that involving the victim in criminal proceedings will further delay and overburden the system. While any major change might result in initial implementation problems, there is evidence that prosecutors, defense attorneys and victim representatives will be able to develop procedures to help them operate more efficiently than they do now. One study on the effects of victim participation in "pretrial settlement hearings" leading to guilty pleas indicates that victim participation can increase the efficiency of the court process.[60] Commenting on the Heinz and Kerstetter study, Goldstein noted:

> There was as an overall reduction in the length of time it took to process the case . . . and a greater proportion of the test cases were closed on or before the scheduled trial date—apparently because the victim's presence facilitated communication among interested parties and crystallized views earlier as a result.[61]

2. Will this impair defendants' rights?

One issue that has generated significant discussion is whether "adding" rights for victims takes away the rights of the defendant. This is an important concern, but it does not necessarily follow that more rights for victims means fewer rights for defendants. Furthermore, the role of the victim as a party might vary from stage to stage of the criminal proceeding so as to protect the defendant's right to a fair trial.[62] In fact, the primary effect will probably be felt by the prosecutor, who will have to adjust to the presence of a victim whose interests may differ from the public's. Nonetheless, it will be important to effect this change that rights given to victims do not diminish the defendant's rights or limit the prosecutor's right to protect the public interest.

Concern also has been expressed that the presence of victims at the trial and at sentencing would add an emotional element to the proceedings to the defendant's disadvantage.[63] Most states, though, already permit victims the right of allocation at sentencing.[64] The detrimental effect on the defendant might actually be decreased if a more specifically defined role were prescribed for victim involvement.

---

[60] A. Heinz and W. Kerstetter, *"Pretrial Settlement Conference: An Evaluation* (Law Enforcement Assistance Administration, U.S. Department of Justice, 1979).

[61] Abraham S. Goldstein, "Victim and Prosecutorial Discretion: The Federal Victim and Witness Protection Act of 1982," *Law & Contemp. Probs.* 47 (Autumn 1984): 244.

[62] Ken Eikenberry, "Victims of Crime/Victims of Justice," *Wayne L. Rev.* 34 (Fall 1987): 29-49.

[63] *See* Kelly, *supra* note 41.

[64] "Currently, 35 states have enacted legislation providing for victim allocation or other ways of directly presenting a victim's opinion." National Organization for Victim Assistance, *Victim Rights and Services: A Legislative Directory*, 1987, 10.

3. Should victims be given appointed counsel?

A victim's status as a party in criminal proceedings can be compared to an intervenor in a civil case. A third party is allowed to intervene in a civil action if that party has an interest in the subject of the action and "the disposition of the action may as a practical matter impair or impede his ability to protect that interest."[65] Viewed in this light, the interest of victims in the criminal case is sufficient to give them the status of a third party, and thus the right to counsel.

Who should pay for the victim's attorney? Indigent defendants are assured of free counsel under the Constitution; should indigent victims receive the same? Perhaps, but this need not be a requirement for at least two reasons. First, defendants are guaranteed an attorney at trial because they have not been found guilty, and, until they are, they are presumed innocent. The Supreme Court has recognized that the availability of appointed counsel is important to guarantee a fair trial and to avoid unjust convictions (with the attendant threat of punitive sanctions). Second, if the victims' right to participate in criminal cases is understood as giving them an alternative to civil action, it would be reasonable to extend the civil court's right to an attorney—the right for victims to obtain attorneys at their own cost or to represent themselves. Therefore, the right to counsel available to a crime victim in the civil process should also be available to the victim seeking restitution in the criminal process. The "contingent fee" arrangement available in civil cases could make attorneys accessible to those who cannot pay immediately.

4. What about vengeful victims?

Some argue that one of the principal accomplishments of separating the civil from the criminal law is this: Victims who might want to "take the law into their own hands" may not determine the offender's punishment. There is little doubt that victims and the public want offenders held accountable for their actions through some form of redress. However, recent studies have shown that victims are primarily interested in wholeness, not revenge. Indeed, while victims have frequently been portrayed as vindictive and angry souls bent on exacting harm, a growing body of literature challenges this perception and suggests that crime victims are most concerned with fairness in applying sanctions. For example, Umbreit[66] found that lengthy incarceration is not high on the agenda of many victims, but rather that justice and fairness be grounded in a preference for treatment and rehabilitation.[67]

---

[65] Eikenberry, *supra* note 62, at 38-39.

[66] Mark Umbreit, "Crime Victims Seeking Fairness, Not Revenge: Toward Restorative Justice," *Federal Probation* 53(3) (1989).

[67] Umbreit reports that the concern about fairness most frequently expressed by victims of burglary by juveniles was the rehabilitation of their offenders. Restitution was the second most frequent concern.

Research on victim-offender reconciliation programs reveals that victims and offenders are overwhelmingly satisfied with these meetings. Of those who participated in the program, 83 percent of offenders and 80 percent of victims were satisfied or somewhat satisfied.[68] In another study, victims participating in pretrial negotiations, contrary to some expectations, did not recommend that the prosecutor "throw the book" at offenders.[69]

A system that allows victims to confront their offenders and play an active role in the pursuit of restitution may prove therapeutic for the victims.[70] An active role, not revenge or complete exclusion, may be exactly what victims most desire. Of course, there will be exceptions. Judicial oversight and guidelines will be needed to prevent abuse.

5. Should victims be compelled to file?

Just as victims are not compelled to file a civil action, so they should not be compelled to file a civil claim in criminal proceedings. The difficulty and length of civil proceedings certainly is a strong disincentive for victims to file. Allowing victims to file in criminal proceedings can be made relatively simple. In France the victim may simply send a registered letter to the court indicating that the victim wishes to commence an *action civile* alongside the criminal proceeding.

Conclusion

The question concerning victim participation in the criminal justice system is not *whether* they should take part but *how*. They are already involved as citizens and (possibly) witnesses, and the rise of restitution orders, victim impact statements and other victim rights initiatives has already begun to give the victim a quasi-party role. A goal that is highly consistent with a restorative response to crime might be to expand and formalize a party role for the victim who wishes to pursue restitution. Such a goal would have at least five practical implications to the criminal justice system.

First, the victim would need access to legal representation separate from that currently provided by the prosecutor for those stages of the criminal justice process that relate to the victim's pursuit of restitution or personal protection. This would avoid a potential con-

---

[68] Kelly, *supra* note 41.

[69] Heinz and Kerstetter, *supra* note 60.

[70] Campbell, *supra* note 42.

flict of interest that may impair the prosecutor's ability to fully represent the government as well as the victim, and it would symbolically and practically demonstrate a change in criminal procedure.

Second, the decision to prosecute would probably remain with the prosecutor, as it is that office that is charged with protecting the public's interest, and for practical reasons of efficiency and fairness. However, because the victim's interests are affected by that decision, there should be an avenue for appeal open to the victim who disagrees with the prosecutor's decision.

Third, sentences would be constructed so as to increase the likelihood of restitution being ordered and paid. In other words, restitution would be normative without a compelling, overriding reason not to order it.

Fourth, care must be taken that rights given to victims do not diminish the defendant's rights or limit the prosecutor's duty to protect the public interest.

Finally, the right to counsel available to a crime victim in the civil process would probably also be available to the victim seeking restitution in the criminal process.

These principles provide a basis for expanding the criminal justice system to include a formal role for victims to pursue restitution. Victim participation addresses the injustice of excluding from the court proceedings those directly harmed by the crime; it moves the criminal justice system toward a more restorative focus.

Chapter Nine

Planning for Restorative Justice

Can the current practices of criminal justice really be changed? It often seems that the overwhelming weight of inertia has entrenched for good the old ways of thinking and doing in criminal justice. In fact, restorative justice has begun taking hold in visible ways at the local and national levels. For example, in a groundbreaking move, Minnesota's Department of Corrections established the position of Restorative Justice Planner in November 1993 to help implement restorative justice approaches throughout the state. Subsequently, in February 1994, Minnesota launched a Restorative Justice Initiative. Its stated purpose is to "promote and support the use of criminal justice practices, policies and programs which focus on repairing the harm of crime and strengthening communities in all jurisdictions around the state."[1] The state of Vermont, in the mid-1990s, began to implement a reform of the state's correctional structures with explicit reference to restorative justice. At the county level, movement has begun in places as diverse as California, Oregon, Florida and Pennsylvania, with other reforms afoot in North Carolina and South Carolina.[2]

In the spring of 1996, the U.S. Department of Justice's National Institute of Justice and Office for Victims of Crime hosted a three-day symposium exploring restorative justice, its applications and its

---

[1] Kay Pranis, "Restorative Justice Initiative," *Ideas that Work: Crime and Public Safety* (Washington, DC: National Governors Association, 1996).

[2] Justice Fellowship is working in these states, for example, to mobilize citizen leadership. They assess the state's criminal justice needs and build a "Plan for Restoring Justice," involving legislative and policy reforms, as well as community-based programs.

future. Attending that symposium were more than 200 practitioners and policymakers from the United States.

Nor has this movement been confined to the United States. According to two observers, restorative justice has become such a significant factor in criminological discussions in many Western countries that it can no longer be dismissed or disregarded.[3] A growing number of countries have begun significant national action to explore implementation of restorative structures and programs. In fact, international interest has advanced to the point that the United Nations Alliance of Nongovernmental Organisations (NGOs) on Crime Prevention and Criminal Justice has established a working party on restorative justice to prepare recommendations for the UN's Crime Congress in the year 2000.

Restorative justice is entering the mainstream parlance of criminal justice. Given this, there is an open door for moving ahead to apply the vision to practice at every level, but that application will not come automatically. What carries restorative justice from theory to practice? We suggest the following "building blocks" to restorative practice. These will help advocates set a course toward restorative justice, generate momentum, offer mid-course corrections and create opportunities to widen the circle of influence for restorative justice action.

Gain Support for Restorative Justice

Public support for restorative justice in many ways begins with public education. Although the term "restorative justice" has become fairly common in the media as well as in criminal justice circles, the term cannot be said to be truly familiar or widely understood. In fact, in light of the political rhetoric and policies aimed to demonstrate a "get tough" attitude about lawbreakers as a response to the social disintegration represented by crime, one might well wonder whether the public, in fact, is likely to take any interest in a restorative response to crime. Yet public opinion surveys suggest that when people are given options, they are strongly inclined to favor

[3]   Heinz Messmer and Hans-Uwe Otto, eds., "Restorative Justice: Steps on the Way Toward a Good Idea," *Restorative Justice on Trial: Pitfalls and Potentials of Victim Offender Mediation—International Research Perspectives* (Dordrecht, The Netherlands: Kluwer Academic Publishers, 1992), 4-5.

responses to crime that are restitutionary, rehabilitative and sensitive to victim issues.[4]

Kay Pranis, Minnesota's Restorative Justice Planner, has written that "[a] restorative response to crime is a community building response."[5] Pranis has written about and demonstrated principles, strategies and methods for gaining public and community support for policies and programs that promote restorative justice. It is notable that the values that undergird a restorative response to crime also inform and shape the process of building a restorative response. In Pranis's words, "victims must have a voice, the community must be involved" and "the work of promoting and supporting the use of restorative practices . . . must be carried out across multiple systems and the community. . . . [P]rogress toward a restorative approach requires engaging voluntary participation and interest."[6]

Engagement of the community requires mechanisms to raise awareness of crime and justice issues in a restorative context. Because every community involves many groups clustered around neighborhoods, religious, professional or recreational affiliations, advocacy interests, and so on, there are a wide variety of opportunities to educate and engage people. While it is important to present the conceptual framework of restorative justice, real life stories— especially those that have local connections—make the concepts more concrete. Credible leadership from those who can speak from experience helps to create an open climate for consideration of new ways to view crime and justice. These approaches are key whether the objective is to gain support in a neighborhood or to gain momentum in policymaking. Policymakers need and want the "cover" of citizen support to advocate change. This may be especially true when it comes to crime and justice. Despite public opinion polls showing wide public support for correctional programs that rehabilitate, policy-

---

[4] Mark Umbreit cites a 1992 Minnesota statewide public opinion survey conducted by the University of Minnesota. The survey used a sample of 825 Minnesota adults, reflecting the demographic and geographic balance of the state population. The survey did not specifically mention restorative justice, but rather included three questions that relate to a restorative approach. The survey found that 71 percent of the sample favored restitution combined with probation over jail for burglary, even where there has been one previous conviction. The survey further found that 80 percent of the sample believed that more money spent on education, job training and community programs would have a greater impact on crime reduction than money for more prisons. Finally, the survey found that 82 percent of the sample said that if they were victims of nonviolent property crimes, they would be very or somewhat likely to participate in a mediation session with their offender. Mark Umbreit et al., *Victim Meets Offender: The Impact of Restorative Justice and Mediation* (Monsey, NY: Criminal Justice Press, 1994), 9-13. Other public opinion research also supports the assumption that the public, if given a choice, tends to support restorative options. *See* Public Agenda Foundation, *Crime and Punishment: The Public's View* (1987); *Punishing Criminals: The Public's View, An Alabama Survey* (1989); and *Punishing Criminals: The People of Delaware Consider the Options* (1991), all published by the Edna McConnell Clark Foundation. *See also* other surveys on crime and punishment cited in the information packet titled, *Seeking Justice: Crime And Punishment in America* (Edna McConnell Clark Foundation, 1995).

[5] Kay Pranis, "Building Community Support for Restorative Justice: Principles and Strategies," in Burt Galaway and Joe Hudson, eds., *Restorative Justice: International Perspectives* (Monsey, NY: Criminal Justice Press, 1996).

[6] Ibid.

makers greatly fear the perception of being "soft on crime." Because of this, it is very helpful to identify allies across the political spectrum. Restorative justice is neither a conservative nor a liberal agenda. It makes sense to political conservatives, through its emphasis on personal accountability and clarity about the limitations of government's role, but political liberals find common ground with its emphasis on community-building and communities' role in the restoration of damaged lives. Presentations of restorative justice can honestly appeal to the public and to policymakers across traditional lines. Indeed, they must do so.

Develop a Credible Coalition

In order to be credible, those planning and working for restorative justice must seek out and reflect the concerns of victims, offenders and the community. The support of law enforcement officials and organizations can also be of great help. This is true for two reasons. First, the particular restorative programs for a locality are often best designed by the members of that locality. Involvement by people representing diverse interests but sharing a common interest in restorative justice will generate creative ideas tailored to local circumstances. Second, proposals made by such a broad-based coalition will have far more credibility than those urged by single interest groups alone. This is particularly true in the area of criminal justice, in which advocacy groups concerned about the needs of victims or offenders have little occasion to find common cause.

Many crime victim groups are cautious about restorative justice, fearing that it is actually less concerned about victim issues than about offender rehabilitation. This is certainly reasonable inasmuch as some restorative justice advocates come directly from judicial or correctional agencies whose role has always been offender-oriented. Some nonprofit advocacy groups also have emerged from previously offender-oriented backgrounds. It is worthwhile for restorative justice proponents to evaluate themselves on this point. As Pranis observes, "[V]ictims have historically been left out of the criminal justice process. Victims groups have had to fight the system for nearly every gain they have achieved. Consequently, many are skeptical."[7] Not all are, however. In 1995, the National Organization for Victim Assistance (NOVA) presented a paper calling for what it calls *restorative community justice* at their national conference. The vic-

---

[7]   Ibid.

tims movement was also well represented at the U.S. Department of Justice symposium on restorative justice mentioned earlier. Leadership from the victims movement will continue to be important, both in presenting restorative justice and in keeping restorative justice in focus from the victims' perspective.

Pursue Strategic Goals

The failure of contemporary criminal justice is not one of technique but of purpose; what is needed is not simply new programs but a new pattern of thinking. The current way of thinking about crime is simply as an offense against government—as lawbreaking. Consequently, criminal law does not recognize the harms to the victim, to the community or to the offender. The offender's punishment seldom redresses the harm done to the victim or ameliorates the conditions that may have contributed to the crime in the first place. Victims have no legal standing in criminal court; their role is limited to assisting the prosecution (when necessary) in convicting the offender (although they may also be allowed to provide an "impact statement" prior to sentencing).

Given the challenges and impediments to implementing a restorative approach, moving forward will require careful thought and a clear strategy. In developing such a strategy, it is important to distinguish between the restorative justice vision itself and the strategies for implementing that vision. Restorative justice is a continuum, not a destination. Intermediate goals must be set but not confused with the ultimate objective; their value depends ultimately on whether they bring the system closer to a total societal response to crime that reflects the restorative justice vision. A physician conducts surgery not because that is the essence of health, but because it can lead to health.

Therefore, intermediate goals are set in order to help redress the current imbalance in criminal justice, with its focus on government and offenders, and begin to build policy and practice on new, more balanced goals. Because they emphasize aspects of justice that are currently missing, these goals may appear as unbalanced as the system they are meant to remedy. They do, however, offer a place to start. We have selected four intermediate strategic goals that, we suggest, will help build a response to crime that is guided by a new, restorative pattern of thinking about crime and justice. Two of these goals address the formal criminal justice system, and two address the informal community-based response to crime. The goals emerge from the restorative values discussed in the last four chapters.

*Strategic Goal #1: Victims and offenders in every community will have opportunities for reconciliation through **encounter** programs.*

Many victims express a desire to confront their offenders, to ask questions, express feelings and—in some cases—to reconcile with and even forgive them. Such encounters cannot, and must not, be forced on victims, but the healing potential has been proven to be enormous for many of those who take the opportunity. This experience is consistent with restorative justice emphasis on the importance of establishing community peace, and even more, peace between the two parties in direct conflict, the victim and offender. Victim-offender encounter programs offer a structured opportunity for victims and offenders (and in some programs, representatives of the families and community) to meet, discuss the crime and work out an acceptable agreement toward making things right. Sometimes this meeting leads to others and moves the victim and offender well beyond the level of basic restitution. Participation in victim-offender reconciliation meetings has been shown to benefit both victims and offenders in several ways. It enables each to become an active participant in the justice process. Victims usually receive restitution; they report a higher degree of satisfaction with the justice process after such an encounter.[8] Offenders are given an opportunity to make amends and perhaps receive forgiveness; they learn how their crime injured people, not just an impersonal system.[9] If opportunities for encounter become a prevalent resource for individuals and communities, then crime's injuries would more often be addressed and would be more likely to heal.

*Strategic Goal #2: Nondangerous offenders will be accountable for **reparation** as a sentencing priority, and given community-based sentences rather than prison.*

Few prisoners have the resources to repay their victims, and prisons rarely prepare them to be productive after release. Few victims can reasonably expect to receive redress under the present system. Because of this, offenders who do not present a serious risk to the community should be sentenced to adequate supervision in settings that permit them to work, repay their victims, avoid the debilitating conditions in prison and save the community the tax burden of unnecessary incarceration.

Three factors should be considered in sentencing decisions. The *seriousness of the offense* should determine the amount of the sanction. The extent of *harm to victims* should determine the form of the

---

[8] Daniel McGillis, *Crime Victim Restitution: An Analysis of Approaches* (National Institute of Justice, U.S. Department of Justice, December 1986).

[9] *See* Chapter Five.

sanction, ensuring an emphasis on reparation. The *risk* the offender poses to the community should be a limiting factor influencing the degree of control exerted by the government during the length of the sanction. Objective criteria need to be established to identify those offenders deemed too dangerous to stay in the community, using a standard such as high likelihood of seriously threatening criminal behavior. Even categories as arbitrary as "violent/nonviolent" reveal that a substantial portion of those now in prison might be sentenced differently under this goal. Nearly one-half the people sent to prison have been convicted of nonviolent crimes.[10] There are undoubtedly many more offenders who could be sentenced to a reparative sanction with appropriate supervision.[11] Further, criminal justice systems should be as accountable for the reparations paid to victims as they are for the care and recidivism of offenders. This accountability would be strengthened by the participation of victims in the formal process.

*Strategic Goal #3: Victims will receive reparation for the primary harms resulting from the crime, and will be offered **participation** in the criminal justice process to ensure that their harms are addressed.*

Although this would be a complete departure from criminal justice practice in the United States, it is similar to the rights offered to crime victims in several European countries.[12] It offers at least three advantages over the current criminal/civil distinction in American law:

- first, the criminal process is more speedy and less costly than the civil process,

- second, it recognizes programmatically that crime harms victims, and

- third, it helps policymakers and parties to distinguish the legal interests of the victim from those of the government.[13]

*Strategic Goal #4: Both victims and offenders have access to services to assist them in the process of **reintegration**.*

Most crime victims need assistance of some kind from the moment a crime is committed. Sometimes they receive it from informal networks of family, friends or church, but often they go without. The immediate and long-term effects of crime can be devastating, but are reduced if immediate aid is available. Crisis intervention pro-

---

[10] Charles W. Colson and Daniel W. Van Ness, *Convicted: New Hope for Ending America's Crime Crisis* (Westchester, IL: Crossway Books, 1989).

[11] *See* Chapter Six.

[12] *See* Chapter Eight.

[13] *See* Chapters Four and Eight.

grams providing services such as emergency shelter, financial assistance, child care and referrals to social service agencies already exist throughout the country. However, most are unable to provide the comprehensive help that is needed due to staff and funding shortages. Communities must augment these system-based victim assistance programs.

Offenders also need help in reintegrating into the community. This need is particularly acute when the offender has been imprisoned, but exists for those who have been sentenced to community-based sanctions as well. In addition to the barriers to successful participation in society that the offender may have faced before, he or she now carries the stigma and (in many cases) the legal disabilities that come with being a convicted felon.

Faith communities are a community resource through which victim and offender assistance might be offered: almost every community has local churches (in some urban communities they are virtually the only viable nongovernmental institution available) or other faith groups, and service to victims and offenders is consistent with their missions.[14] They are currently a largely unused resource in criminal justice, but the factors that have contributed to that underuse may be overcome.

Encounter and reintegration require mobilization of community resources and institutions, and are significant ways for the community to help foster relationships characterized by peace and safety. Reparation and participation require governmental action to realign the official system response to crime from a narrow punishment model to a fuller, restorative model. Though punishment has a place, emphasis on reparation and participation increases the likelihood that the punishment imposed would serve to restore the harm caused by the crime. If these four strategic goals are creatively pursued and progress on them is charted and evaluated, the pattern of thinking that shapes our society's response to crime will begin to change. Both the system responses and the community responses will open up to new possibilities, by considering victim harms and how offenders may be accountable for delivering reparations, by facing up to the personal dimensions of crime and ways to honor them, and by recognizing the need and opportunity for both victims and offenders to grow into healthier lives through reintegrative programs and community relationships.

---

[14] *See* Chapter Seven.

Revisit the Vision

Work toward intermediate goals to help restore balance to the system may nonetheless produce programs that fail to reflect restorative principles. For example, victim involvement in criminal trials is a strategic goal, but if such involvement increased the isolation of victims from offenders it would end up conflicting with the restorative goals of reconciliation and restoration. It is important, then, to regularly evaluate policies and programs both in terms of their success at redirecting society's response to crime and the extent to which they help assure restoration of victims, offenders and communities.

One approach to such evaluation is to cast the basic foundations of restorative justice in the form of questions that probe the practical tendencies of the policy or program and help focus on issues for which measurements may be designed. Remember the propositions for restorative justice described in Chapter Three:

1. Justice requires that we work to restore victims, offenders and communities who have been injured by crime.

2. Victims, offenders and communities should have opportunities for active involvement in the restorative justice process as early and as fully as possible.

3. In promoting justice, government is responsible for preserving order and the community is responsible for establishing peace.

The following questions may help frame approaches to evaluating whether a policy or program is promoting in practice what it set out to do in principle.[15]

1. Does the program pursue the goal of restoration?

    Does it promote restoration of all parties?

    Do its social controls interfere as little as possible with the restoration of the victim and offender?

2. Does the program meet the needs of victims?

    Does it help make right the harm to victims?

    Does it enable the victim to participate fully?

    Does it protect victims who are less powerful?

    Does it provide standing and dignity to victims?

---

[15] These are adapted from a similar list compiled in Howard Zehr, *Changing Lenses: A New Focus for Crime and Justice* (Scottsdale, PA: Herald Press, 1990), 230-231.

3. Does the program meet the needs of offenders?

    Does it enable and encourage offenders to accept respon-
    sibility for their actions?

    Does it enable the offender to participate fully?

    Does it avoid dehumanizing offenders?

    Does it protect the less powerful offender?

    Does it help make right the harm to offenders?

4. Does the program meet the needs of the community?

    Does it enable the community to participate fully?

    Does it make right the harm to the community?

    Does it address the community's need for safety?

5. Does the program facilitate effective community-government
    cooperation?

    Does it effectively coordinate public and private resources?

    Does it impose the least drastic government intervention
    possible?

6. Does the program successfully maintain the restorative vision
    as it encounters adverse political and institutional forces?

    Do new leaders and staff understand and act upon the
    original mission and vision?

    Do the procedures and policies interfere as little as possi-
    ble with the accomplishment of reparative and/or reinte-
    grative goals?

    Are measurable objectives set and tracked, objectives that are
    directly related to the restorative purposes of the program?

    Does analysis of program data give an honest picture of
    the program's restorative nature and activities, and are
    reports available to others seeking to build restorative
    justice?

Policies and legislation are difficult to keep focused, subject as they
are to a wide range of pressures and changes. However, restorative justice advocates who are working in this arena are wise to analyze the
status quo, and revisit previously enacted policies and their results.
One very practical reason is that arguments for restorative justice in
the policy arena depend on practical examples and arguments of cost
and benefit. Future arguments rest on the credibility of past accomplishments; and past accomplishments are only as strong as their practical outcomes. Therefore, an ongoing commitment to evaluation

based on the basics of the restorative justice vision builds the necessary research and experience base for the future of restorative justice. [16]

Evaluate for Impact

Impact evaluations may be highly formal or fairly simple, but they are the only way to establish whether a program or policy is, in fact, what it set out to be. Commitment to such evaluations begins with program design, guides the development of ideas into actions and provides an objective framework for testing whether the features produce the intended benefits or outcomes. Far from being a "threat" to programs (as one can feel when undergoing an evalua-tion that asks tough questions about the translation of principles into practice), evaluation is the backbone of a healthy movement toward a new "pattern of thinking." It provides the opportunity to constantly improve on program strengths and correct unsatisfactory performance before it weakens the whole program. Evaluation data are the best "proof" to funders, professional associates and even crit-ics who want some objective verification of the benefits of the pro-gram or policy.

Evaluation is easily accomplished when clear goals and measur-able objectives have been assigned. The discipline of careful planning is a great advantage. The principle of "go slow to go fast" is applic-able to those charting the course for restorative justice in practice. We may be eager to accomplish change, but we will only know what we have accomplished if we know what we set out to do, how our methods relate to our goals and what measures tell us if we are mak-ing progress. For restorative justice to take root and bear fruit, its policies, practices and programs must be observably and measurably connected to the vision—and this must remain true through the inevitable process of growth and change with changing times, new challenges and fresh opportunities.

---

[16] We know of several assessment tools that have been designed to help with more informal analysis of the status quo or of new programs. Justice Fellowship's "Evaluating Your Criminal Justice System" (1996) presents several sets of questions addressed to various phases in the justice process. Contact Justice Fellowship, P.O. Box 16069, Washington, DC 20041-6069 (Phone: 703/904-7312). Restorative Justice Ministry's "Measuring Restorative Justice" identifies factors that should be considered in assessing how individual restorative programs might be made more restorative. Contact Restorative Justice Ministries, Fresno Pacific University, 1717 S. Chestnut Avenue, Fresno CA 93702 (Phone: 209/453-2064).

Realign Vision and Practice

As stated above, evaluation provides a link between vision and practice that tests and establishes the restorative value of policies and program. The process of change is constant and inevitable, with changing political, economic and social realities. Restorative justice is inherently interested in the well-being of persons and communities. Our arguments for its "rightness" must stand the reality test. Proponents of the penitentiary believed fervently that the penitentiary was the logical, moral and humane response to lawbreaking—especially in contrast to the prevailing practices of the day. In practice, though, the penitentiary failed to match the vision from which it sprang. The history of American corrections is, in many ways, an example of dogged adherence to one dimension of the penitentiary—confinement—while the concomitant features have shifted and changed according to various social, psychological and practical currents over time. Although the penitentiary has not delivered the desired results, confinement has remained a dominant feature of the corrections landscape. As a society we have only rarely and recently questioned the value of confinement as the "normative" mode of punishment for any crime deemed serious. There is a lesson here. For the Quakers, confinement was a practical way for penitents to focus on their wrongs and change their lives apart from the pressures, temptations and distractions. Instead it became a means of isolating wrongdoers from their communities. In restorative justice practice, we must be prepared to be creative, flexible and nondogmatic about program features while holding firmly to the vision and intents of restorative justice theory.

Stay Connected

Since the late 1980s, when we first began drawing together working sessions of diverse individuals to draw out our propositions for restorative justice, the concept has gained momentum with a wide variety of proponents.[17] These range from representatives of the correctional system, advocating a better way from the system side of things (in Minnesota and Vermont, for example), to those deeply committed to community-based, nonsystem justice. If restorative jus-

---

[17] See "Forward."

tice may be called a "movement," it is clearly not a parochial one. Within the boundaries of the restorative justice vision, much may be gained by learning, growing, collaborating with and challenging each other as well as those with other visions and agendas. Restorative justice will continue to be relevant and vital only if it stays in touch with its vision, tests its practice, stretches its applications and grows with the diversity and creativity of its proponents. Otherwise, this new pattern of thinking and its practical applications will become insulated and marginalized.

Take Obstacles Seriously

As planners work toward turning restorative justice theory into practice, there are several issues that immediately present themselves. These issues are not rhetorical, but in fact represent serious obstacles. We will treat some of the most obvious of these in turn. They are:

1. Unsolved crimes;

2. Social, economic and political inequalities in society;

3. Politics as usual.

Obstacle 1: Unreported/Unsolved Crimes

Some failures of the current criminal justice system are due not to its lack of a restorative focus, but from deeply rooted systemic problems facing government and the community. Because these will not disappear with the adoption of restorative vision, they must be confronted as structural impediments to achieving the vision. One of the most serious of these is the attrition rate as cases enter and pass through the criminal justice system; it is difficult for society to ensure that victims and offenders are restored when the parties are not known. Only one out of three crimes is reported to the police; police make an arrest in only 20 percent of the cases that are reported; and convictions result in only 50 percent of those cases.[18] This means that for every 1,000 crimes, around 70 result in an arrest and about 35 result in a conviction.

This attrition rate poses serious problems for current criminal justice, predicated as it is on the power of deterrence and incapaci-

---

[18] Colson and Van Ness, *supra* note 10.

tation to reduce crime. It poses equally serious problems under a restorative justice model concerned with addressing the harm caused by crime; the possibility of restitution is automatically foreclosed if no offender is found.

Restorative justice programs may address this obstacle in two ways: by *reducing* it and by *compensating* for it. We reduce the obstacle by reducing the number of unreported crimes, the number of uncleared cases and the number of offenders who are not prosecuted. There are several reasons why restorative justice programs might help bring about these reductions. First, restorative justice's emphasis on a community-government partnership in establishing safe communities is a strategy likely to increase the likelihood of crimes being reported and suspects identified, while simultaneously reducing the incidence of crime. Community organizing, storefront police facilities and neighborhood foot patrols—all of which emphasize collaboration between the community and civil government—have been effective in reducing both the fear of crime and the incidence of crime.[19] Second, it has frequently been noted that victims are more inclined to report crimes if they believe that the inconvenience of reporting and assisting with prosecution will be offset by recovery of their losses. As restitution is a central element of restorative justice, it is reasonable that programs predicated on that model could expect increased participation by victims.

While restorative justice programs may be able to reduce the attrition rate, they will not end it entirely.[20] It will be necessary to design ways to compensate for it as well. One way this could be done is by broadening and substantially funding victim compensation programs to help address the harm suffered by victims whose offenders are unknown or unable to pay. Funding for these programs could come in part from the "surplus" restitution paid when the sentence imposed on the offender reflects not only the actual damages to the victim but the seriousness of the offender's conduct and ability of the offender to pay.[21] Furthermore, victim compensation should be given priority over other monetary penalties such as fines and supervision fees, given the preeminence of the goal of addressing victim harm. While assessing fees to cover the system costs of processing offenders has become increasingly popular, the overarching goal of reparation must remain preeminent or the conversion of restitution to victims into fines for government coffers (which took place in the days of King Henry I) will happen again.

---

[19] Lawrence Sherman, *Neighborhood Safety.* Crime File Study Guide Series. (Washington, DC: National Institute of Justice).

[20] Nor should they, since there will presumably continue to be occasions when suspects are charged who are not guilty, and who should therefore be acquitted.

[21] As discussed in Chapter Six.

Obstacle 2: Social, Economic and Political Inequalities in Society

Imbalances of power among the parties in a criminal justice proceeding exist at many levels. One that has received official recognition, the disproportionate power of civil government over individual defendants, has resulted in a panoply of procedural protections designed to protect defendants' human rights.[22] But there are other imbalances as well, such as those that result from poverty. Accused defendants with abundant financial resources receive substantially better representation than do indigent defendants who are assigned overworked, underpaid public defenders. The pithy title of Jeffrey Reiman's book *The Rich Get Richer and the Poor Get Prison*[23] underscores this point. Poverty creates imbalances among victims as well, the majority of whom are as poor and powerless as their offenders. While there has been a steady growth of services to victims over the last 15 years, disenfranchised crime victims—especially those who are members of racial minority groups—are not benefiting from them as much as wealthier, more powerful victims.[24] A third example of a power imbalance is the disparity that may exist between victims and offenders caused by social, economic and political inequities,[25] and by a pre-existing relationship that may have existed between the two (a particular problem in the case of domestic violence cases). As negotiation and mediation become standard fare in resolving disputes, this particular imbalance will become increasingly important for restorative justice practitioners to recognize and address.

The existence of social, political and economic inequities challenges any society that values justice and fairness, but under the restorative justice model it poses a special challenge to communities who are responsible for creating peace, and to governments who are charged with providing order that protects the disenfranchised. There has been long and heated debate over the extent to which these inequities either cause crime (by reducing the honorable choic-

---

[22] This official legal response to the potential abuse of governmental power has been a distinguishing characteristic of the Anglo-American adversarial systems when compared with continental inquisitorial systems (*see, e.g.,* Mirjan Damaska, "Evidentiary Barriers To Conviction and Two Models of Criminal Procedure: A Comparative Study," *U. Pa. L. Rev.* 121 (1973): 506, 583) and the Japanese legal system (*see, e.g.,* Daniel H. Foote, "The Benevolent Paternalism of Japanese Criminal Justice," *Cal. L. Rev.* 80 (1992): 317, 322-328). Within Anglo-American jurisprudence it has been described as a fundamental dividing line between "crime control" and "due process" ideologies (Herbert L. Packer, *The Limits of the Criminal Sanction* (Stanford: Stanford University Press, 1968), 149-173).

[23] Jeffrey H. Reiman, *The Rich Get Richer and the Poor Get Prison: Ideology, Class, and Criminal Justice* (New York: John Wiley & Sons, 1979).

[24] Holly Metz, "The Illusion of Victim Rights," *Student Lawyer* 17(7) (1989): 16-23.

[25] While most victims and offenders come from similar backgrounds, not all do.

es available to the offender) or produce unfairness in the criminal justice system.[26] Because the discussion has been linked to issues of offender responsibility and accountability, it has become highly polarized. While a society may determine that such inequities do not reduce or deny individual responsibility, their existence creates a moral obligation for that society to respond. Just as individuals must accept responsibility for their acts, so societies must assume some responsibility for the inequalities that plague them.

One way to do this is to use mechanisms such as grand juries, inquests or legislative hearings to explore and address larger societal issues surrounding patterns of offenses or offenders. The agency conducting the hearing could be given not only investigative and fact-finding authority but also the power necessary to implement reforms. While this would not solve the problem of inequities, it would at least partly ameliorate the effects of these inequities on the practice of justice.

Obstacle 3: Politics as Usual

Many of the themes of restorative justice are appealing. In fact, what restorative programs seek—redress for victims, recompense by offenders, the development of peaceful communities, increased participation in criminal justice by victims, offenders and communities, reintegration and reconciliation—will have wide appeal (if not dismissed by initial skepticism). But *wide* appeal is not the same as *deep* appeal—and that can have a significant impact on the success of restorative programs.

Restitution is a good example. These programs enjoy almost universal support from victim rights and prisoner rights interest groups, liberals and conservatives, Republicans and Democrats. While this makes it a highly attractive feature for restorative justice advocates, countervailing political forces may in the end be more powerful than restitution. As Harland and Rosen noted:

> If winning popular support for the system is a rationale for
> using the criminal justice process to compensate victims,
> however, questions arise again as to the likely fate of resti-
> tution when it conflicts with other powerful items on the
> public popularity agenda. How, for example, are individ-
> ual decisionmakers and policymakers to rank public sup-
> port for victims against the omnipresent mandate to get

---

[26] See, for example, Lawrence Friedman, *Crime and Punishment in American History* (New York: Basic Books, 1993); Reiman, *supra* note 23; William J. Bennett, John J. Dilulio, Jr. and John P. Waters, *Body Count: Moral Poverty . . . And How to Win America's War Against Crime and Drugs* (New York: Simon and Schuster, 1996); and William Wilbanks, *The Myth of a Racist Criminal Justice System* (Monterey, CA: Brooks/Cole Publishing Company, 1987).

> tough on crime, if imprisoning more offenders means
> destroying or deferring for long periods whatever earning
> capability they may have had to repay their victims?[27]

This phenomenon is apparent with regard to other aspects of restorative justice programs as well. Although substantial evidence exists that the public supports rehabilitation of offenders[28] and community-based corrections over massive prison construction,[29] that same public also votes for politicians who use "get tough" rhetoric at election time. Consequently, the support for a program can dissipate rapidly if it becomes a point of political controversy. The challenge to restorative justice advocates is to use existing public support to establish programs that reflect restorative justice ideals while at the same time using those programs to promote deeper public commitment to those ideals.

The criminal justice system, like any bureaucratic system, resists change.[30] Just as modern prosecutors are agency administrators with their own political and administrative agendas, so too are all other parts of the criminal justice system, from law enforcement to corrections. Each has its own interests, which are at least as important to it as an overall societal objective for the system. For this reason it has become commonplace to observe that the criminal justice system is not a "system" at all, and instead is a series of departments and agencies linked programmatically. Staff of those departments not only report to different branches of the government, they may actually have differing objectives. For example, if the police demonstrate success by clearing reported cases, they may have a high tolerance for arrests later determined to be based on inadequate evidence of guilt. Because prosecutors show success through a high conviction rate, they may err on the other side by refusing to file charges in order to avoid a high acquittal rate.

---

[27] Alan T. Harland and Cathryn J. Rosen, "Impediments to the Recovery of Restitution by Crime Victims," *Violence and Victims: Special Issue on Social Science and Victim Policy* 5(2) (1990). Howard Zehr raised a similar concern in his discussion of how visions become distorted: "If we speak language that the system understands, the language of punishment, the punitive may come to overshadow the restorative. If we refuse to speak the language of punishment, chances are that we will remain marginal, a non-essential for "minor" cases." Zehr, *supra* note 15, at 233.

[28] Francis T, Cullen and Karen E. Gilbert, *Reaffirming Rehabilitation* (Cincinnati: Anderson Publishing Co., 1982).

[29] Sandra E. Skovron, Joseph E. Scott and Francis T. Cullen, "Prison Crowding: Public Attitudes Toward Strategies of Population Control," *Journal of Research in Crime and Delinquency* 25(2) (1988): 150-169.

[30] Machiavelli counseled the Prince:
> And one should bear in mind that there is nothing more difficult to execute, nor more dubious of success, nor more dangerous to administer than to introduce a new order of things; for he who introduces it has all those who profit from the old order as his enemies, and he has only lukewarm allies in all those who might profit from the new. (Niccolò Machiavelli, *The Prince*, Peter Boudanella and Mark Musa, trans., (New York: Oxford University Press, 1984), 21.

Conclusion

Restorative justice will not just happen on its own. However, two things (at least) are occurring to create an openness to a "new pattern of thinking." First, the sheer cost of incarceration is creating a budgetary crisis. In the attempt to contain the rising costs, correctional programs are being squeezed. However, innovation—particularly if it can demonstrate better results than the status quo—is viewed with interest. Second, people are better connected through online services and other communication technologies that offer instant information and the ability to discuss it in a wide variety of forums.

We have made a case for restorative justice in this book, and others are doing the same. We have made suggestions for policy and practice, for opening up possibilities to balance the interests and needs of victims, communities, offenders and the government. We have presented information about what the various parties' interests and needs are, and how they might be better balanced. For example, since the goal of restorative justice includes restoration of victims and not simply holding offenders accountable, reparation can be accomplished through restitution, where possible, and through compensation funds for victims whose offenders do not make restitution either because they are not apprehended and convicted or because they are financially unable to pay. The key is to make this a priority of the justice process, and not an afterthought.

As restorative programs and approaches are developed for responding to individual crimes, they must anticipate and compensate for the pressures and realities of social change. They must put themselves to the test, to see whether they do, in fact, deliver what they promised and if the outcomes are indeed restorative. If not, they must be open to change and not entrench themselves (as it is so easy to do when a hard-won program has become established). The ultimate test of any policy or program will be whether it helps achieve the overarching goal of restoration—on a case-by-case basis; and in terms of its influence in the wider social process. We believe the changes now underway demonstrate the promise of restorative justice. Furthermore, we believe much, much more is possible.

Chapter Ten

Transformation

In 1968, Herbert Packer wrote of two approaches to criminal justice, the crime control model and the due process model.[1] While acknowledging the limitations of such polarities, he suggested that examining criminal justice in this way would reveal "two separate value systems that compete for priority in the operation of the criminal process. Packer's dual models have been both widely accepted and widely criticized.[2] One of the more intriguing criticisms was raised by John Griffiths. He contended that rather than providing two models, Packer had really only offered one, which Griffiths called the battle model. ". . . Packer consistently portrays the criminal process as a struggle—a stylized war—between two contending forces whose interests are implacably hostile: the Individual (particularly, the accused individual) and the State. His two models are nothing more than alternative derivations from that conception of profound and irreconcilable disharmony of interest."[3]

John Griffiths was not particularly interested in advocating alternative approaches to Packer's adversarial paradigm of justice, but he did want to demonstrate how ideological preconceptions can blind

---

[1] Herbert L. Packer, *The Limits of the Criminal Sanction* (Stanford: Stanford Univresity Press, 1968), 153.

[2] For a review of this debate, *see* Peter Arenella, "Rethinking the Functions of Criminal Procedure: The Warren and Burger Courts' Competing Ideologies," *Geo. L.J.* 72 (1983): 185; Mirjan Damaska, "Evidentiary Barriers to Conviction and Two Models of Criminal Procedure: A Comparative Study," *U. Pa. L. Rev.* 121 (1973): 506; and John Griffiths, "Ideology in Criminal Procedure or A Third 'Model' of the Criminal Process," *Yale L.J.* 79 (1970), 359.

[3] Griffiths, *supra* note 2, at 367.

us to the possibilities that lie outside our purview.[4] In order to do that, he posited what he called the "family" model.[5] Whereas Packer's adversarial models assumed disharmony and fundamentally irreconcilable interests amounting to a state of war, Griffiths proposed assuming "reconcilable—even mutually supportive—interests, a state of love."[6] This would, he argued, significantly change our concepts of crime and the criminal. Crime would be seen as only one of a variety of relationships between the state and the accused, just as disobedience by children is only one dimension of their relationships with their parents.[7] Furthermore, crime would be treated as normal behavior, expected even if not condoned.[8] Criminals would be viewed as people just like us, not members of a special and deviant class of people.[9] Furthermore, there would be an emphasis on self-control rather than on the imposition of external controls.[10] Consequently, the family model would consider the criminal process as having an educational function, teaching those who participate in and observe it by *what* it does and *how* it does it.[11] In other words, the family model is a personal model that assumes an existing constructive relationship between the offender and the community; the adversarial model is impersonal and assumes a destructive relationship between offender and community, one that justifies declaring a war on criminals.

Whatever his purposes in outlining the family model, Griffiths has illustrated the deep differences between it and the battle model.

---

[4] The alternative presented is not especially novel, nor is it one to which I necessarily subscribe. My purpose is merely to explore the problem of ideology in criminal procedure, and to that end the self-conscious posing of an alternative is justified by its heuristic value. (Griffiths, *supra* note 2, at 360.)

In an article on the history of the Critical Legal Studies movement, Mark Tushnet has described the firing of six professors at Yale (including Griffiths) as follows:
To many of the senior faculty, the junior faculty's lack of judgment was demonstrated as well by their scholarship. . . . Griffiths did a certain type of doctrinal scholarship, but not one that the senior faculty was comfortable with. Griffiths' major work, prior to his firing, amounted to a powerful assault on the prevailing view in criminal law scholarship, developed by Herbert Packer, that society faced a choice between a "due process" model and a "crime control" model. Griffiths argued that Packer had identified only a single model of the criminal process; Griffiths offered instead what he called, necessarily but misleadingly, a "third" model, which today would be viewed as an interesting communitarian-feminist approach to criminal procedure but which then was seen as wildly totalitarian. In many ways the reaction to Griffiths' articles can be understood as a model of the whole process. Not only were they severely critical of what many on the senior faculty regarded as the culmination of a life's work by a major figure in the field; they also had a tone suggesting that Griffiths could not believe that anyone with an ounce of intellectual integrity could take Packer's work seriously, let alone write it. Even worse, they were published almost contemporaneously with the massive stroke that ultimately led Packer to commit suicide. If Griffiths didn't exactly cause the stroke, for the senior faculty his behavior—which his hypercritical tone exemplified—was typical of the sort of thing that led men of their generation to have strokes. (Mark Tushnet, "Critical Legal Studies: A Political History," *Yale L.J.* 100 (1991): 1515, 1532.)

[5] Griffiths, *supra* note 2, at 371ff.

[6] Ibid., 371.

[7] Ibid., 373.

[8] Ibid., 376.

[9] Ibid., 374.

[10] Ibid.

[11] Ibid., 389.

We have argued for a similar new pattern of thinking about criminal justice. Restorative justice recognizes the *persons* involved—not just the *laws* involved. Such a recognition is inherently transformational. That is, it transforms (rather than merely reforming) the nature of the justice process and our expectations for the outcome of that process. To use Howard Zehr's analogy, many things look different when we view them through a new lens.[12] Old problems, issues and solutions fade in importance as new ones come into perspective. Structures that once made sense are now recognized as inadequate; formulations that once seemed to be the essence of wisdom are transparently foolish. Over time we begin to see new implications, to ask new questions, to uncover new inadequacies with the status quo and to qualify and deepen our initial impressions. A hallmark of restorative justice, then, should be transformation.

In the previous chapter we discussed the tension between the vision of restorative justice and the incremental steps that need to be taken to move toward it. We proposed steps that can be taken in planning programs, policies and laws from a restorative perspective. In this chapter we would like to explore the elements of transformation—the metamorphosis needed to bring into reality a restorative system—at three levels: (1) transformation of perspective, (2) transformation of structures, and (3) transformation of persons.

Transformation of Perspective

Patterns of thinking shape what we "know" to be true. They make it possible for us to function in our daily lives, but they do so by blinding us to conflicting or irrelevant data.[13] Once we recognize that limitation, often when we are forced to confront the inadequacy of our existing pattern of thinking, we are faced with the need to move to an alternative. But how can that be done when we are so entrenched in the ruts of conventional approaches that we can neither see nor evaluate alternatives? Edward de Bono has observed that it can actually be misleading to look to previous situations in which our pattern of thinking changed dramatically. This is because every "creative thought must always be logical in hindsight."[14] We must always connect a creative insight with current reality in order to make use of it. As soon as we have cut the path from the creative

---

[12] Howard Zehr, *Changing Lenses: A New Focus for Crime and Justice* (Scottsdale, PA: Herald Press, 1990), 178.

[13] *See* discussion in Chapter One.

[14] Edward de Bono, *Conflicts: A Better Way to Resolve Them* (New York: Penguin Books, 1991), 14.

idea to our present situation, we discover that the path moves both ways. We now can understand the logic of the new idea, and we conclude that what we needed all along was better logic. When confronted with the need for new creative insights, we remember our past conclusion and attempt to be "logical again." But, in fact, he argues, it was not logic that produced the insight; it was creativity.[15]

This, then, is one element of a transformation of perspective: creativity. It entails risk. We attempt something because it makes sense, or because we must under the circumstances, but not because we know it will work. It is interesting that victim-offender reconciliation and family group conferencing did not begin with a theory and move from there to programmatic expression, but in fact did the reverse. It was as early program staff and observers began to ask themselves why results were so different from what they had anticipated that they began to understand the psychological, theological, criminological and philosophical implications of what they observed.[16]

A second element that can lead to transformation of perspective is to ask others to help us approach a situation for which we have a conventional pattern of thinking by using a different pattern. This is the approach offered by the Alternatives to Violence Project in helping prisoners accustomed to dealing with conflict through violence to learn nonviolent responses instead.[17] In the course of two three-day workshops, participants learn through presentation, discussion and experience that violence need not be treated as a given. It is possible to convert hostility, destructiveness, aggression and violence into cooperation and community. Participants are taught conflict resolution skills and are given opportunities to practice these. The effect of these workshops, however, is more fundamental than simply skill-enhancement:

> It is enlivening to observe, much less experience, the process at work: affirmation, love, openness, honesty, laughter, respect, diligence, genuineness. At the outset of a workshop, participants seem wary and guarded. Some feign nonchalance with nervous laughter and chatter; others sit cautiously expressionless, arms crossed, registering everything; others engage in conversation, filling this unfamiliar space with something, anything; still others feign aloofness, exuding an air of superiority. By workshop's end, however, there is a deeply abiding sense of goodwill

---

[15] Ibid.

[16] *See* John Braithwaite, "Thinking Harder About Democratising Social Control," in Christine Alder and Joy Wundersitz, eds., *Family Conferencing and Juvenile Justice: The Way Forward or Misplaced Optimism?* (Canberra: Australian Institute of Criminology, 1994), 213.

[17] The following description is drawn from Lila Rucker, "Peacemaking in Prisons," in Harold E. Pepinsky and Richard Quinney, eds., *Criminology as Peacemaking* (Bloomington: Indiana University Press, 1991), 172-180.

that permeates the atmosphere. People look at one another rather than through one another or at the floor. Laughter and joking fill the air. Faces are soft. Eyes sparkle. Smiles abound. Ancient doors have creaked open. Tears spill down radiant cheeks. Heads are on straight; bodies erect. Voices are clear and strong. People approach rather than avoid each other; they connect.[18]

Third, we can look to other places, times or traditions to find new ways of looking at familiar problems. One of the hallmarks of restorative justice to date has been the interest of its advocates in looking outside their own present cultures for inspiration and ideas.[19] Considering how crime has been handled in the past or how it is resolved in other cultures, helps pull us out of the troughs of our current patterns of thinking about crime. While what we see in the past or in other cultures cannot be transferred directly to our own contemporary situations, it may spur us to new ideas and possibilities.

Fourth, consider alternatives to approaches that we take for granted. For example, the adversarial paradigm of crime has resulted in significant implications in our thinking about criminal justice. A statue of the goddess Justicia stands above the Old Bailey law courts in London; she is blindfolded as she holds the scales of justice. This reminds us that justice must not be skewed by the status of, relationship to or hope of reward from one of the parties to a dispute. *Impartial* justice has become equated with mechanically (and sometimes mechanistically) applying rules to determine an outcome. *Dispassionate* justice has become equated with indifference concerning that outcome. We are preoccupied with what Jonathan Burnside has called "an antiseptic construal of justice," one that values "objectivity, impartiality and the fair application of rules."[20] That, he argues, must be balanced by "a passionate construal of justice [which] would emphasise love, compassion and the vindication of the weak."[21]

Under such a "passionate construal" of justice, the goddess might throw off her blindfold and draw her sword in righteous anger or open her arms in a merciful embrace. We may agree that a law court with *that* sort of statue over it would dispense justice differently, but in what ways? What outcomes would we expect? How would its processes be different? How would the architecture of the building

---

[18] Ibid., 177-178.

[19] *See, e.g.,* Heinz Messmer and Hans-Uwe Otto, eds., *Restorative Justice on Trial: Pitfalls and Potentials of Victim Offender Mediation—International Research Perspectives* (Dordrecht, The Netherlands: Kluwer Academic Publishers, 1992).

[20] Jonathan Burnside and Nicola Baker, eds., "Tension and Tradition in the Pursuit of Justice," *Relational Justice: Repairing the Breach* (Winchester, UK: Waterside Press, 1994), 43.

[21] Ibid.

change? Or the demeanor of those who staff it? Reflection on this sort of question can prepare us for a transformation of perspective.

Another example is the premise that criminal law expresses in a symbolic way the norms of a society.[22] One alternative to explore is the hypothesis that criminal law, because it is maintained by force, expresses in a symbolic way the *lack of consensus* concerning the norms of a society. We might ask why it is that so many of us are disinclined to behave in the prescribed way, so many that governments spend billions of dollars to investigate, punish and attempt to deter that behavior. This leads into extended and important political, sociological and theological discussions.

An alternative hypothesis concerning criminal law and societal norms might be the following: A society's norms are best revealed in the course of conversation. Under this perspective, law might be considered the conclusion of a kind of conversation (the lobbying and deliberative process that precedes its adoption), but there are other forms of conversation as well. We might look at the nature of discourse in the media, in entertainment or in art for clues concerning what is important to our society. We might conclude that because those sorts of discourse are carried on by representatives (e.g., elected representatives who pass laws, columnists or talk show hosts who find topics that will interest their audiences, artists and producers who need to make money), they give us skewed and inaccurate perceptions of our norms and values. For a more accurate picture we would need to look at more intimate discussions carried on by the participants themselves, not by representatives. Out of those conversations we may discern a different set (or a different formulation of the same set) of norms. This certainly carries with it important implications for the criminal justice process, and in particular our interest in justice dispensed by professionals versus justice determined by the participants themselves.

Transformation of Structures

Transformed perspectives will have only academic value if there is not structural transformation as well. Here we face a serious challenge, for as M. Kay Harris has pointed out, proposals for change tend to fall into one of two approaches. The first is what she calls the "systems-improvement" approach, which "takes for granted exist-

---

[22] *See, e.g.,* Kai-D. Bussmann, "Morality, Symbolism, and Criminal Law: Chances and Limits of Mediation Programs," in Heinz Messmer and Hans-Uwe Otto, eds., *Restorative Justice on Trial* (Dordrecht, The Netherlands: Kluwer Academic Publishers, 1992), 317-326.

ing political, economic, and social institutional structures as well as the values that undergird them, assuming that they are proper or, at least, unlikely to be changed within the foreseeable future."[23] The other is the "crime-prevention/social-reform" approach, which emphasizes "the social and economic underpinnings of crime and the need to address them through policies and programs focused on families, neighborhoods, schools, and other institutions."[24] Neither approach is particularly attractive to those interested in restorative structures. The first implies incremental change that at best may ameliorate problems confronting those caught up in criminal justice, and the second requires a change in society that is so widescale that it is highly unlikely. One seems achievable but hardly worth pursuing; the other, worth pursuing but impossible to achieve.

Confronted with such a dilemma, how do we proceed? One strategy is to skirt the two alternatives just mentioned by considering how to apply visionary approaches to discrete problems: in other words, transform a small part of existing criminal justice structures.[25] One example of this is the work of Dennis Wittman and others in Genesee County, New York. This program operates out of the sheriff's office and organizes community service, community reparations, reconciliation, victim assistance, presentence diversion, intervention in child abuse situations, victim-directed sentencing and other programs. It has grown to this scale only after years of operation; it was started in 1980 as a relatively modest diversionary program. By asking questions about larger dimensions of justice, by recognizing the needs of the particular victims, offenders and community members in that county, and by being willing to take responsible risks, the program has become an intriguing and stimulating model of a restorative response to crime.[26]

A second strategy is to think in terms of dual tracks: that is, a restorative system paralleling the criminal justice system. We discussed this in Chapter Four in dealing with the problem of community and governmental cooperation. Herman Bianchi commends this approach for two reasons. First, it will reassure those who fear violence that the familiar criminal justice process is available and hence

---

[23] M. Kay Harris, "Moving Into the New Millennium: Toward a Feminist Vision of Justice," The Prison Journal 67, 2 (1987): 83.

[24] Ibid., 84.

[25] Martin Wright proposes a similar approach:
In the transitional phase there would, as we have seen, be tension with the traditional retributive philosophy of the courts. A vital key to progress would be to remove this dichotomy by encouraging the courts to move towards a restorative philosophy. Initially this might be done in relation to juvenile offenders; it could be extended to adults whose crime arose out of a relationship, and then to crimes by adult strangers. Finally the legislature could set the seal on the changeover. There would then no longer be two or even three principles pulling in different directions. (Martin Wright, "Victim-Offender Mediation as a Step Towards a Restorative System of Justice," in Heinz Messmer and Hans-Uwe Otto, eds., Restorative Justice on Trial (Dordrecht, The Netherlands: Kluwer Academic Publishers, 1992), 535.)

[26] For more information, contact Dennis Wittman, Genesee County Sheriff's Office, County Building 1, Batavia, NY 14020 (716/344-2550, ext. 226).

it undercuts one objection to the development of a more restorative process. Second, the existence of two systems, side by side, increases the likelihood that each will limit the power of the other. He observes that the presence of conflict resolution mechanisms will not prevent individuals from attempting to abuse power: "One of the disputing parties, either plaintiff or defendant, might, if motivated by human malice, consider the abuse of power as a workable reality. . . . If two systems keep an eye on one another, they can keep each other in order."[27] Martin Wright adds that this permits opportunities for experimentation in the restorative track with the possibility of adoption later by the criminal justice system.[28]

As we mentioned earlier, we have identified four strategic goals for implementation of restorative approaches. Of these, two addressed the formal criminal justice system:

- *Victims will receive reparation for the primary harms resulting from the crime, and will be offered **participation** in the criminal justice process to ensure that their harms are addressed.*

- *Nondangerous offenders will be accountable for **reparation** as a sentencing priority, and given community-based sentences rather than prison.*

The other two addressed the need for an informal community-based response:

- *Victims and offenders in every community will have opportunities for reconciliation through **encounter** programs.*

- *Both victims and offenders will have access to services to assist them in the process of **reintegration**.*

A third strategy is to identify practices and institutions in the criminal justice system that, because of their history or structure, may be amenable to modification to make them more restorative. There are a number of possibilities here. For example, when they were developed, juries were intended to be a community voice in the criminal justice process.[29] There are a number of ways in which their deliberation might be made more restorative: have them hold their discussion in the presence of the victim and the defendant,[30] seek

---

[27] Herman Bianchi, *Justice as Sanctuary: Toward a New System of Crime Control* (Bloomington: Indiana University Press, 1994), 96.

[28] Wright, *supra* note 25, at 535.

[29] Daniel W. Van Ness, "Preserving a Community Voice: The Case for Half-and-Half Juries in Racially-Charged Criminal Cases," *John Marshal L. Rev.* 28 (1994): 1.

[30] Bianchi, *supra* note 27, at 86.

ways to increase the diversity of the persons on the jury,[31] permit and encourage juries to ask questions of witnesses, lawyers and the judge,[32] and so on.

Transformation of Persons

In this book we have used words not usually heard in contemporary debate over criminal justice policy: healing, reconciliation, negotiation, vindication, transformation. They are words that rest uneasily on current structures. We have attempted to show that they resonate within our legal and social traditions, that they are professed by major segments of our societies and that they are being demonstrated in programs around the world. They are *catalytic* words, reminding us of the passionate side of justice, which appears to be neglected as we move into the twenty-first century.

They are also *convicting* words. It is easier to hypothesize the "family model" of justice, with its assumption of a state of love, than to live it. It is more orderly to design systems than to encounter living, breathing people. It is simpler to edit a chapter into its final form than to deal with the contradictions and complexities of human relationships.

It is not surprising that encounter has been a hallmark of the restorative justice movement. In victim-offender reconciliation meetings, family group conferences and victim-offender panels, real people confronting specific crimes have met to understand the dimensions of the injustice done, the harm that resulted and the steps that must be taken to make things right. Those meetings permit participants to deal with the relational and passionate dimensions of crime, and to seek more satisfying responses than antiseptic justice can offer.

Crime and injustice are moral problems at root.[33] A criminal act's nature as wrongdoing is important to the participants and to their communities. Its nature as lawbreaking answers a jurisdictional question: will this case be heard in criminal courts? It also represents a violation of legal norms designed (in theory) to uphold the common good. Its nature as wrongdoing has personal and social consequences that surpass questions of procedure but still go to the heart of "common good."

---

[31] *See, e.g.,* Van Ness, *supra* note 29; George P. Fletcher, *With Justice for Some: Victims' Rights in Criminal Trials* (New York: Addison-Wesley Publishing Company, 1995): 250-251.

[32] Fletcher, *supra* note 31, at 253-254.

[33] *See, e.g.,* Charles Colson and Daniel Van Ness, *Convicted: New Hope for Ending America's Crime Crisis* (Westchester, IL: Crossway Books, 1989), 55-64; William J. Bennett, John J. Dilulio, Jr. and John P. Walters, *Body Count: Moral Poverty . . . And How to Win America's War Against Crime and Drugs* (New York: Simon and Schuster, 1996).

A danger, however, in recognizing that crime has moral roots is that it can lead us into hypocrisy. "Crime has moral roots; therefore criminals are immoral. I am not a criminal; therefore. . . ." Our glib assertions lead us into another "us/them" dichotomy and intensifies, often without our realizing it, the existing state of war against criminals. Charles Colson has remarked that there are two kinds of criminals: those who get caught and the rest of the human race.[34] Jerome Miller has said that there are two kinds of criminologists: those who view criminals as different from themselves and those who do not.[35] Furthermore, this locates the moral problem squarely and solely with individuals, begging the question of social morality and its relation to crime's milieu.

Hypocrisy, injustice and indifference are moral problems. The ancient rebuke (made to "good" people) warned that when we are angry at others without cause we have committed murder in our hearts, and that when we think of them as fools we have condemned ourselves.[36] When we fail to respond to crime victims as our neighbors[37] and offenders as our brothers and sisters,[38] we ignore the injustice they experience and escape our own responsibility. Where, then, shall we find the resources for transformation of ourselves and of the world? This, Richard Quinney reminds us, is a spiritual issue:

> All of this is to say, to us as criminologists, that crime is suffering and that the ending of crime is possible only with the ending of suffering. And the ending both of suffering and of crime, which is the establishing of justice, can come only out of peace, out of a peace that is spiritually grounded in our very being. To eliminate crime—to end the construction and perpetuation of an existence that makes crime possible—requires a transformation of our human being. . . . When our hearts are filled with love and our minds with willingness to serve, we will know what has to be done and how it is to be done.[39]

Where can we go to have our hearts and minds so filled? This is a question each person must answer for himself or herself. Many find this place within the reintegrating community we spoke of in Chapter Eight (i.e., faith communities). That has been our experience. We have encountered, within our churches, in the presence of "One" who

---

[34] Colson has used this line regularly in speeches and conversations, although to our knowledge it has not been included in any of his publications.

[35] Pepinsky and Quinney, *supra* note 17, at 303.

[36] Matt. 5:21-22.

[37] *See* Luke 10:25-37.

[38] *See* Luke 19:1-10.

[39] Pepinsky and Quinney, *supra* note 17, at 11, 12.

came to preach the gospel to the poor, to heal the brokenhearted, to preach deliverance to captives and recovery of sight to the blind, to set at liberty those who are oppressed, and to proclaim Jubilee.[40] One who speaks to our own brokenness: "I have loved you with an everlasting love; I have drawn you with loving-kindness. I will build you up again and you will be rebuilt."[41] One who calls on us to "let justice roll on like a river, righteousness like a never-failing stream."[42]

A hallmark of restorative justice must be ongoing transformation: transformation of perspective, transformation of structures, transformation of people. It begins with transformation of ourselves, for we too have recompense to pay, reconciliation to seek, forgiveness to ask and healing to receive. We look not only for justice "out there," but must turn the lens on ourselves as well—on our daily patterns of life and on our treatment of and attitudes toward others. Restorative justice is an invitation to renewal in communities and individuals as well as procedures and programs. Transformation of the world begins with transformation of ourselves.

---

[40] Luke 4:18-19.

[41] Jer. 31:3-4.

[42] Amos 5:24.

Selected Bibliography

Abel, Charles F. and Frank H. Marsh. *Punishment and Restitution: A Restitutionary Approach to Crime and the Criminal.* Westport, CT; London: Greenwood Press, 1984.

Alder, Christine and Joy Wundersitz, eds. *Family Conferencing and Juvenile Justice: The Way Forward or Misplaced Optimism?* Canberra: Australian Institute of Criminology, 1994.

Alschuler, Albert W. "The Failure of Sentencing Guidelines." *University of Chicago Law Review* 58 (1991).

American Bar Association. *Resolution 101B, Victim Offender Mediation/Dialogue* (adopted by the House of Delegates), August 1994.

————. *Guidelines Governing Restitution to Victims of Criminal Conduct* (including commentary on the guidelines), 1988.

Anderson, Dennis B., Randall E. Schumacker and Sara L. Anderson. "Releasee Characteristics and Parole Success." *Journal of Offender Rehabilitation* 17 (1991).

Andrews, Arlene B. "Crisis and Recovery Services for Family Violence Survivors." In *Victims of Crime: Problems, Policies, and Programs,* edited by Arthur Lurigio et al. Newbury Park, CA: Sage Publications, 1990.

Ankerich, Michael. "GDC's MH/MR Work Program Transforms Inmates' Attitudes." Georgia Department of Corrections *Newsbriefs* (July 1990).

Arenella, Peter. "Rethinking the Functions of Criminal Procedure: The Warren and Burger Courts' Competing Ideologies." *Georgetown Law Journal* 72 (1983): 185, 209-228.

Ashworth, Andrew. "Some Doubts about Restorative Justice." *Criminal Law Forum* 4, 2 (1993): 277.

————. "Criminal Justice and Deserved Sentences." Paper presented at the annual conference of the Society for the Reform of Criminal Law, Ottawa, Ontario, August 1988.

Atkeson, B.M. et al., "Victims of Rape: Repeated Assessment of Depressive Symptoms." *Journal of Consulting and Clinical Psychology* 50 (1982).

185

The Attorney's Victim Assistance Manual: A Guide to the Legal Issues Confronting Victims of Crime and Victim Service Providers. Prepared for The Sunny von Bulow National Victim Advocacy Center in cooperation with the Attorney's Victim Assistance Project of the American Bar Association, Criminal Justice Section, 1987.

Auerbach, Barbara. *Work in American Prisons: The Private Sector Gets Involved.* National Institute of Justice, Issues and Practices. National Institute of Justice, U.S. Department of Justice, 1988.

Auerbach, Jerold S. *Justice Without Law?* New York: Oxford University Press, 1983.

Bacon, G. Richard et al. *Struggle for Justice: A Report on Crime and Punishment in America.* New York: Hill and Wang, 1971.

Baker, Nicola. "Mediation, Reparation and Justice." In *Relational Justice: Repairing the Breach*, edited by Jonathan Burnside and Nicola Baker. Winchester, United Kingdom: Waterside Press, 1994.

Bakker, Mark W. "Repairing the Breach and Reconciling the Discordant: Mediation in the Criminal Justice System." *North Carolina Law Review* 72 (1994): 1479.

Bard, Morton and Dawn Sangrey. *The Crime Victim's Book.* 2d ed. Secaucus, NJ: Citadel Press, 1986.

Barnett, Randy E. and John Hagel, eds. *Assessing the Criminal: Restitution, Retribution, and the Legal Process.* Cambridge, MA: Ballinger Publishing Co., 1977.

Bazemore, Gordon and Mark Umbreit. "Rethinking the Sanctioning Function in Juvenile Court: Retributive or Restorative Responses to Youth Crime." *Crime and Delinquency* 41, 3 (1995): 296-316.

Beattie, J.M. *Crime and the Courts in England: 1660-1800.* Princeton, NJ: Princeton University Press, 1986.

Bennett, William J., John J. DiIulio, Jr. and John P. Walters. *Body Count: Moral Poverty . . . And How to Win America's War Against Crime and Drugs.* New York: Simon and Schuster, 1996.

Bera, Walter. "Victim-Sensitive Offender Therapy with a Systemic and Attributional Analysis." In *The Use of Victim Offender Communication in the Treatment of Sexual Abuse: Three Intervention Models*, edited by James Yokley. Orwell, VT: Safer Society Press, 1990.

Berman, Harold. *Law and Revolution: The Formation of the Western Legal Tradition.* Cambridge, MA: Harvard University Press, 1983.

Bianchi, Herman. *Justice as Sanctuary: Toward a New System of Crime Control.* Bloomington: Indiana University Press, 1994.

Black, Hartzell L., Pam G. Turner and James A. Williams. "There Is Life After Prison: Successful Community Reintegration Programs Reduce Recidivism in Illinois." *Common Ground* (Spring 1993).

Black, Henry C. et al. *Black's Law Dictionary.* 4th ed. St. Paul, MN: West Publishing, 1968.

Boal, John. "Helping Prison Work." *The American Way* (January 7, 1987): 38.

Boecker, Hans J. *Law and the Administration of Justice in the Old Testament and Ancient East.* Translated by J. Moiser. Minneapolis: Augsburg Publishing House, 1980.

Boland, Barbara et al. *The Prosecution of Felony Arrests, 1986.* U.S. Department of Justice, Bureau of Justice Statistics, June 1989.

de Bono, Edward. *Conflicts: A Better Way to Resolve Them.* New York: Penguin Books, 1991.

Braithwaite, John. "Conditions of Successful Reintegration Ceremonies." *British Journal of Criminology* 34, 2 (1994): 139-171.

———. "Thinking Harder About Democratising Social Control." In *Family Conferencing and Juvenile Justice: The Way Forward or Misplaced Optimism?*, edited by Christine Alder and Joy Wundersitz. Canberra: Australian Institute of Criminology, 1994.

———. "Shame and Modernity." *British Journal of Criminology* 1 (1993).

———. *Crime, Shame, and Reintegration.* New York: Cambridge University Press, 1989.

Bureau of Justice Statistics, U.S. Department of Justice. *Criminal Victimization 1987.* Washington, DC: U.S. Government Printing Office, October 1988.

Burney, Elizabeth. *Magistrate, Court and Community.* London: Hitchinson, 1979.

Burnside, Jonathan and Nicola Baker, eds. *Relational Justice: Repairing the Breach.* Winchester, United Kingdom: Waterside Press, 1994.

Bussmann, Kai-D. "Morality Symbolism, and Criminal Law: Chances and Limits of Mediation Programs." In *Restorative Justice on Trial*, edited by Heinz Messmer and Hans-Uwe Otto. Dordrecht, The Netherlands: Kluwer Academic Publishers, 1992.

Cameron of Lochbroom QC, The Rt. Hon. Lord. "Future Trends in Sentencing Policy—The Satisfaction of the Individual Victim within a System of Public Prosecution." Unpublished paper presented at the annual conference of the Society for the Reform of the Criminal Law, Ottawa, Ontario, August 1988.

Campbell, Patrick. "A Comparative Study of Victim Compensation Procedures in France and the United States: A Modest Proposal." *Hastings International and Comparative Law Review* 3, 2 (1980): 321-348.

Caplan, Gerald. "Criminal Justice in the Lower Courts: A Study in Continuity." *Michigan Law Review* 89 (1991).

Cardenas, Juan. "The Crime Victim in the Prosecutorial Process." *Harvard Journal of Law and Public Policy* 9 (1986).

Carr, G. Lloyd. "Shalom." In *Theological Wordbook of the Old Testament*, edited by R.L. Harris, G.L. Archer, Jr. and B.K. Waltke. Chicago: Moody, 1980.

Christie, Nils. *Limits to Pain.* Oslo-Bergen-Tromsø: Universitetsforlaget, 1981.

———. "Conflict as Property." *British Journal of Criminology,* 17, 1 (1977): 1-14.

Chupp, Mark. "Reconciliation Procedures and Rationale." In *Mediation and Criminal Justice*, edited by Martin Wright and Burt Galaway. Newbury Park, CA: Sage Publications, 1989.

The Church Council on Justice and Corrections, *Satisfying Justice: Safe Community Options that Attempt to Repair Harm from Crime and Reduce the Use or Length of Imprisonment*. Ottawa, Ontario. The Church Council on Justice and Corrections, 1996.

Claassen, Ron and Howard Zehr. "VORP Organizing: A Foundation in the Church." Elkhart, IN: Mennonite Central Committee U.S. Office of Criminal Justice, 1989.

Clear, Todd. "Statistical Prediction in Corrections." *Research in Corrections* 1, 1 (1988): 1-39.

Coates, Robert and John Gehm. "An Empirical Assessment." In *Mediation and Criminal Justice*, edited by Martin Wright and Burt Galaway. Newbury Park, CA: Sage Publications, 1989.

Colson, Charles W. "Towards an Understanding of the Origins of Crime," and "Towards an Understanding of Imprisonment and Rehabilitation." In *Crime and the Responsible Community: A Christian Contribution to the Debate About Criminal Justice*, edited by John Stott and Nick Miller. London: Hodder and Stoughton, 1980.

Colson, Charles W. and Daniel H. Benson. "Restitution as an Alternative to Imprisonment." *Detroit College of Law Review* 2 (1980): 523-598.

Colson, Charles W. and Daniel W. Van Ness. *Convicted: New Hope for Ending America's Crime Crisis*. Westchester, IL: Crossway Books, 1989.

Conference Report: Reform of the Criminal Law. *Criminal Law Forum* 1 (1989).

Consedine, Jim. *Restorative Justice: Healing the Effects of Crime*. Lyttelton, New Zealand: Ploughshares Publications, 1995.

Coyle, Andrew. "My Brother's Keeper: Relationships in Prison." In *Relational Justice: Repairing the Breach*, edited by Jonathan Burnside and Nicola Baker. Winchester, United Kingdom: Waterside Press, 1994.

Cragg, Wesley. *The Practice of Punishment: Towards a Theory of Restorative Justice*. New York: Routledge, 1992.

Cullen, Francis T. and Karen E. Gilbert. *Reaffirming Rehabilitation*. Cincinnati: Anderson Publishing Co., 1982.

Dagger, Richard. "Restitution, Punishment, and Debts to Society." In *Victims, Offenders, and Alternative Sanctions*, edited by Joe Hudson and Burt Galaway. Lexington, MA: Lexington Books, 1980.

Damaska, Mirjan. "Evidentiary Barriers to Conviction and Two Models of Criminal Procedure: A Comparative Study." *University of Pennsylvania Law Review* 121 (1973): 506, 574-577.

Davis, Robert C. "Crime Victims: Learning How to Help Them." *NIJ Reports: Research in Action*. National Institute of Justice, U.S. Department of Justice, May-June 1987.

Davis, Robert C. and Madeline Henley. "Victim Service Programs." In *Victims of Crime: Problems, Policies, and Programs*, edited by Arthur Lurigio et al. Newbury Park, CA: Sage Publications, 1990.

Day, Frank B. and Robert R. Gallati. *Introduction to Law Enforcement and Criminal Justice*. Springfield, IL: Charles C Thomas, 1978.

Delaplane, David W. *Clergy In-Service Training Manual*. Sacramento, CA: The Spiritual Dimension in Victim Services, 1990.

Denton, A.R. "Victims of Violent Crime." In *Baker Encyclopedia of Psychology*, edited by David G. Benner. Grand Rapids, MI: Baker Book House, 1985.

DiMascio, William M. et al. *Seeking Justice: Crime and Punishment in America*. New York: Edna McConnell Clark Foundation, 1995.

Dünkel, Frieder and Dieter Rössner. "Law and Practice of Victim/Offender Agreements." In *Mediation and Criminal Justice*, edited by Martin Wright and Burt Galaway. Newbury Park, CA: Sage Publications, 1989.

Durham, Alexis M., III. "The Justice Model in Historical Context: Early Law, the Emergence of Science, and the Rise of Incarceration." *Journal of Criminal Justice* 16 (1988).

Eglash, Albert. "Beyond Restitution: Creative Restitution." In *Restitution in Criminal Justice*, edited by Joe Hudson and Burt Galaway. Lexington, MA: D.C. Heath and Company, 1977.

Eikenberry, Ken. "Victims of Crime/Victims of Justice." *The Wayne Law Review* 34 (Fall 1987): 29-49.

Elias, Robert. "Which Victim Movement? The Politics of Victim Policy." In *Victims of Crime: Problems, Policies, and Programs*, edited by Arthur Lurigio et al. Newbury Park, CA: Sage Publications, 1990.

―――――. *The Politics of Victimization: Victims, Victimology and Human Rights*. New York: Oxford University Press, 1986.

―――――. *Victims of the System: Crime Victims and Compensation in American Politics and Criminal Justice*. New Brunswick, NJ: Transaction Books, 1983.

Ellis, Richard E. *The Jeffersonian Crisis: Courts and Politics in the Young Republic*. New York: Oxford University Press, 1971.

Evans, T.D. et al. "Religion and Crime Reexamined: The Impact of Religion, Secular Controls, and Social Ecology on Adult Criminality." *Criminology* 33 (1995).

Faulkner, David. "Relational Justice: A Dynamic for Reform." In *Relational Justice: Repairing the Breach*, edited by Jonathan Burnside and Nicola Baker. Winchester, United Kingdom: Waterside Press, 1994.

Feinberg, Joel. *Harm to Others*. New York: Oxford University Press, 1984.

Finn, Peter and N.W. Beverly Lee. *Issues and Practices in Criminal Justice: Serving Crime Victims and Witnesses*. National Institute of Justice, U.S. Department of Justice, June 1987.

Fletcher, George P. *With Justice for Some: Victims' Rights in Criminal Trials*. New York: Addison-Wesley Publishing Company, 1995.

Foote, Daniel H. "The Benevolent Paternalism of Japanese Criminal Justice." *California Law Review* 80 (1992).

Fortune, Marie M. *Domestic Violence and Its Aftermath*. Elkhart, IN: Mennonite Central Committee U.S. Office of Criminal Justice, 1989.

France, Kenneth. *Crisis Intervention: A Handbook of Immediate Person-to-Person Help*. Springfield, IL: Charles C Thomas, 1982.

Freeman, Richard B. and Holzer, Harry J. "Who Escapes? The Relation of Church-going and Other Background Factors to the Socio-Economic Performance of Black Male Youths From Inner City Tracts." In *The Black Youth Employment Crisis*, edited by Richard B. Freeman and Harry J. Holzer. Chicago: University of Chicago Press, 1986.

Friedman, Lawrence. *Crime and Punishment in American History*. New York: Basic Books, 1993.

Fry, Margery. "Justice for Victims." *London Observer* (7 July 1957).

Galaway, Burt. "Victim Offender Reconciliation Project (VORP) Evaluation Issues." Unpublished paper presented at the Third National Conference on Peacemaking and Conflict Resolution, 1986.

Galaway, Burt and Joe Hudson, eds. *Restorative Justice: International Perspectives*. Monsey, NY: Criminal Justice Press, 1996.

————. *Criminal Justice, Restitution and Reconciliation*. Monsey, NY: Criminal Justice Press, 1990.

Gartner, J., D.B. Larson and G.E. Allen. "Religion Commitment and Mental Health: A Review of the Empirical Literature." *Journal of Psychology and Theology* 2 (1991).

German, Steve. "Knowledge Is Not Enough: Addressing Client Needs in Probation and Parole." *Community Corrections*. American Correctional Association Monographs, Series 1, Vol. 5. Laurel Lakes, MD: American Correctional Association, 1981.

Gest, Ted and Pamela Ellis-Simons. "Victims of Crime." *U.S. News and World Report* (31 July 1989): 16-19.

Gittler, Josephine. "Expanding the Role of the Victim in a Criminal Action: An Overview of Issues and Problems." *Pepperdine Law Review* 11 (1984): 117-182.

Goldstein, Abraham S. "Victim and Prosecutorial Discretion: The Federal Victim and Witness Protection Act of 1982." *Law and Contemporary Problems* 47 (Autumn 1984): 225-248.

————. "Defining the Role of the Victim in Criminal Prosecution." *Mississippi Law Journal* 52, 3 (September 1982): 515-562.

Goolsby, Deborah Gatske. "Using Mediation in Cases of Simple Rape." *Washington and Lee Law Review* 47 (1990).

Gottfredson, Don M. and Stephen D. Gottfredson. "Stakes and Risks in the Prediction of Violent Criminal Behavior." *Violence and Victims: Special Issue on the Prediction of Violent Criminal Behavior* 3, 4 (1988): 247-262.

Griffiths, Curt T. and Ron Hamilton. "Sanctioning and Healing: Restorative Justice in Canadian Aboriginal Communities." In *Restorative Justice: International Perspectives*, edited by Burt Galaway and Joe Hudson. Monsey, NY: Criminal Justice Press, 1996.

Griffiths, John. "Ideology in Criminal Procedure or a Third 'Model' of the Criminal Process." *Yale Law Review* 79 (1970).

"Guidelines Governing Restitution to Victims of Criminal Conduct." American Bar Association, Criminal Justice Section, Approved as ABA policy by the ABA House of Delegates, 1988.

Gustafson, David L. and Henk Smidstra. "Victim Offender Reconciliation in Serious Crime." A report on the feasibility study undertaken for the Ministry of the Solicitor General (Canada) by Fraser Region Community Justice Initiatives Association, Langley, British Columbia, May 1989.

Gyandoh, Samuel O. "Tinkering With the Criminal Justice System in Common Law Africa." *Temple Law Review* 62 (1989): 1131.

Hairston, Creasie F. "Family Ties During Imprisonment: Important to Whom and for What?" *Journal of Sociology and Social Welfare* 18 (1991).

Haley, John O. "Confession, Repentance and Absolution." In *Mediation and Criminal Justice*, edited by Martin Wright and Burt Galaway. Newbury Park, CA: Sage Publications, 1989.

Harland, Alan T. "Monetary Remedies for the Victims of Crime: Assessing the Role of the Criminal Courts." *UCLA Law Review* 30 (1982): 52.

————. "Court-Ordered Community Service in Criminal Law: The Continuing Tyranny of Benevolence?" *Buffalo Law Review* 29 (1980): 425-486.

Harland, Alan T. and Cathryn J. Rosen. "Impediments to the Recovery of Restitution by Crime Victims." *Violence and Victims: Special Issue on Social Science and Victim Policy* 5, 2 (1990): 127, 132.

————. "Restitution to Crime Victims as a Presumptive Requirement in Criminal Case Dispositions." In Albert R. Roberts, *Helping Crime Victims: Research, Policy, and Practice*. Newbury Park, CA: Sage Publications, 1990.

Harris, M. Kay. "Alternative Visions in the Context of Contemporary Realities." In *New Perspectives on Crime and Justice: Occasional Papers of the MCC Canada Victim Offender Ministries Program and the MCC U.S. Office of Criminal Justice*, Issue 7. Elkhart, IN: Mennonite Central Committee U.S. Office of Criminal Justice, February 1989.

————. "Moving Into the New Millennium: Toward a Feminist Vision of Justice." *The Prison Journal* 67, 2 (1987): 27-38.

Haugk, Kenneth C. *Christian Caregiving: A Way of Life*. Minneapolis: Augsburg Publishing House, 1984.

Hay, Douglas and Francis Snyder, eds. *Policing and Prosecution in Britain 1750-1850*. Oxford: Clarendon Press, 1989.

Heinz, A. and W. Kerstetter. *Pretrial Settlement Conference: An Evaluation*. Law Enforcement Assistance Administration, U.S. Department of Justice, 1979.

Herrington, Lois H. "Victim Rights and Criminal Justice Reform." *The Annals of the American Academy of Political and Social Science* (November 1987).

Hetherington, Thomas. *Prosecution and the Public Interest.* Old Tappan, NJ: Waterlow/Macmillan, 1989.

Hoebel, E. Adamson. *The Law of Primitive Man: A Study in Comparative Legal Dynamics.* New York: Atheneum, 1973.

Hudson, Joe and Burt Galaway. "Financial Restitution: Toward an Evaluable Program Model." *Canadian Journal of Criminology* 31 (1989): 1-8.

Hudson, Joe and Burt Galaway, eds. *Restitution in Criminal Justice.* Lexington, MA: D.C. Heath and Company, 1977.

————. *Considering the Victim.* Springfield, IL: Charles C Thomas, 1975.

Idler, E.L. and S.V. Kasl. "Religion, Disability, Depression, and the Timing of Death." *American Journal of Sociology* 97 (1992).

Irwin, John and James Austin. *It's About Time: America's Imprisonment Binge.* New York: Oxford University Press, 1994.

Jacob, Bruce. "The Concept of Restitution: An Historical Overview." In *Restitution in Criminal Justice*, edited by Joe Hudson and Burt Galaway. Lexington, MA: D.C. Heath and Company, 1977.

Jacoby, Joan. *The American Prosecutor: A Search for Identity.* Lexington, MA: Lexington Books, 1980.

Joutsen, Matti. "Listening to the Victim: The Victim's Role in European Criminal Justice Systems." *The Wayne Law Review* 34 (Fall 1987): 95-124.

Karmen, Andrew. *Crime Victims: An Introduction to Victimology.* 2d ed. Pacific Grove, CA: Brooks/Cole Publishing Company, 1990.

Keeton, George W. *The Norman Conquest and the Common Law.* New York: Barnes and Noble, 1966.

Kelly, Deborah. "Victim Participation in the Criminal Justice System." In *Victims of Crime: Problems, Policies, and Programs*, edited by Arthur Lurigio, et al. Newbury Park, CA: Sage Publications, 1990.

————. "How Can We Help the Victim without Hurting the Defendant?" *Criminal Justice* 2, 2 (1987): 14-17, 38-41.

Kilpatrick, Dean G. "The Mental Health Impact of Crime: Fundamentals in Counseling and Advocacy." In supporting materials from the *1996 National Victim Assistance Academy* sponsored by the U.S. Department of Justice Office for Victims of Crime in conjunction with Victims Assistance Legal Organization, California State University-Fresno, and the National Crime Victims Research and Treatment Center, July 1996.

Klein, Andrew R. *Alternative Sentencing, Intermediate Sanctions and Probation.* 2d ed. Cincinnati: Anderson Publishing Co., 1997.

————. *The Earn It Story.* Published by the author, 1981.

Koppel, Herbert. *Lifetime Likelihood of Victimization.* U.S. Department of Justice, Bureau of Justice Statistics Technical Report, March 1987.

Kratcoski, Peter C. "Volunteers in Corrections: Do They Make a Meaningful Contribution?" *Federal Probation* 46, 2 (1982): 30-35.

Lamborn, LeRoy L. "Victim Participation in the Criminal Justice Process: The Proposals for a Constitutional Amendment." *The Wayne Law Review* 34 (Fall 1987): 125-220.

Lane, Roger. *Policing the City: Boston 1822-1885.* Cambridge, MA: Harvard University Press, 1967.

LaPrairie, Carol. "Conferencing in Aboriginal Communities in Canada: Finding Middle Ground in Criminal Justice?" *Criminal Law Forum* 6 (1995): 576.

Laub, John H. "Patterns of Criminal Victimization in the United States." In *Victims of Crime: Problems, Policies, and Programs,* edited by Arthur Lurigio et al. Newbury Park, CA: Sage Publications, 1990.

Lauen, Roger J. *Community-Managed Corrections and Other Solutions to America's Prison Crisis.* College Park, MD: The American Correctional Association, 1988.

Launay, Gilles and Peter Murray. "Victim/Offender Groups." In *Mediation and Criminal Justice,* edited by Martin Wright and Burt Galaway. Newbury Park, CA: Sage Publications, 1989.

Lerner, Melvin J. *The Belief in a Just World: A Fundamental Delusion.* New York: Plenum Press, 1980.

Lilly, J. Robert, Francis T. Cullen and Richard A. Ball. *Criminological Theory: Context and Consequences.* 2d ed. Thousand Oaks, CA: Sage Publications, 1995.

Llewellyn, Karl N. *Jurisprudence: Realism in Theory and Practice.* Chicago: University of Chicago Press, 1962.

Lord, Janice H. *Victim Impact Panels: A Creative Sentencing Opportunity.* Mothers Against Drunk Driving (MADD), 1990.

Lurigio, Arthur J. and Patricia A. Resick. "Healing the Psychological Wounds of Criminal Victimization: Predicting Postcrime Distress and Recovery." In *Victims of Crime: Problems, Policies, and Programs,* edited by Arthur Lurigio et al. Newbury Park, CA: Sage Publications, 1990.

Lurigio, Arthur J., Wesley G. Skogan and Robert C. Davis, eds. *Victims of Crime: Problems, Policies, and Programs.* Newbury Park, CA: Sage Publications, 1990.

Machiavelli, Niccolò. *The Prince,* translated by Peter Boudanella and Mark Musa. New York: Oxford University Press, 1984.

Mackey, Virginia. "Restorative Justice: Toward Nonviolence." Discussion paper on Crime and Justice, Presbyterian Justice Program, Presbyterian Church U.S.A., March 1990.

———. "Punishment: In the Scripture and Tradition of Judaism, Christianity and Islam." A paper presented to the National Religious Leaders Consultation of Criminal Justice, Claremont, CA, September 1981.

Macneil, Ian R. "Bureaucracy, Liberalism, and Community—American Style." *Northwestern University Law Review* (1984-1985).

Maguire, Mike and Joanna Shapland. "The 'Victims Movement' in Europe." In *Victims of Crime: Problems, Policies, and Programs,* edited by Arthur Lurigio et al. Newbury Park, CA: Sage Publications, 1990.

Maguire, Mike, Rod Morgan and Robert Reiner. *The Oxford Handbook of Criminology.* New York: Oxford University Press, 1994.

Mann, Kenneth. "Punitive Civil Sanctions: The Middleground Between Criminal and Civil Law." *Yale Law Journal* 101 (1992): 1795.

Massaro, Toni. "Shame, Culture, and American Criminal Law." *Michigan Law Review* 89 (1991).

Matthews, Roger, ed. *Informal Justice?* Newbury Park, CA: Sage Publications, 1988.

Maxwell, Gabrielle and Allison Morris. "The New Zealand Model of Family Group Conferences." In *Family Conferencing and Juvenile Justice: The Way Forward or Misplaced Optimism?*, edited by Christine Alder and Joy Wundersitz. Canberra: Australian Institute of Criminology, 1994.

Maxwell, Joe. "Getting Out, Staying Out," *Christianity Today,* 22 July 1991, 36.

McDonald, William F. *Criminal Justice and the Victim.* Beverly Hills, CA: Sage Publications, 1976.

————. "Towards a Bicentennial Revolution in Criminal Justice: The Return of the Victim." *American Criminal Law Review* 13, 4 (1976): 649-673.

McElrea, Fred. "Justice in the Community: The New Zealand Experience." In *Relational Justice: Repairing the Breach*, edited by Jonathan Burnside and Nicola Baker. Winchester, United Kingdom: Waterside Press, 1994.

McGillis, Daniel. *Crime Victim Restitution: An Analysis of Approaches.* National Institute of Justice, U.S. Department of Justice, December 1986.

McHugh, Gerald A. *Christian Faith and Criminal Justice: Toward A Christian Response to Crime and Punishment.* New York: Paulist Press, 1978.

McKelvey, Blake. *American Prisons: A History of Good Intentions.* Montclair, NJ: Patterson Smith, 1977.

McMurray, Harvey L. "High Risk Parolees in Transition from Institution to Community Life." *Journal of Offender Rehabilitation* 19 (1993).

Meek, Theophile J., trans. "Hammurabi, Law 8." In *The Ancient Near East: Vol. 1. An Anthology of Texts and Pictures*, edited by J.B. Pritchard. Princeton, NJ: Princeton University Press, 1958.

Mercer, Dorothy, Rosanne Lorden and Janice Lord. *Drunken Driving Victim Impact Panels: Victim Outcomes.* Paper presented to the American Psychological Association, August 1995.

Messmer, Heinz and Hans-Uwe Otto, eds. *Restorative Justice on Trial: Pitfalls and Potentials of Victim Offender Mediation—International Research Perspectives.* Dordrecht, The Netherlands: Kluwer Academic Publishers, 1992.

Metz, Holly. "The Illusion of Victim Rights." *Student Lawyer* 17, 7 (1989): 16-23.

Miller, Marc and Norval Morris. "Predictions of Dangerousness: An Argument for Limited Use." *Violence and Victims: Special Issue on the Prediction of Interpersonal Criminal Violence* 3, 4 (1988): 263-283.

Miller, Rod, George E. Sexton and Victor J. Jacobsen, *Making Jails Productive.* National Institute of Justice Report #223, January/February 1991.

Mockler, Richard S. "Confronting Crime: Strategies from Catholic Social Thought." Unpublished paper, 1989.

Mollica, Richard F. et al. "A Community Study of Formal Pastoral Counseling Activities of the Clergy." *American Journal of Psychiatry* 143, 3 (1986): 323-328.

Moore, David. "Evaluating Family Group Conferences." In *Criminal Justice Planning and Coordination: Proceedings of a Conference Held 19-21 April 1993, Canberra*, edited by David Biles and Sandra McKillop. Canberra: Australian Institute of Criminology, 1994.

————. "Shame, Forgiveness and Juvenile Justice." *Criminal Justice Ethics* 12, 1 (1993): 3-25.

Moore, D.B. and T.A. O'Connell. "Family Conferencing in Wagga Wagga: A Communitarian Model of Justice." In *Family Conferencing and Juvenile Justice: The Way Forward or Misplaced Optimism?*, edited by Christine Alder and Joy Wundersitz. Canberra: Australian Institute of Criminology, 1994.

Morris, Norval and Michael Tonry. *Intermediate Punishments*. New York: Oxford University Press, 1989.

Morris, Norval and David Rothman, eds. *The Oxford History of the Prison: The Practice of Punishment in Western Society*. New York: Oxford University Press, 1995.

Morris, Ruth. *A Practical Path to Transformative Justice*. Toronto: Rittenhouse, 1994.

Murphy, Jeffrie G. "Retributive Hatred: An Essay on Criminal Liability and the Emotions." Paper read at the Liability in Law and Morals conference, at Bowling Green State University, April 1988.

National Associations Active in Criminal Justice. "A Social Responsibility Approach to Criminal Justice." Unpublished discussion paper, February 1988.

A National Charter of Victims' Rights: Minimising the Risk of Victimisation and Recognition of Victims' Rights as Fundamental Tenets of Crime Prevention. Paper prepared for the South Australian Commissioner of Police, D.A. Hunt, for presentation at the Australian Policy Ministers' Council, November 1989.

National Council on Crime and Delinquency (NCCD). "Illusory Savings in the War Against Crime." San Francisco: NCCD, July 1988.

National Organization for Victim Assistance. *Victim Rights and Services: A Legislative Directory 1987*. U.S. Department of Justice, Office of Justice Programs, Office for Victims of Crime, 1987.

Neiderbach, Shelley. *Invisible Wounds: Crime Victims Speak*. New York: Harrington Park Press, 1986.

Neighbors Who Care: A Christian Ministry to Victims of Crime. *Getting Started: Building Your Chapter*. Washington, DC: Neighbors Who Care, 1994.

Nielsen, Marianne O. "A Comparison of Developmental Ideologies: Navajo Peacemaker Courts and Canadian Native Justice Committees." In *Restorative Justice: International Perspectives*, edited by Burt Galaway and Joe Hudson. Monsey, NY: Criminal Justice Press, 1996.

Northey, Wayne. *Justice is Peacemaking: A Biblical Theology of Peacemaking in Response to Criminal Conflict*. Akron, PA: Mennonite Central Committee U.S. Office of Criminal Justice, 1992.

Nsereko, Daniel D.N. "Compensating the Victims of Crime in Botswana." Paper presented at the conference of the Society for the Reform of Criminal Law, at Ottawa, Ontario, August 1988.

Packer, Herbert. *The Limits of the Criminal Sanction.* Stanford: Stanford University Press, 1968.

Pelikan, Christa. "Conflict Resolution Between Victims and Offenders in Austria and the Federal Republic of Germany." In *Crime in Europe*, edited by Frances Heidensohn and Martin Farrell. London; New York: Routledge, 1991.

Pepinsky, Harold E. and Richard Quinney, eds. *Criminology as Peacemaking.* Bloomington: Indiana University Press, 1991.

Peritz, Ingrid. "On the Outside, Lifers Struggle to Pick Up the Pieces," *Montreal Gazette*, 14 March 1993, A1.

Perkins, Craig et al. *Criminal Victimization in the United States, 1993.* Bureau of Justice Statistics, U.S. Department of Justice, May 1996.

Petersilia, Joan. "A Crime Control Rationale for Reinvesting in Community Corrections." *The Prison Journal* 75, 4 (December 1995).

————. *Expanding Options for Criminal Sentencing.* Santa Monica, CA: The Rand Corporation, 1987.

Petersilia, Joan, and Susan Turner. "Reducing Prison Admissions: The Potential of Intermediate Sanctions." *The Journal of State Government* 62, 2 (1989): 65-69.

Petersilia, Joan, Susan Turner and Allan Abrahamse. *Intermediate Sanctions: Their Potential for Reducing Prison Crowding.* Santa Monica, CA: The Rand Corporation, 1989.

Petersilia, Joan, Susan Turner and Joyce Peterson. *Prison versus Probation in California: Implications for Crime and Offender Recidivism.* Santa Monica, CA: The Rand Corporation, 1986.

Pilcher, Dan. "State Correctional Industries: Choosing Goals, Accepting Tradeoffs." *National Conference of State Legislatures* (June 1989).

Pollack, Frederick. "English Law Before the Norman Conquest." *Law Quarterly Review* 14 (1898).

Pranis, Kay. "Building Community Support for Restorative Justice: Principles and Strategies." In *Restorative Justice: International Perspectives*, edited by Burt Galaway and Joe Hudson. Monsey, NY: Criminal Justice Press, 1996.

————. "Restorative Justice Initiative." In *Ideas That Work: Crime and Public Safety*. Washington, DC: National Governors Association, 1996.

Pratt, John. "Colonization, Power and Silence: A History of Indigenous Justice in New Zealand Society." In *Restorative Justice: International Perspectives*, edited by Burt Galaway and Joe Hudson. Monsey, NY: Criminal Justice Press (1996).

President's Task Force on Victims of Crime. 1982. Final Report. Washington, DC: U.S. Government Printing Office, December 1982.

Public Agenda Foundation. *Punishing Criminals: The People of Delaware Consider the Options.* Edna McConnell Clark Foundation, 1991.

————. *Punishing Criminals: The Public's View, and Alabama Survey.* Edna McConnell Clark Foundation, 1989.

————. *Crime and Punishment: The Public's View.* Edna McConnell Clark Foundation, 1987.

Reiman, Jeffrey H. *The Rich Get Richer and the Poor Get Prison: Ideology, Class, and Criminal Justice.* New York: John Wiley & Sons, 1979.

Reppetto, Thomas. *The Blue Parade.* New York: Free Press, 1978.

Resnick, H.S. et al. "Prevalence of Civilian Trauma and PTSD in a Representative National Sample of Women." *Journal of Consulting and Clinical Psychology* 61, 6 (1993).

Richardson, Greg D. "Victim-Offender Reconciliation." *Wisconsin Bar Criminal Law News* (August 1989).

Riggs, David S. and Dean G. Kilpatrick. "Families and Friends: Indirect Victimization by Crime." In *Victims of Crime: Problems, Policies, and Programs,* edited by Arthur Lurigio et al. Newbury Park, CA: Sage Publications, 1990.

Rivera, Carla. "Guiding Ex-Offenders Back into Society," *Los Angeles Times,* 11 December 1991, B2.

Roberts, Albert R. *Helping Crime Victims: Research, Policy, and Practice.* Newbury Park, CA: Sage Publications, 1990.

Robins, Carl. "Finding Jobs for Former Offenders," *Corrections Today,* August 1993, 140.

Robinson, Clay. "Jobs for Ex-Offenders a Crime Issue, Too," *Houston Chronicle,* 17 July 1994, 2.

Robinson, Paul H. "Hybrid Principles for the Distribution of Criminal Sanctions." *Northwestern University Law Review* 82, 1 (1987): 19-42.

Rotman, Edgardo. *Beyond Punishment: A New View of the Rehabilitation of Criminal Offenders.* Westport, CT: Greenwood Press, 1990.

Rowland, Judith A. "Illusions of Justice: Who Represents the Victim?" Unpublished article, 1989.

————. "Representation of Victims' Interests within the Criminal Justice System." In *The Attorney's Victim Assistance Manual: A Guide to the Legal Issues Confronting Victims of Crime and Victim Service Providers.* Prepared for The Sunny von Bulow National Victim Advocacy Center in cooperation with the Attorney's Victim Assistance Project of the American Bar Association, Criminal Justice Section, 1987.

Rucker, Lila. "Peacemaking in Prisons." In *Criminology as Peacemaking,* edited by Harold E. Pepinsky and Richard Quinney. Bloomington: Indiana University Press, 1991.

Ruth-Heffelbower, Duane. "What Does It Mean to Be Church-Based?" In *VORP Organizing: A Foundation in the Church,* by Ron Claassen and Howard Zehr. Elkhart, IN: Mennonite Central Committee U.S. Office of Criminal Justice, 1989.

Sank, Diane and David I. Caplan, eds. *To Be a Victim: Encounters with Crime and Injustice.* New York: Insight Books/Plenum Publishing Corporation, 1991.

Schafer, Stephen. *Victimology: The Victim and His Criminal*. Reston, VA: Reston, 1968; 1977.

_____. "The Restitutive Concept of Punishment." In *Considering the Victim*, edited by Joe Hudson and Burt Galaway. Springfield, IL: Charles C Thomas, 1975.

_____. *Compensation and Restitution to Victims of Crime*. Montclair, NJ: Patterson Smith, 1970.

_____. "Victim Compensation and Responsibility." *Southern California Law Review* 43 (1970): 55.

Schauer, Frederick. "Community, Citizenship, and the Search for National Identity." *Michigan Law Review* (1986).

Schluter, Michael and David Lee. *The R Factor*. London: Hodder and Stoughton, 1993.

Sexton, George E. et al. *Developing Private Sector Prison Industries: From Concept to Start-Up*. National Institute of Justice, U.S. Department of Justice, 1991.

Seymour, Anne, Christine Edmunds and Jane N. Burnley. "Crisis Intervention" in materials prepared for the *1996 National Victim Assistance Academy* sponsored by the U.S. Department of Justice Office for Victims of Crime, July 1996.

Shapiro, Joseph. "Can Churches Save America?" *U.S. News and World Report* (September 9, 1996).

Shaw, Roger. "Prisoners' Children: Symptoms of a Failing Justice System." In *Relational Justice: Repairing the Breach*, edited by Jonathan Burnside and Nicola Baker. Winchester, United Kingdom: Waterside Press, 1994.

Sherman, Lawrence. *Neighborhood Safety*. Crime File Study Guide Series. Washington, DC: National Institute of Justice.

Skogan, Wesley G., Arthur J. Lurigio and Robert C. Davis. "Criminal Victimization." In *Victims of Crime: Problems, Policies, and Programs*, edited by Arthur Lurigio, et al. Newbury Park, CA: Sage Publications, 1990.

Skolnik, Howard L. and John Slansky. "A First Step in Helping Inmates Get Good Jobs after Release." *Corrections Today* (August 1991).

Skovron, Sandra E., Joseph E. Scott and Francis T. Cullen. "Prison Crowding: Public Attitudes Toward Strategies of Population Control." *Journal of Research in Crime and Delinquency* 25, 2 (1988): 150-169.

Smith, Barbara E., Robert C. Davis and Susan W. Hillenbrand. *Improving Enforcement of Court-Ordered Restitution: Executive Summary*. A Study of the American Bar Association Criminal Justice Section Victim Witness Project, August 1989.

Spader, Dean J. "Megatrends in Criminal Justice Theory." *American Journal of Criminal Law* 13, 2 (1986): 157-198.

Stark, J.H. and H.W. Goldstein. *The Rights of Crime Victims*. New York: Bantam Books (in conjunction with the American Civil Liberties Union), 1985.

Steinberg, Allen. *The Transformation of Criminal Justice: Philadelphia, 1800-1880*. Studies in Legal History. Chapel Hill: University of North Carolina Press, 1989.

————. "From Private Prosecution to Plea Bargaining: Criminal Prosecution, the District Attorney, and American Legal History. *Crime and Delinquency* 30 (1984).

Stephen, James F. *A History of the Criminal Law of England.* London: Macmillan, 1883.

Stott, John and Nick Miller, eds. *Crime and the Responsible Community.* London: Hodder and Stoughton, 1980.

Stripling, Sherry. "A Life of Opening Doors, Hearts—Herb Smith Helped Former Prisoners Through Respect," *Seattle Times,* 7 November 1991, E1.

Stuart, Barry. "Circle Sentencing: Turning Swords into Ploughshares." In *Restorative Justice: International Perspectives,* edited by Burt Galaway and Joe Hudson. Monsey, NY: Criminal Justice Press (1996).

Sullivan, John L. *Introduction to Police Science.* New York: McGraw-Hill, 1971.

Thorvaldson, Sveinn. "Restitution and Victim Participation in Sentencing: A Comparison of Two Models." In *Criminal Justice, Restitution, and Reconciliation,* edited by Burt Galaway and Joe Hudson. Monsey, NY: Criminal Justice Press, 1990.

Trenczek, Thomas. "A Review and Assessment of Victim-Offender Reconciliation Programming in West Germany." In *Criminal Justice, Restitution, and Reconciliation,* edited by Burt Galaway and Joe Hudson. Monsey, NY: Criminal Justice Press, 1990.

Trubek, David M. "Turning Away From Law?" *Michigan Law Review* 82 (1984).

Tushnet, Mark. "Critical Legal Studies: A Political History." *Yale Law Journal* 100 (1991).

Umbreit, Mark. "Restorative Justice Through Mediation: The Impact of Programs in Four Canadian Provinces." In *Restorative Justice: International Perspectives,* edited by Burt Galaway and Joe Hudson. Monsey, NY: Criminal Justice Press, 1996.

————. "Restorative Justice: What Works?" Paper presented to the International Community Corrections Association Conference, September 1996.

————. "Holding Juvenile Offenders Accountable: A Restorative Justice Perspective." *Juvenile and Family Court Journal* (Spring 1995): 31-42.

————. *Mediating Interpersonal Conflicts: A Pathway to Peace.* West Concord, MN: CPI Publishing, 1995.

————. "Mediating Victim-Offender Conflict: From Single-Site to Multi-Site Analysis in the U.S." In *Restorative Justice on Trial,* edited by Heinz Messmer and Hans-Uwe Otto. Dordrecht, The Netherlands: Kluwer Academic Publishers, 1992.

————. "The Meaning of Fairness to Burglary Victims." In *Criminal Justice, Restitution and Reconciliation,* edited by Burt Galaway and Joe Hudson. Monsey, NY: Criminal Justice Press, 1990.

————. "Victim-Offender Mediation with Violent Offenders." In *The Victimology Handbook: Research Findings, Treatment, and Public Policy,* edited by Emilio Viano. New York: Garland, 1990.

————. "Crime Victims Seeking Fairness, Not Revenge: Toward Restorative Justice." *Federal Probation* 53, 3 (1989): 52-57.

————. "Violent Offenders and their Victims." In *Mediation and Criminal Justice: Victims, Offenders and Community*, edited by Martin Wright and Burt Galaway. Newbury Park, CA: Sage Publications, 1989.

————. "Mediation of Victim Offender Conflict." *The Missouri Journal of Dispute Resolution* (Fall 1988): 85-105.

————. "Victim Offender Mediation in Urban/Multi-Cultural Settings." Manuscript 1986.

————. *Crime and Reconciliation: Creative Options for Victims and Offenders.* Nashville: Abingdon Press, 1985.

Umbreit, Mark S. and Mike Niemeyer. "Victim-Offender Mediation: From the Margins Toward the Mainstream." American Probation and Parole Association *Perspectives* (Summer 1994).

Umbreit, Mark S. et al. *Victim Meets Offender: The Impact of Restorative Justice and Mediation.* Monsey, NY: Criminal Justice Press, 1994.

Van Ness, Daniel W. "Restorative Justice and International Human Rights." In *Restorative Justice: International Perspectives,* edited by Burt Galaway and Joe Hudson. Monsey, NY: Criminal Justice Press, 1996.

————. "Anchoring Just Deserts." *Criminal Law Forum* 6, 3 (1995).

————. "Preserving a Community Voice: The Case for Half-and-Half Juries in Racially-Charged Criminal Cases." *John Marshall Law Review* 28, 1 (1994).

————. "New Wine in Old Wineskins." *Criminal Law Forum* 4, 2 (1993).

————. "Christians and Prison Reform." In *Dictionary of Christianity in America*, edited by Daniel Reid et al. Downers Grove, IL: InterVarsity Press, 1990.

————. "Restorative Justice." In *Criminal Justice, Restitution, and Reconciliation*, edited by Burt Galaway and Joe Hudson. Monsey, NY: Criminal Justice Press, 1990.

————. *Crime and Its Victims: What We Can Do.* Downers Grove, IL: InterVarsity Press, 1986.

Van Ness, Daniel W. et al. *Restorative Justice: Theory, Principles, and Practice.* Washington, DC: Justice Fellowship, 1989; 1990.

Viano, Emilio, ed. *The Victimology Handbook: Research Findings, Treatment, and Public Policy.* New York: Garland, 1990.

Victims' Rights: Opportunities for Action. National Victim Center, March 1989.

Villmoare, Edwin and Jeanne Benvenuti. *California Victims of Crime Handbook.* Sacramento: Victims of Crime Resource Center, McGeorge School of Law, University of the Pacific, 1988.

Villmoare, Edwin and Virginia V. Neto. *Victim Appearances at Sentencing Hearings under the California Bill of Rights: Executive Summary.* National Institute of Justice, U.S. Department of Justice, March 1987.

von Hirsch, Andrew. *Censure and Sanctions.* Oxford: Clarendon Press, 1993.

————. *Doing Justice: The Choice of Punishments.* New York: Hill and Wang, 1976.

Wachtel, Ted. "Family Group Conferencing: Restorative Justice in Practice." *Juvenile Justice Update* 1, 4 (1995).

Wagatsuma, Hiroshi and Arthur Rosett. "The Implication of Apology: Law and Culture in Japan and the United States." *Law and Society Review* 20 (1986).

Walker, Samuel. *Popular Justice: A History of American Criminal Justice*. New York: Oxford University Press, 1980.

Waller, Irvin. "International Standards, National Trail Blazing, and the Next Steps." In *Victims of Crime: A New Deal?*, edited by M. Maguire and J. Pointing. Philadelphia: Open University Press, 1988.

Weiner, Neil A. "Editorial." *Violence and Victims: Special Issue on the Prediction of Violent Criminal Behavior* 3, 4 (1988): 243-246.

Weitkamp, Elmar. "Can Restitution Serve as a Reasonable Alternative to Imprisonment? An Assessment of the Situation in the U.S.A." In *Restorative Justice on Trial*, edited by Heinz Messmer and Hans-Uwe Otto. Dordrecht, The Netherlands: Kluwer Academic Publishers, 1992.

Wilkinson, Henrietta and William Arnold. *Victims of Crime: A Christian Perspective*. Presbyterian Criminal Justice Program of the United Presbyterian Church U.S.A., 1982.

Worth, Dave. "Mediation and Values." *Accord, A Mennonite Central Committee Canada Publication for Victim Offender Ministries* 8, 3 (1989).

Wright, Martin. "Victim-Offender Mediation as a Step Towards a Restorative System of Justice." In *Restorative Justice on Trial*, edited by Heinz Messmer and Hans-Uwe Otto. Dordrecht, The Netherlands: Kluwer Academic Publishers, 1992.

————. *Justice for Victims and Offenders*. Philadelphia: Open University Press, 1991.

————. "Introduction." In *Mediation and Criminal Justice*, edited by Martin Wright and Burt Galaway. London: Sage Publications, 1989.

————. *Making Good: Prisons, Punishment, and Beyond*. London: Burnett Books, 1982.

Wright, Martin and Burt Galaway, eds. *Mediation and Criminal Justice: Victims, Offenders, and Community*. Newbury Park, CA: Sage Publications, 1989.

Yazzie, Robert. "'Life Comes From It': Navajo Justice Concepts." *New Mexico Law Review* 24 (1994): 175.

Yazzie, Robert and James W. Zion. "Navajo Restorative Justice: The Law of Equality and Justice." In *Restorative Justice: International Perspectives*, edited by Burt Galaway and Joe Hudson. Monsey, NY: Criminal Justice Press (1996).

Young, Marlene A. *Restorative Community Justice: A Call to Action*. Washington, DC: National Organization for Victim Assistance, 1995.

Zedner, Lucia. "Victims." In *The Oxford Handbook of Criminology*, edited by Mike Maguire, Rod Morgan and Robert Reiner. New York: Oxford University Press, 1994.

Zehr, Howard. *Changing Lenses: A New Focus for Crime and Justice*. Scottsdale, PA: Herald Press, 1990.

————. "VORP Dangers." *Accord, A Mennonite Central Committee Canada publication for Victim Offender Ministries* 8, 3 (1989).

————. "The Subversion of Visions." *Network Newsletter* (January-February-March 1988).

————. *Retributive Justice, Restorative Justice.* Akron, PA: Mennonite Central Committee U.S. Office of Criminal Justice, 1985.

————. "Retributive Justice, Restorative Justice." In *New Perspectives on Crime and Justice: Occasional Papers of the MCC Canada Victim Offender Ministries Program and the MCC U.S. Office of Criminal Justice*, Vol. 4. Elkhart, IN: Mennonite Central Committee U.S. Office of Criminal Justice, 1985.

Zehr, Howard and Earl Sears. *Mediating the Victim-Offender Conflict.* Elkhart, IN: Mennonite Central Committee U.S. Office of Criminal Justice, 1980.

Appendix A:
Restorative Justice Resources / Programs

Balanced and Restorative Justice Project
University of Minnesota School of Social Work
386 McNeal Hall, 1985 Buford Avenue
St. Paul, MN 55108-6144
612/624-4923
E-mail: ctr4rjm@che2.che.umn.edu

Campaign for Equity-Restorative Justice
111 High Street
Brattleboro, VT 05301-3018
E-mail: jwlmrdng@sover.net
Web Page: http://www.cerj.org

Center for Peacemaking and Conflict Studies
Fresno Pacific University
1717 S. Chestnut Avenue
Fresno, CA 93702
209/453-2064
E-mail: pacs@fresno.edu
Web Page: http://www.fresno.edu.pacs/

Center for Restorative Justice and Mediation
University of Minnesota School of Social Work
386 McNeal Hall, 1985 Buford Avenue
St. Paul, MN 55108-6144
612/624-4923
E-mail: ctr4rjm@che2.che.umn.edu

The Church Council on Justice and Corrections
507 Bank Street
Ottawa, Ontario K2P 1Z5
Canada

Community Service Foundation, Inc.
P.O. Box 283
Pipersville, PA 18947

Conflict Transformation Program
Eastern Mennonite University
Harrisonburg, VA 22801
504/432-4490
Fax: 540/432-4449
E-mail: ctprogram@emu.edu

Criminal Justice Program
Presbyterian Church (USA)
100 Witherspoon Street
Louisville, KY 40202-1396
502-569-5810

Forum for Initiatives in Reparation and Mediation (FIRM)
19 London End
Beaconsfield
Bucks HP9 2HN
England

Fresno Pacific University
1717 S. Chestnut Avenue
Fresno, CA 93702
209/453-2064
E-mail: rjm-vorp@vorp.org
Web Page: http://www.fresno.edu.pacs/rjm.html

Genesee Justice Program
Genesee County Sheriff's Department
County Building 1
Batavia, NY 14020
716/344-2550

The Institute for Economic and Restorative Justice
P.O. Box 262
Voorheesville, NY 12186
518/765-2468

Jubilee Centre
3 Hooper Street
Cambridge CB1 2NZ
England

Justice Fellowship
P.O. Box 16069
Washington, DC 20041-6069
703/904-7312
Web Page: http://www.pfm.org/jf.htm

Mennonite Central Committee U.S.
Office on Crime and Justice
21 South 12th Street, Box 500
Akron, PA 17501
717/859-3889

Murder Victims' Families for Reconciliation
P.O. Box 208
Atlantic, VA 23303-0208
804/824-0948

National Criminal Justice Reference Service (NCJRS)
Topical Bibliography and Search on Restorative/Community Justice
Box 6000
Rockville, MD 20849-6000
800/851-3420

National Organization for Victim Assistance
1757 Park Road NW
Washington, DC 20010
202/232-6682
E-mail: NOVA@access.digex.net

Neighbors Who Care
P.O. Box 16079
Washington, DC 20041
703/904-7311
Web Page: http://www.neighborswhocare.org
            http://www.pfm.org/nwc.htm

Prison Fellowship—England and Wales
P.O. Box 945
Chelmsford
Essex CM2 7RD
England
E-mail: fi34@dial.pipex.com

Prison Fellowship International
P.O. Box 17434
Washington, DC 20041
703/481-0000
E-mail: info@pfi.org
Web Page: http://www.prisonfellowshipintl.org

REALJUSTICE
P.O. Box 500
Pipersville, PA 18947
610/807-9221
E-mail: realjust@aol.com

Restorative Justice Association
Oregon Council on Crime and Delinquency
2530 Fairmount Boulevard
Eugene, OR 97403
541/484-2468

Restorative Justice Initiative
Minnesota Department of Corrections
1450 Energy Park Drive, Suite 200
St. Paul, MN 55108-5219
612/642-0338

Restorative Justice Institute
P.O. Box 16301
Washington, DC 20041-6301
703/404-1246
E-mail: grichardjd@aol.com or bprestonjd@aol.com

Restorative Justice Ministries
Fresno Pacific University
1717 S. Chestnut Avenue
Fresno, CA 93702
209/453-2064
E-mail: rjm-vorp@vorp.org
Web Page: http://www.fresno.edu.pacs/rjm.html

Restorative Justice Network
P.O. Box 33-135
Christchurch 8030
New Zealand

Transformative Justice Association
115 Curlewis Street
Bondi Beach NSW 2026
Australia
61/2/9130/2481 (phone and fax)

Victim Offender Mediation Association
777 South Main Street, Suite 200
Orange, CA 92668
714/836-8100
E-mail: vorpoc@ige.apc.org
Web Page: http://igc.org/voma

Victim Offender Ministries
Mennonite Central Committee Canada
P.O. Box 2038
Clearbrook, British Columbia V2T-3T8
Canada

Prison Fellowship International sponsors the Restorative Justice Forum. To subscribe, send E-mail to: MAISER@PFI.ORG; in the body of the message (not subject line), type: SUBSCRIBE JCENTRE YourFirstName YourLastName

Appendix B:
Discussion Questions

Overall book:

1. Compare restorative justice to the main practices and assumptions of American criminal justice in the twentieth century. What is different about restorative justice?

2. What are the main principles required for criminal justice to be fair and effective? How does restorative justice measure up?

3. What do crime victims most want, in terms of justice? What are victims' claims and their responsibilities in a just response to crime?

4. Why have crime victims been given a secondary role in modern criminal justice practices? What are the advantages and disadvantages, in terms of justice, to giving victims a primary role?

5. Is retribution enough to satisfy justice for offenders? Why or why not?

6. What are the advantages and disadvantages of involving communities as "players" in the criminal justice process and in the nonprocedural aspects of justice (such as in programs to assist victims, offenders and their families)?

7. What does it take to change a society's approach to justice? Think in terms of both attitudes and practices.

By chapter:

Chapter One

1. What is a paradigm shift? How is it different from a new pattern of thinking?

2. What forces prompted the shift in thinking about crime that took place during the Middle Ages? What forces have prompted other similar shifts in other fields? What forces in contemporary society might lead to fundamental shifts in thinking in criminal justice?

3. Why does it matter what pattern of thinking is adopted within the justice system?

Chapter Two

1. Are there similarities among the movements that the authors suggest have led to restorative justice theory? Are there contradictions or tensions among them that restorative justice will need to resolve?

2. The authors explain the source of the term "restorative justice" as well as giving alternative names that have been suggested from time to time. What is the significance of choosing one term over another?

Chapter Three

1. Define restorative justice, outlining several key differences from current practice.

2. The authors present three propositions concerning restorative justice. Explain ways contemporary criminal justice appears to share those propositions. In what ways are they not shared?

3. What should the role of government be in relation to specific restorative programs? Can government funding, oversight and/or referrals limit the extent to which these are authentic community-based responses? How might that potential impediment be addressed?

Chapter Four

1. In what ways does restorative justice theory raise the objections noted in this chapter?

2. What does restorative justice offer to a victim, offender or community that is not already available in criminal and civil courts?

3. It has often been observed that the criminal justice system is not a system at all. Do the proposals made in this chapter make it more or less likely that it will become more of a system? Why?

Chapter Five

1. Several of the earliest proponents of restorative justice developed their ideas while working with victim-offender reconciliation programs. Why is encounter, as described in this chapter, so central to restorative justice?

2. Are understanding and agreement really possible given the diversity and mobility of contemporary, urbanized society?

3. Victims and offenders who participate in encounter programs report high levels of satisfaction when they have finished. But some victims and offenders choose not to participate. Assuming that their refusal is not based on a misunderstanding of the process, what are some reasons for either or both parties deciding not to encounter the other? What implications might this have for restorative justice theory?

Chapter Six

1. How feasible is it to quantify into dollars the injuries that result from a crime? In what other governmental agencies or private businesses is this done? Can approaches used there be applied to reparation?

2. The authors argue that reparation and effective management of risks and stakes are feasible, and that what is needed is a commitment to fund and use programs that bring them into fruition. What arguments are likely to be most successful to the public and to policymakers in gaining that commitment?

3. The previous chapter noted that offenders who meet with their victims in an encounter program are more likely to complete restitution payments. Why do you think that is, and what does that suggest for increasing compliance with restitution orders?

4. The authors discuss monetary restitution, but also note that there are other forms of reparation besides restitution. What are some of those other ways of repairing harm?

Chapter Seven

1. The authors argue that in urbanized, individualized societies the difficulties with reintegration are more important to restorative practitioners than the difficulties with shaming. Why would that be?

2. Self-help affinity groups (motivated in part by shared experiences of alienation) and faith communities (motivated by spiritual commitments) are two groups that might serve as reintegrating communities for victims or offenders. What other groups or institutions might play that role? What are their motivations?

3. Why is reintegration important in a restorative response to crime?

Chapter Eight

1. Imagine a courtroom with three counsel's tables—one for the prosecutor, one for the defendant and the defendant's attorney, and one for the victim and the victim's attorney. The victim's role would be limited to seeking financial restitution, but the victim would have all the rights and privileges ordinarily provided to a party. How might this change affect courtroom dynamics? Would the result be more or less restorative?

2. The opportunities for victim participation in informal proceedings were discussed earlier in the chapter on encounter. In those programs, the offender has an increased chance to participate directly as well. Are there changes to the formal judicial process that could increase the defendant's direct participation?

3. Why is participation important in a restorative response to crime?

Chapter Nine

1. With (apparently) uniquely restorative programs becoming available to practitioners—such as victim-offender reconciliation programs, family group conferencing, restitution, and so on—why is it necessary to evaluate how effective they are? Do you think it is enough to just use and expand those programs?

2. What reasons might there be for restorative programs to place a low priority on evaluation?

3. The authors argue that broad-based support is important for restorative programs. This is, of course, valuable for any criminal justice program. What aspects of restorative justice make it easier to gain support for its programs? What aspects make it harder?

Chapter Ten

1. Creative thinking is one means of spurring transformation of perspectives and structures. What are some impediments to creativity in the criminal justice system? What dynamics might stimulate and support it?

2. Is there a "normal" pattern of transformation? For example, does transformation of people lead to new perceptions and new structures? Or do structures change perceptions and then people? What are the implications of beginning with one and moving from there to the other two?

3. The authors quote Richard Quinney on the spiritual dimension of a restorative transformation. Is this a necessary component of restorative justice, or simply a dimension of experience that seems to be important to some of its practitioners? If you think it is necessary, explain why. If you think it is not necessary, what significance is there in the spiritual interests (and discussion) of many of its proponents?

Subject Index

Page numbers followed by "n" indicate that the term appears or is included in a footnote.

Name Index

Page numbers followed by "n" indicate that the term appears or is included in a footnote.